SET YOURSELF FREE

*Live the Life
YOU Were Meant
to Live!*

by

Jean Walters

Robert D. Reed Publishers

Robert D. Reed Publishers
P.O. Box 1992
Bandon, OR 97411
Phone: 541-347-9882; Fax: -9883
E-mail: 4bobreed@msn.com
Website: www.rdrpublishers.com

Editor: Anne Cote
Cover Designer: Cleone Reed
Cover Photo: "Flight of Pelicans" (taken where the Tárcoles River meets
the Pacific Ocean in Costa Rica, 1915), by Cleone Reed
Author Photo: David Rabon
Book Designer: Susan Leonard

Soft Cover: ISBN 13: 978-1-944297-03-9
eBook: ISBN 13: 978-1-944297-04-6

Library of Congress Number: 2016953536

Designed and Formatted in the United States of America

I dedicate this book to all those who seek the Light.
May you be inspired in your search!

ACKNOWLEDGMENTS

I acknowledge the thousands of people who have allowed me to dip into my soul and share my Truth with them. I have felt privileged to participate in your growth and you have most definitely been part of mine.

I am so grateful to all those amazing people who shared their stories with me. You knew that I would include them in my writing and your adventures would inspire many people. Thank you for your kind generosity.

I also acknowledge the enthusiastic and tireless efforts of my editor, Anne Cote. Her suggestions and guidance made this book possible. I deeply appreciate the brilliant assistance of Cleone Reed in getting this manuscript ready for publication—especially her reminder to keep having fun.

As you now know, I have been fortunate to have many angels in my life that made the way easier. I am ever so grateful to each of you and even to those who were challenging. I have learned many great and powerful lessons through our interactions.

Most assuredly I am grateful to the Light within that I recognized as a child. It has inspired me, spurred my desire to know more, and given me the courage to press on even during the most trying of times.

TABLE OF CONTENTS

FOREWORD

When I was a little girl (around nine years old), I saw the Light. I was throwing a ball against the front steps of my house and catching it. I noticed a Light that ran through my body from the top of my head to the bottom of my feet. It resembled a fluorescent bulb. As I observed it, the Light seemed joyful and different from the *me* that was throwing the ball. Yet, I knew it was also me. I studied it for a bit, went on to do something else, and then forgot about it. I noticed that whenever I wanted to, I could think about the Light and it was there in my mind, shining through my body all the way to my toes.

Being curious, I started experimenting with it. For instance, when I fell, skinned my knee, and cried in pain, I quickly checked to see if the Light was distraught. It wasn't. It was the same as always: joy-filled. Hem! No matter what was happening, the Light was constant and joyful.

It occurred to me that perhaps I could stay in the Light and not get involved with the hurts of the world. At nine years of age, I was unable to figure out how to do that. Thus, this idea became a precursor for my life. For here I am, a mature woman, learning how to live in the Light and teaching others to do the same.

You might say that living in the Light is what this book is about. I have studied metaphysics, the Bible, the Bhagavad Gita, The Course in Miracles, The Life and Teachings of the Masters of the Far East, the works of Paramahansa Yogananda and a myriad of other authors, teachers, and resources. I have meditated for most of my life. I have been a Spiritual and Personal Growth Consultant and psychic for over thirty-five years. I have discovered truth in many forms and teachings.

This book represents my truth. It follows the life of Jesus and his journey and teachings to illustrate the principle of transformation. Jesus, as a teacher, prototype, and model, instructs us through his example as to what we are to do and be in order to ascend to Higher Consciousness and live in the Light of God. Through our actions, we will be known.

In this book, I track his journey and convert much of what he taught into everyday examples. This is for those who have ears to hear and eyes to see. This book outlines personal transformation. It is our destiny.

We are here in the earth to know the truth and to be set free. The teachings are simple, the practice more difficult. Why? Because we are undoing a lot of ideas that have been programmed into the software of our minds since infancy. However, the truth is always with us, and we will find it as we release the errors of the ego. So you must decide, for only you know the time of your transformation.

I offer this information with an open heart. May you receive it the same way. My wish for you is that you use the tools in this book and live the life you were meant to live!

Jean Walters

INTRODUCTION

I have been a truth-seeker my whole life. Early on, I searched for answers. *If God is love, how could there be a holocaust?* I believed that God is love. I could feel it. But the pieces were not coming together for me. I asked anyone I thought might know the answers to no avail. It was clear. *I am on my own and I will have to figure this out myself.*

My need to *know* brought me to metaphysics. Metaphysics is the study of that which lies beyond the physical realm. It is the study of energy, the mind, the Universe, and Universal Laws. Along the way, my quest has led me to many holy books: *The Bible, The Bhagavad Gita, Vedas, A Course in Miracles, The I Am Dialogues, Life and Teachings of the Masters of the Far East,* and many other resources and courses. In the process, I learned to concentrate my attention and meditate, and I unlocked the mystery of dreams and intuition. I became a psychic reader, transformational coach, and teacher. The world opened up for me.

The pieces to the puzzle came together. This is what I share with you in this book. I call it *Set Yourself Free: Live the Life YOU Were Meant to Live!* because within its pages, you will learn how to move beyond the limitation of the ego and discover the greater realm of the mind and then beyond.

Many people seek the truth to make sense of the seeming chaos of the world. Throughout history, there have been those in every culture and situation seeking peace and harmony. Perhaps peace has come in fleeting moments, or even extended periods. Yet eventually, the

1

restlessness returns, and again there is doubt, fear, insecurity, or guilt. What gets in the way? What is it that uproots serenity? And is there a way to loosen the grip of apprehension and rid it forever? These are the questions of a truth-seeker.

Yes, you can find meaning and purpose in life, and discover the answers you seek. In this manuscript, I provide tools to assist you in your pursuit.

Turning to the quiet space within begins the journey. Learning to listen to the still small voice of intuition is a must. We have a master and teacher to help us find our way. In the Bible, Jesus is our example, prototype, and model. He came into the earth to instruct in mastership. His path is our path. He modeled for us how to live life and how to bring our energy and awareness to a high vibratory level that we might move from the darkness of fear and limitation to the Light to love.

In this book, I use Jesus' example to illustrate the journey. He led the way that we might follow. We have the same Christ Consciousness. His was developed and ours is in process. As we follow his model, we are led to the freedom that is our inheritance as a child (offspring or spark) of God. He made this promise:

> *Verily, verily, I say unto you, he that believeth on me, the works that I do shall he do also; and greater works than these shall he do; because I go unto the Father.* John 14:12

By closing your eyes to the material world and turning inward to the spirit within, you will discover truth and come to recognize your true Identity. This is how you engage your intuition. You were made in God's image and likeness. Thus, you possess the internal blueprint to set yourself free from false beliefs and ego-restrictions. In this book, you will explore your inner wisdom and discover your birthright.

> *Jesus answered them, 'Is it not written in your law, I said, ye are gods?'* John 10:34

The physical world offers an exciting place to learn and a vast array of opportunity. As we address each experience and challenge, we learn to love and develop into enlightened beings. The requirement is self-cleansing and forgiveness. That means we willingly release fear so we can return to love. It requires action.

Our world instructs us with rules, dogma, and shoulds. You should give more than you receive; be humble, self-sacrificing; you must not acknowledge your merits; or make waves; always share; never complain; be polite, etc. The dictates go on and on. They are distractions. Yet, as we advance to adulthood, the program is set. Anything fun or expansive is taboo, illegal, immoral, fattening, restrictive, or socially unacceptable.

If you have acquiesced to man-made rules and superstitions, you have likely closed down natural avenues of expression, intuition, and creativity. Concern over public scrutiny renders self-expression frightening and leads to self-rejection, darkness, depression, and feeling lost.

As humans, we have basic needs. The most important of which is freedom. But what is freedom? We had freedom to express as babies, yet with time and mental programming, we lost touch with this inherent need. Thus, the question remains: how to become our authentic selves?

It is no wonder teenagers rebel. After repeated years of *don't do that; you mustn't want that; what will the neighbors think; it's bad to be or do that; repress, suppress, hold back*, the only path remaining is rebellion.

Rebellion is a way to find ourselves. Yet, stepping from the restrictive box in which we were raised, risks us being cast from our *tribes*, represented by our religious, social-ethnic groups, the people we grew up with, our families. This change carries either gloom and despair or excitement and adventure. Either way, it is an evolutionary step.

Most everything we have been taught is other-oriented: be polite, don't cause trouble or inconvenience, don't rock the boat, don't be rude or too honest and, for heaven's sake, don't hurt anyone's feelings. The rebellion is against society and leads to unorthodox behavior: boys wear earrings and pants around their knees; girls have nose rings and wild, revealing costumes; and both use their bodies as canvasses broadcasting their specialness and sameness. All of this activity is pointed outward toward the world and is, essentially, ineffective. The ideal gets lost. With this kind of rebellion, we still operate at the level of form: the ego.

Yet, through all of this, the desire to explore one's uniqueness can be achieved. Perhaps that is the point.

Through these pages, you will discover your natural, God-given expression, the Light of your being, and your freedom.

Adjusting your psyche to eliminate ideas that are not only meaningless, but harmful and disrespectful to your authentic self, is a dynamic step toward transformation. For example, being nice to people who are rude and inconsiderate is ludicrous. In the same sense, holding back to become a doormat for someone else is futile. Not stating what you want wastes time. These are unproductive behaviors stemming from erroneous beliefs and programs, and they are based on protecting the fragile ego.

You are not here to be cookie-cutter perfect. When you do not acknowledge your rights as a spiritual being, you grow to hate yourself. Eventually, you are called to throw off repression and addiction to outer-world focus, to reclaim your innate birthright as a powerful spiritual being.

Throughout this book, you will find stories of people who have done just that. There are others who remain stuck. I hope you find inspiration and motivation in these testaments. Please note that, in many of the stories, the names have been changed to protect identities.

Nature is ordered and rhythmic and so are we. Are you ready to decree your right to harmony? If so, the cause, process, and direction for control will be revealed to you in the pages of this manuscript. We will explore selfhood and what is required to reclaim your birthright as a divine expression of the Creator.

Putting this in perspective, imagine you are the offspring of a king. Your father possesses vast riches and unlimited resources. At the snap of a finger, he can command any situation, call for what he wants, and send servants scurrying. Would he ignore his position to sit back passively and let others rule his kingdom? Never!

As the child of this monarch, you also have rights and responsibilities. You are liable to learn to manage yourself so that you may command your own universe. It is unseemly for you, an exalted being, to proceed head down and shoulders slumped, pretending to be nothing. It would be foolish and wasteful for you to toil while your servants twiddled their thumb when your real work is to develop the authority to command them and create your earthly kingdom. Your servants are the Universal Laws. We will discuss them in full in this manuscript. Learning to direct them is a matter of education and experimentation. To use them well requires balance, discipline, good judgment, vision, and responsible action.

You are the offspring of this monarch. You have a heavenly parent who is the King of the Universe and you are in His direct lineage. It is time to train for your position of leadership.

True royalty is not concerned with other people's judgments, nor do they sulk if things don't go their way. Contrarily, a prince stands with dignity, holding his vision while accepting responsibility for results and outcomes with grace and maturity. And he takes loving action. You are this being. As you emulate these noble ways, you learn to manage your own universe: yourself.

This book is about being your true Self. Its purpose is to give you the tools you need to assume your rightful place, thus freeing yourself from ego, fear, false beliefs, and their resultant conditioning and limitations.

What do you want to do with your life? What is holding you back? Keep these questions in mind while reading this book and your way will crystallize. With vision comes motivation. Motivation guides you to the right steps to achieve your goal.

The word definitions are taken from the *Metaphysical Bible Dictionary*, published by Unity Publications, and the Bible quotes are taken from the *American Standard Bible*.

Thank you for taking this journey with me. May you discover your brilliance as you move along your spiritual path.

CHAPTER 1

JESUS, OUR PROTOTYPE

W e are all part of the revolution taking place in the world. It started with Jesus, a spiritual revolutionary, 2000 years ago. More recently, self-improvement expert, Dr. Wayne Dyer, mentioned during a seminar that spiritual teacher, Madame Blavatsky, made a prediction in the early1900's that, in the last twenty-five years of this century, there would be a profound worldwide spiritual revolution that would create massive changes in the consciousness of all people.

When the Mayan calendar emerged some years ago, the news agencies reported that the calendar ended in December 2012. This put a fright into many people who interpreted it to mean the world would end. As it turned out, the calendar ended at that date because the ancient Mayans knew there would be a new evolutionary period beginning and they did not know how to predict this New Age. What they did know was that it would be a time of openhearted, nurturing energy, a shift from the patriarchal tempo of the past centuries to a softer energy of femininity and compassion.

In the later part of the twentieth century, we learned of an event called the Harmonic Convergence, which consisted of a shift to a higher energy that was felt round the world. I personally remember the day in August 1987. I was filled with energy, a noticeable change for me, and I washed windows and zoomed around my house like a wild woman completing tasks. Other people noticed that time seemed to go faster. Indeed, there was a speeding up of evolution.

This shift in energy was the beginning of the transformation that Madame Blavatsky spoke of in her writings. She also predicted that the leaders in this transformation would be ordinary people. Thus, folks like Marianne Williamson, a former nightclub singer, Wayne Dyer, a former school teacher, Zig Ziglar, a former preacher, and Brian Tracy, a salesman, all started teaching as they reached out to the multitudes in new ways of thinking and being.

It is my thought that we are all teachers. As we venture through life, we leave our energy with the people and situations we touch. When we approach life from the point of view of unconditional love, non-judgment, openness, and forgiveness, we create a profound and progressive ripple effect in the world. We literally transform our lives and the energy in which we all function.

We can compare this change to placing drops of colored dye, representing love, in the universal sea of energy in which we live, breath, and have our being. We will call this sea the Quantum Field. As more and more people release their love, their unique color of dye, this Quantum Field takes on a new hue, resulting in an energy shift that affects everyone and everything. As this process continues, we will be living in a sea of love to which we have all contributed. There is now more kindness and compassion in the world, and this will continue to build.

Transformation requires looking *inside* instead of focusing on the material world and depending on the five physical senses of sight, taste, touch, hearing, and smell to inform us of reality. We have spent an inordinate amount of time looking *out there*, when the truth lies *in here*, in the stillness of our hearts and minds.

People are always telling me about the *real* world. They think their material reality is *real*. Yet, if this were true, why is it so unstable and unpredictable? Jobs, relationships, homes, and friends are here today and gone tomorrow. All are transforming. Change, as it turns out, is the only constant.

The only thing that is *real* is that which is unchangeable and stable. That is God, the Universe, the Quantum Field, Spirit. Thus, we should make our claim for the stability of our spiritual domain.

The great teacher Jesus provided deep, clear, and specific instructions on how to live *in* the world but not *of* it. His work reveals the process of transformation. He offers methods for affecting change. He is still our teacher and guide, and his message is for those who have ears to hear and eyes to see. This is not about religion. It is about connecting with our spiritual center, Love, and living from a place of authenticity. In this book, I have extracted Jesus' practical approach to self-awareness and self-healing.

And he said, 'Who hath ears to hear, let him hear.' And when he was alone, they that were about him with the twelve asked of him the parables. And he said unto them, 'Unto you is given the mystery of the kingdom of God: but unto them that are without, all things are done in parables: that seeing they may see, and not perceive; and hearing they may hear, and not understand; lest they should turn again, and it should be forgiven them.'
Mark 4:9-12

Jesus is more than a teacher and healer. He is an example and prototype. In his ministry, he was clear that he was in the earth to show the way and that we are to follow his example and demonstrate our own God-given talents. He stated often that we are to do greater things than he has done.

Jesus never lost his focus, no matter how dismal the situation appeared to be. He consistently maintained the divinity of man and sought the opportunity to share, to heal, and to demonstrate truth in every circumstance. We will read about many of his acts in these pages. He never deemed the task too great to handle. Even in the Garden of Gethsemane, before he was handed to Roman troops, he did not stray from his path, vision or truth. In fact, his prayer to God was:

And he went forward a little, and fell on his face, and prayed, saying, 'My Father, if it be possible, let this cup pass away from me: nevertheless, not as I will, but as thou wilt.' Matthew 26:39

After these words, he surrendered to the event at hand.

Jesus, called the *Wayshower*, points the way to the true Self. His instruction is thus:

> *If ye abide in my word, then are ye truly my disciples; and ye shall know the truth, and the truth shall make you free.*
> John 8:31-32

The name Jesus means *safety, salvation, deliverance through Jehovah, God*. Jesus, the man, symbolizes the conscious mental state of man struggling and succeeding in revealing an inner, directive power: God.

As Jesus evolved through his earthly life, he grew to trust his inner voice of guidance. By opening to the flow of divine energy, he became a channel for healing and teaching. He stated,

> *Even so let your Light shine before men; that they may see your good works, and glorify your Father who is in heaven.*
> Matthew 5:16

As we raise our energy, we will radiate Divine Light and be a model for others. We can use our everyday events and encounters to practice love and forgiveness. In so doing, we raise our consciousness and our expression changes. We let go of rigidity, become non-reactive, more stable, non-judgmental, and happier.

Self-discipline necessitates consistency in disengaging from ego needs for approval, attention, and fitting-in. The focus instead, will be on the purity of love and the choice to see the Light in every person we encounter. In this on-going effort, we learn to see with new *eyes* and are, therefore, set free from worldly limitations.

In the scriptures, Jesus used the term *Son of Man*, referencing his physical identity. This phrase was used to encourage people to focus beyond the physical being of Jesus to his message of love. He acknowledged the God-power within as the source of his ability and that he was but a channel for it. In fact, every act of creativity in the world is a result of the same flow of divine energy. Each creation (building, painting, book, workshop, drawing, television show) is the result of divine, creative energy expressed through a human channel.

All people—author, architect, auto mechanic, teacher, engineer, factor worker, handyman, or parent—are channels for this incredible energy. Jesus, our prototype, called this energy I AM. It is the principle and energy we each possess that guides us from the wilderness of earthly life to awareness of our inner reality. It is ever-present. We but need to open our hearts to receive it.

When I am in the world, I am the light of the world. John 9:5

I am the way, the truth, and the life; no man cometh unto the Father, but by me. John 14:6

When you lift up the Son of Man you will come to realize that I Am and that I do nothing by myself. I say only what the Father has taught me. John 8:28

The *Son of Man* refers to the physical representation of the person. Lifting the consciousness of man means to raise our mental state to a high vibratory level. This indicates that our feeling-thinking state be poised in love. This is accomplished through the discipline of meditation, contemplation, entering the stillness, unconditional love, and forgiveness.

And Jesus said, 'Father, forgive them; for they know not what they do.' And parting his garments among them, they cast lots. Luke 23-34

More currently, here is a true story of a man who put his own safety aside so that he could follow the intuitive urgings of his Higher Self. This is an example of following the model of Jesus and listening to your Higher Guidance.

One day, an odd-looking truck was rushing at high speed down Highway 85 near Greenville, South Carolina. The truck was engulfed in flames. Except for the driver, nearly everyone on the road realized the truck was on fire and in risk of exploding. No motorist seemed willing to hazard getting close enough to let the driver know what was happening.

An improbable hero, Jack Pace of Greer, South Carolina, a man crippled with rheumatoid arthritis for years, happened along. He had worked diligently to be able to drive and use crutches to get around.

When he recognized the emergency of the burning truck, he put his own safety aside, spun his car across the median strip, and accelerated to 115 miles-an-hour, shooting past backed-up traffic. He caught up with the rig, raced ahead of the truck, and stopped his car. Astonishingly, he threw himself bodily onto the highway. With everything he had, his crippled body crawled into the middle of the road.

The shocked truck driver saw the man lying on the highway and screeched his burning truck to a halt.

Pace shouted to the driver to jump, and the man did.

Emergency workers found the two men huddled safely in a ditch. There had been no explosion. But no one had known that in advance.

The grateful driver cried as he blurted, *Mr. Pace, I don't know you, but I'll sure never forget you. And I thank God for you. But how could you do this?*

Jack Pace shook his head. *I didn't know that I could. But I told the Lord that you had to be saved. And the Lord told me that I had to save you.*

This is a story of courage and overcoming obstacles that stemmed from Jack Pace listening to the inner voice of God. He did the impossible. He is an example of what all of us can do, given our willingness. He did not see himself as a hero. He simply felt he had to do what was necessary.

Perhaps that is all any of us has to do: Follow your heart and let it lead you to great things.

Perfection: What Is It?

Jesus affirms repeatedly man's inherent right to perfection. Perfection denotes *wholeness*. In other words, aligning to the totality of our potential and purpose, clear, visionary, unlimited, and living as *I AM*. As we accept, without resistance, our intuitive insight, we function as Sons of God, as perfected open channels for our inner creative power. Jack Pace's actions in following his inner voice of God are prime examples of this perfection.

There is symbolism in Jesus' attempts to work with his disciples to create unity of mind, body, and spirit under one purpose. Jesus, as leader, teacher, and directing intelligence shepherded his disciples. As we look to the symbolism of the disciples, we find they represent the twelve major faculties of man. Jesus' struggle and their lack of discipline and self-doubt, illustrate our own internal battle to keep our minds centered on God.

Here is a rundown of the twelve major faculties represented by Jesus' disciples. These are our faculties, and it is our assignment to bring them into alliance so that our focus on Spirit will be complete. See if you recognize yourself in these descriptions.

> *Now the names of the twelve apostles are these: The first, Simon, who is called Peter, and Andrew his brother; James the son of Zebedee, and John his brother;*
>
> *Philip, and Bartholomew; Thomas, and Matthew the publican; James the son of Alphaeus, and Thaddeus; Simon the Cananaean, and Judas Iscariot, who also betrayed him.*
>
> *These are the names of the twelve apostles: first, Simon, who is called Peter, and his brother Andrew; James, son of Zebedee, and his brother John; Philip and Bartholomew; Thomas and Matthew, the tax collector; James, son of Alphaeus, and Thaddeus; Simon the Zealot and Judas Iscariot, who betrayed him.* Matthew 10:2-4

Following is the metaphysical interpretation of each of the disciples, starting with Peter. Peter is referred to as the *rock* because he represents the *faculty of faith*. When we couple Peter with Simon, as in Simon Peter, it signifies the ability to hear, which denotes *receptivity*. This concerns our ability to listen faithfully to our inner voice, the voice of God. Jesus indicated Peter when he stated, *I will build my church on this rock*. In other words, I will build my church on faith.

Faith is one of the first spiritual faculties to be called into expression. Peter, *faith*, starts off unsteadily, yet ever-desiring to know the truth. Steadiness of faith comes as we grow in our capacity to love.

Andrew means *strong and manly*. The brother of Simon Peter, he represents *strength of mind*. This is exemplified when Andrew exclaims, *We have found the Messiah*.

Strength and *faith* are brothers. They illustrate a bond of unity that can carry one through difficult times.

James, Son of Zebedee, represents *the faculty of judgment*, which relates to justice and discrimination. It carefully weighs a question and draws a conclusion. From a physical point of view, this faculty relates to caution, fearfulness, criticism, and condemnation. When we use it as a spiritual faculty, it expresses as guidance and good judgment regarding spiritual understanding.

You can see by this that each faculty can be used in a negative or positive manner. As we develop in understanding, we make the choice to use our faculties toward our highest purpose. We always get to choose how this is done.

The family name Zebedee, means *Jehovah is giver of life*. It represents the idea that life is spiritual and God's gift to man. The wife of Zebedee tried to gain the promise that her two sons, James and John, *wisdom* and *love*, would sit with Jesus in the Kingdom of Heaven. This introduces the idea of the supremacy of love and wisdom in man's development.

John means *Jehovah bestows mercifully* or *compassion, fruitfulness, love*. Essentially, John is the spiritual *faculty of love*. Love is the dominant theme of his teaching and writing. Unifying all other faculties helps to develop a spiritual basis for love.

James, son of Alphaeus, was called James, the less. He represents *order*. Alphaeus means *a successor, leader, chief*. The metaphysical interpretation regards this leadership as the spirit in each of us. Our spiritual insight brings order to our lives.

Jude means *praise Jehovah*. He is the brother of the other James and his surname is Thaddeus. He represents the *faculty of elimination*. Thaddeus also means *large-hearted, warm-hearted*, and *courageous*. He represents our mental ability to eliminate old, ineffective ideas and beliefs that have served their purpose and are no longer relevant. Working together, James and Jude, or Thaddeus, bring leadership and order by letting go of ideas that no longer serve a purpose.

Philip means *lover of horses*. This is the *power faculty* in man. Power comes through our words. *In the beginning was the Word and the Word was with God*. Words are used as creative vehicles. We speak our word and it is so. We affirm or deny. *I am loving. I am angry.* In each case, we exemplify our word.

Nathanael, means *gift of God* or *grace of God*. This is possibly the same person as Bartholomew. Bartholomew may be Nathanael's surname. Nathanael represents the imaging power of the mind or *imagination*. When the soul is lifted with spiritual fervor, the result is art, beauty, and creation. You can see how combining *power* and *imagination* can bring about great work.

Matthew means *gratuity of Jah* or *a gift of God*. As a tax collector, Matthew represents the *will faculty* in man. This faculty controls, directs, teaches, and disciplines the mind. To play his role as a disciple of Jesus, Matthew must withdraw from mercenary occupations and material ambitions that have absorbed his time and attention. Know anyone like this?

Thomas means *joined* or *twin*. Thomas represents the *understanding faculty* in man. Understanding and will must function in unison, which means *joined*. This would be *reason* and *intellectual perception*.

Simon, the Zealot, refers to *one who listens and obeys*. This denotes listening for spiritual guidance. This faculty boils down to *receptivity*.

Judas comes from the word Judah, which means *praise Jehovah, celebrate God*. Judah signifies the spiritual faculty that corresponds to *accumulation or increase in the mental realm*. As we offer prayer as a joyful thanksgiving, we bring energy to the super-conscious or highest mental state.

The metaphysical meaning of Judas Iscariot is *the custodian of life, the unredeemed life forces*. This refers to the element in humanity that has caught the higher vision of life, yet still resorts to underhanded methods to meet its obligations. Judas carried the moneybag and betrayed Jesus for thirty pieces of silver. Afterward, Judas hanged himself, which illustrates the remorse of putting material wealth before spiritual abundance.

Judas Iscariot was the disciple of Jesus who refers to the life faculty in man. The life faculty at this phase of overcoming is not fully redeemed from carnal thoughts and desires.

The disciples of Jesus symbolically paint a picture of the faculties we shape and the discipline needed to achieve enlightenment. Faith, receptivity, will, judgment, love, order, release, power, discrimination, and intellectual perception must work together to illuminate the mind of man. After one has been awakened to truth, the desire is to express and to go forth in ministry, be it a business leader, housewife, lawyer, artist, bookkeeper, or whatever. There is no implication that secular industry be abandoned, but it does signify that the mind should make the dissemination of truth the most important goal of life.

The symbolic example of the disciples and their specific faculties within man illustrates our work to unify within the Cosmic Light of God. In the Foreword, when I described the Light that appeared as a fluorescent bulb running through my body, it was an introduction to the I AM Light. However, the faculties were unfocused as was my child-self when I wondered how I was to live in the Light, yet also deal with the challenges of earth life.

Jesus continually worked with his disciples and they eventually unified in recognition of the Master, I AM. As we examine our own journeys, we are to do the same. We are to unify our faculties in the pursuit of spiritual awareness, to be of one mind. This is the process we explore through these pages.

No man can serve two masters; for either he will hate the one, and love the other; or else he will hold to one, and despise the other. Ye cannot serve God and mammon. Matthew 6:24

You can serve the ego or you can serve Spirit. You can not do both.

In summary, our work, then, is to create the inner harmony that allows us to live in the Light of Christ Consciousness, to let go of that which is no longer relevant so that we can direct our will and imagination to greater heights of spiritual awareness, to develop the power and strength of faith along with love and wisdom, and to cultivate our inner authority so that we are living exalted lives as Sons of the Creator.

There are many examples of people who decided to turn from the ego and use their talents to serve others. Here are a few men who were transformed by their prison experiences:

Former Nixon aid, Charles Colson, pleaded guilty to obstruction of justice and spent a year in federal prison for his involvement in the Watergate scandal. After serving his time, Colson started *Prison Fellowship*, the world's largest prison outreach organization. Colson founded this organization because he *could not forget those he had left behind prison walls.*

Stephen Richards spent nine years in prison for selling marijuana. While in prison, he faced a tough wake-up call as he witnessed suicides, beatings, and shootings. These events touched him in such a way that he wanted to transform the system. He started getting an education and received his bachelor's degree while incarcerated. Later, he earned his graduate degree from the University of Wisconsin and his Ph.D. from Iowa State University. He went on to become a professor of criminal justice at the University of Wisconsin, Oshkosh, and published several books on criminology.

Larry Jay Levine was sentenced to ten years in prison for conspiracy charges related to narcotics, securities fraud, obstruction of justice, and possession of automatic weapons. When Levine was released, he made use of his prison experience and knowledge to become a federal prison consultant, providing prison survival education courses and legal services to lawyers and offenders.

A movie called *Catch Me if You Can* captured the story of Frank William Abagnale. Between the ages of sixteen and twenty-one, Abagnale wrote $2.5 million in fraudulent checks and successfully posed as an airline pilot, doctor, lawyer, and college professor. He was later apprehended by the French police and served five years in prison. Abagnale was released early under the condition that he would work with the US government. Now, he runs a fraud-consulting company and has worked with financial institution, corporations, and law enforcement agencies on fraud and securities. He has serviced more than 14,000 companies.

Choosing to serve humanity and committing to spiritual advancement is what we are here to do. We have the faculties and powers to make a difference. We are the product of the Divine Holographic Mind, the Christ. We were made in the image and likeness of God. In other words, Christ is our spiritual leader, guide, and parent.

Jesus said unto him, 'I am the way, and the truth, and the life: no one cometh unto the Father, but by me.' John 14:6

This passage means that Jesus signifies the Christ Consciousness, the energy which is life and is referred to in the Bible as I AM. We attune our minds to the high energy of I AM in order to experience God. We alter our minds through mental discipline in order to rise to a high vibrational state.

If we want to experience a wave, we walk into the ocean. We would feel the wave and become one with it. If we want to experience God, we must *feel* God and become *one* with God. As we elevate our minds, we raise our vibration and energy and, thus, move into the high frequency of the Christ Consciousness. We become one with the Light of God.

As we let go of old ideas such as guilt, shame, regret, resentment, hate, and anger, which keep us from connecting to our higher minds, we basically clean our mental slates. This creates space and allows the mind to reach a fine attunement. This cannot be accomplished if we carry the heaviness of negativity.

Our path winds through various levels of awareness. We start by disciplining our faculties to work in concert with spiritual evolution. We learn what love is and how to experience and share it, and we elevate our consciousness, i.e., raise our energy to the realm of the Christ.

When you walk into a forest, you will notice a calm, serene energy. The trees, shrubs, wild flowers, and animals are at peace. There is no hurry or worry. Slowly, you attune your mind to this energy of serenity and become still. As we meditate, we enter the same stillness and, with practice, we achieve the mental discipline to enter this quiet space whenever we choose. This is what mind-training is all about.

We are made in the image and likeness of God because we are God Energy. There is one energy in the universe. This has been scientifically proven. It goes by various names: the Unified Field, the Quantum Field, the Divine Holographic Mind, or the Divine Mind. All of these denote the same thing. We are in this field and we are made of this field. We *are* this field. The energy and intelligence of God is our energy and intelligence. We are one. There is no separation.

Here is how the Bible describes the process:

When you lift up the Son of Man, you will come to realize that I AM and that I do nothing by myself. I say only what the Father has taught me. John 8:28

In other words, as you lift your consciousness, you become a channel for God. You do nothing by yourself. You are God's vehicle of expression. It goes along with the saying that God needs a body. Each of us is the vehicle-body that God uses to express through.

Raising consciousness refers to our feeling-thinking state. As awareness is expanded through daily practice, we graduate into higher levels of expression. This exercise requires consistent discipline in disengaging from egoic opinions, beliefs, prejudices, and ideas, and turning to the purity, the *Light/Love*, of the Real Self, I AM. Through this effort we are set free from worldly limitations.

The word Christ is defined as *anointed, the messiah*. Messiah denotes *king and deliverer*. Anointed refers to *apply oil*, which indicates *sacredness or reverence*.

Each of these descriptions applies to Jesus, I AM, and conveys the ideas of divinity, sacredness, king, and deliverer. Thus, Jesus symbolizes the Christ Consciousness that is inherent in every person. Sonship, perfection, and completeness are all the same thing.

Our work lies in exploring, developing, and demonstrating the Christ by peeling away erroneous, restrictive beliefs and ideas so that the *Son* shines through. As you read this book you will find many examples of people working through this process.

Man, An Individualized Expression

Observe the ocean. It is vast and magnificent, stretching for thousands of miles, housing a myriad variety of life from tiny microcosms to massive whales and everything in between. It has a rhythm. Each wave, created by wind and the earth's rotation, rises from the ocean body and races across the surface, collapsing onto the beach or against a rock. Each wave is born as an individual creation, and then it merges back into its parent, the ocean.

We can merge with the wave and feel its momentum. We can let it carry us and then, finally, release us into the greater body of the sea. We can feel the power of the ocean. It supports all life, yet has the ability to crush and destroy, too.

Man is an individualized expression of God, represented by the Ocean. The wave expresses the energy and might of the ocean, is dependent upon the ocean, and cannot exist without the ocean. We are the same. The wave, as an extension of its parent, has the same capability, and so it is with us. We *are* the ocean and the wave in our expanded energy. We are vast, without limit. When we live in the Light, we are the power and the magnificence of the universe.

As a child is a product and expression of his earthly parents, he grows and emulates the character, attitudes, and values of his parents. It is a great pride for the parent to observe his child expanding his abilities beyond his own. This is the metaphor we seek to understand.

In our Heavenly Father/earthly son relationship, we have the same power and capacity of our Parent, but we have defused it by identification with the physical world of form. In other words, we see ourselves as bodies and operate within a three-dimensional time continuum. This perception is our limitation.

To be spiritually mature, we must adjust our identification from earth to Spirit. Before we can understand and develop this potential, we must acknowledge ourselves as greater than a tiny material form living in a 24/7 world of other tiny material forms.

The Bible speaks of man as an individualized expression of God:

Who so sheddeth man's blood, by man shall his blood be shed: for in his image of God made he man. Genesis 9:6

This passage not only states that man is made in the image of God but also points out man's important position in God's kingdom. *Made in the image of God* does not mean that our physical attributes resemble our parent. It means that we have the same energy, power, and qualities of the Father. It is up to us to bring these potentials to maturity. We do this by practicing unconditional love, non-judgment, and forgiveness.

Jesus said:

Ye therefore shall be perfect, as your heavenly Father is perfect.
Matthew 5:48

Thus, we are to practice and demonstrate perfection, completeness, and wholeness outwardly in daily life so that we can fulfill the
plan and image of the Father, for that is our birthright.

Mother Teresa, from an early age, worked to fulfill the plan and
image of God. She is the founder of the Order of the Missionaries
of Charities, a Roman Catholic Congregation of Women who are
dedicated to helping the poor. Born in Skopje, Macedonia as Agnes
Bojaxhiu, she taught in India for seventeen years before she experienced her 1946 *call within a call* to devote herself to caring for the sick
and poor.

Agnes was nine when her father died. She became close to her
mother, who instilled in her a deep commitment to charity. By no
means wealthy, Drana Bojaxhiu extended an open invitation to the
city's destitute to dine with her family and taught her daughter to *never
eat a single mouthful unless you are sharing it with others.*

At the age of twelve, Agnes Bojaxhiu first felt a calling to a religious life. In 1928, at eighteen, she decided to become a nun and set off
for Ireland to join the Sisters of Loreto in Dublin. A year later, Sister
Mary Teresa, as she was called, made her first profession of vows and
was sent to Calcutta.

In Calcutta, she was assigned to a school run by the Loreto
Sisters. This school was dedicated to teaching girls from the poorest
Bengali families. She committed herself to alleviating the girls' poverty
through education. Later, as principal of the school, her prayer was,
*Give me the strength to be ever the light of their lives, so that I may lead
them at last to you.*

On September 10, 1946, Mother Teresa experienced a second
calling that would forever transform her life. She was riding on a train
from Calcutta to the Himalayan foothills when Christ spoke to her and
told her to abandon teaching to work in the slums of Calcutta, aiding
the city's poorest and sickest.

She lobbied for release from her convent for a year and a half. Finally, in January 1948, she received approval from the Archbishop. After six months of basic medical training, she voyaged into Calcutta's slums with the goal of aiding *the unwanted, the unloved, and the uncared for.*

She quickly began an open-air school and a home for the dying and destitute in a dilapidated building that she convinced the city government to donate to her cause. In 1950, she started the Missionaries of Charity with a handful of members. Over the course of 1950's and 1960's, she established a leper colony, an orphanage, a nursing home, a family clinic, and a string of mobile health clinics.

By the time of her death in 1997, the Missionaries of Charity numbered more than 4000. In addition, she left behind thousands of lay volunteers working in 610 foundations in 123 countries on all seven continents. For her work *in bringing help to suffering humanity,* Mother Teresa received many awards and honors, including the Nobel Peace Prize.

Mother Teresa said, *I am the pencil and God is the lead.* Her dedication was to follow Jesus' guidance. She was one of God's vehicles, just as we all can be by listening to the Christ within.

Commitment

The story of Mother Teresa illustrates faith and dedication to following her inner voice of the Christ within and offering unconditional love and service to the poorest among mankind.

Jesus taught the same principle. We are in the earth to understand and express love. The life of Jesus exemplifies the mental phases, conditions, attitudes, and changes through which man passes as he evolves. His story illustrates the lessons, temptations, faith, demonstrations, teaching, trials, and challenges that lead us to transformation. Jesus experienced all of this without confusion. He was always focused, clear, and visionary. He knew who he was: *I AM that I AM.*

When I am in the world, I am the light of the world. John 9:5

Jesus determined at the early age of twelve that he had to *be in his Father's house*. Luke 2:49

This means to be with his spiritual Source, to be about his Father's business, to fulfill his purpose. This determination set his path, goal and activity. He was to live in the consciousness of God, his Father.

Committing yourself to your *Father's house* means to focus on your divine purpose, follow your intuition, and learn to love expansively. It also requires discrimination as you learn through each experience, opening to greater possibilities, addressing challenges, and listening for guidance. Ultimately it signals surrendering to your higher God Mind Intelligence.

Each situation and event, be it job, relationship, or home, offers a learning opportunity. If growth is your purpose, you will find it in every experience. Pursue each phase of your development with excitement and enthusiasm. Even death, clouded with the stigma of negative human opinion, can be perceived as closure to a completed event and the onset to a new, fresh experience for the one making the transition, as well as for those left behind.

Commitment to be in the Father's house occurs at different times. Yet, because each person has the inherent potentiality of Sonship, this desire for oneness with the Father always comes. This is how the Bible describes it:

Then shall two men be in the field; one is taken, and one is left: two women shall be grinding at the mill; one is taken, and one is left.

Watch therefore: for ye know not on what day your Lord cometh. But know this, that if the master of the house had known in what watch the thief was coming, he would have watched, and would not have suffered his house to be broken through. Therefore be ye also ready; for in an hour that ye think not the Son of man cometh. Matthew 24:40-44

A man owns a hundred sheep and one of them wanders away; will he not leave the ninety-nine out on the hills and go in search of the stray? If he succeeds in finding it, believe me, he is happier about this one than about the ninety-nine that did not wander away. Just so, it is no part of your heavenly Father's plan that a single one of these little ones shall ever come to grief. Matthew 18: 12-14

Just as the shepherd rejoices in the finding of his lost sheep, the Father rejoices in our return to his flock. The commitment from the Father to his Son is that *I am with you always, even unto the end of times.*

CHAPTER 2

DESIRE EQUALS MOTIVATION

Sometimes people dream outrageous dreams, go for extreme goals, and achieve them. Such was the case for Edwin C. Barnes, a man of no technical skills or money. Barnes had a dream to work with the great inventor, Thomas A. Edison, and nothing could discourage him for the dream's successful completion.

Barnes traveled by freight train to Orange, New Jersey to meet Thomas Edison. He imagined standing in Edison's presence and requesting an opportunity to carry out his life-long consuming desire to work alongside the great man. Barnes did not just *wish* to do this; he had a *burning desire* to do it. He held this denominating thought for several years and by the time he introduced himself to Edison, it had become his obsession.

When he arrived in Orange, he did not say, *I will try to convince Edison to give me a job.* He said, *I will see Edison and put him on notice that I have come to be in business with him.* There was no question in Barnes' mind that he would become Edison's business associate. Starting in a menial position as a floor sweeper held no threat to Barnes, as it represented a chance to show Edison what he could do. Earning Edison's trust and being privy to the way his mind worked was a huge opportunity.

For Edison's part, he saw standing before him a man of ambition and internal drive. He recognized these qualities because he possessed them as well.

Barnes' relentlessness paid off a few years later as he stood before Thomas Edison as his business partner.

Barnes' story illustrates the power of desire. He started without money and rode a freight train, the only manageable transportation, to reach Edison's laboratory. He never lost his determination or changed his mind. His desire was not about money but the opportunity to learn from a genius. He knew they would accomplish great things together, and his willingness to earn Edison's trust was a bygone conclusion. His consistent effort and unbending vision yielded to the accomplishment of his dream.

Desire also played an important part in the ministry of Jesus. As he went among the people casting out demons and healing the sick, he sought those with the desire to be healed. The demons amounted to negative thoughts and beliefs. Self-abasement, self-condemnation, hate, self-pity, and lack of forgiveness were the mental poisons. These demons sapped strength and ultimately reflected in debilitating conditions and dis-ease.

There is a story in Luke about four men who went to great trouble to deliver a paralyzed man to Jesus. They wanted to avail the man of Jesus' healing touch but found it impossible to get through the crowd to reach him. In their inventiveness, the men devised a solution to their problem by cutting a hole in the roof over the spot where Jesus sat. Can you imagine this happening in today's world? It would certainly be on the nightly news.

As they lowered the paralyzed man on his mat through the roof, Jesus saw their faith and spoke to the man, *Son, be of good cheer; thy sins are forgiven.* Matthew 9:2

The man stood, picked up his mat, and went outside in the sight of the crowd. When desire is strong, inventiveness and determination find a solution.

In his healing work, Jesus saw the Christ in each person. Their minds responded to his knowing and the result was the removal of the illness or problem. As we discover the truth that we are made from divine substance and are without flaw, we can mentally shift our focus, and the body, as an extension of the mind, responds.

Desire for change is what motivates people to transform their thinking. The mind is powerful and will produce whatever you desire. Edwin Barnes is a great example of the determination needed to achieve a shift in circumstances. In this chapter, we will explore desire, the release of fear, and healing.

Negativity, which is grounded in fear, is the root cause of all adversity, such as loss of hope, poor relationships, poverty, and all limitations. Knowing the source of dis-harmony or dis-ease, allows us to effect healing. It is in our hands.

Before performing a healing, Jesus would ask an appropriate question. *And when he was come into the house, the blind men came to him: and Jesus saith unto them, 'Believe ye that I am able to do this?' They say unto him, 'Yea, Lord.'* Matthew 9:28

These questions served as a declaration of the patient's faith and willingness to change. Believing in the Christ as our inner state shifts mental-physical energy. Thus, in the case of the two blind men, the externalized symptom, blindness, was eliminated.

Willingness and desire for healing are the most important factors in procuring spiritual wholeness. Whether the condition be allergy, paralysis, cancer, or depression, you must be sincere in your desire. Healing is not possible without desire. This is true of any change. No desire, no change. This is why folks who trade on their infirmities, even with the finest of care, do not get better. The inquiry is, *Do I really want this?*

Readiness Factor

There are a number of unsure but determined people illustrated in the Bible. Moses did not think he had the ability and intelligence to meet with the Egyptian pharaoh to plead for the release of his people, but he did it. He kept stating his case to the pharaoh and steadfastly held to the belief that he deserved what he requested. Whenever he doubted himself, an inner knowing told him to press on. He persevered and eventually crossed the Red Sea with the Israelites.

Joshua is another example of determination. He walked through the desert for forty years before reaching the Promised Land. He would not stop until he arrived at his goal.

Then, of course, there was David, a mere boy who killed a giant with a sling-fired missile. He faced seemingly impossible odds but maintained his faith, commitment, and courage. And he succeeded.

These individuals are examples of *readiness*. They saw a need and responded to it with grit and determination. We may not be visiting the pharaoh or killing a giant, but we have our own challenges to prepare for and meet. We are in the earth to conquer our own giants, be they real or imagined.

Jesus speaks to this readiness factor in Luke.

And being asked by the Pharisees, when the kingdom of God cometh, he answered them and said, 'The kingdom of God cometh not with observation: neither shall they say, Lo, here! or There! for lo, the kingdom of God is within you.' Luke 17:20-21

This tells us we can experience the reign of God *now*.

Readiness is a factor that works with desire, but desire can be lost when the ego rules the mind. For instance, to the ego, illness and other maladies like losing a job, do have rewards. If you're hooked on receiving sympathy and attention, you may enjoy ill health or poverty. If you don't believe you are loveable, it is affirming when others show up to help. If you really don't like working and are not interested in being in control of your life, remaining without skills may prove beneficial in receiving handouts. Sometimes negative conditions give you power over others. You may control through guilt and manipulation. Illness may keep a family together. Out of concern for a disabled member, the family feigns unity and squelches conflict. It is perhaps superficial unification, but it works.

Being ready to make the changes necessary for transformation is important because many naively believe that illness or tough circumstances are happenstance and arrive without cause. Some even blame God when things go badly. Our state of health, whether physical, mental, emotional, or spiritual, is our responsibility.

Yes, health is our natural state, but we can disrupt it. Negative emotional energy, such as anger, fear, guilt, and shame, creates physical rigidity and restricts energy flow in the body. Over time, the body suffers, organs are deprived, dis-ease occurs. Add poor nutrition, lack of exercise, insufficient sleep, and you have a perfect storm.

It all starts in the mental realm, carries to the emotional, and is manifested in the physical body and world. The body is the last place for energy to express and the body never lies. If you are ill, depressed, or lacking funds, something has gone awry in your thinking. Pay attention to stress. When do you get tense? Why?

The physical condition cannot be brought into balance until the mental state is corrected. That means get ready to let go of erroneous beliefs that may have, in the past, brought comfort. This could be blaming others for your troubles or having the idea that, if someone doesn't love you, it is awful. Ideas of this sort are inefficient and impractical. The belief that you can't stand something or someone is also untrue. Marriages end, jobs are lost, houses are destroyed, and life goes on. At the basis of all things is love trying to reveal itself, trying to move us to a greater reality. Rise above it all and look for a higher meaning.

Here is how the Dalai Lama, the leader of Tibet, deals with negative emotion. A reporter once asked him why he didn't hate the Chinese for overtaking Tibet and killing the people. The Dalai Lama answered, *It would be inefficient.*

Let's look at emotional inefficiency. Living with beliefs that produce negative outcomes is certainly inefficient, especially when your desire is for joy, health, and abundance. In our culture, we have many thought patterns that are inefficient. For example, people live in poverty because they hold the belief of not being good enough, smart enough, lacking talent, or being unworthy.

You can also manifest poverty by holding the idea that money taints you. The truth is that money has no power unto itself. The only power it has is what you give it. Thus, accepting this irrational concept is inefficient because it keeps money away from you and you away from money, as well as from all fun things in life. Exposing limiting beliefs for the erroneous thought patterns they are, and having the determination to change them, will alter your life. In other words, abundance is yours if you agree to it.

If you need proof that the universe is abundant, pay attention to nature. Every tree produces millions of leaves every season. They do this with no strain or hurry. They do this through the natural processes of nature. The sun shines on the rich and poor without discrimination. It radiates 24/7 without concern for running out of energy. Nature is abundant with every kind of flower, bird, and animal you could imagine and more. Nature is always bountiful and never considers lack.

Where is your attention? Do you concentrate on how little you have or what is missing? The adage is that *what you focus on increases*, be it abundance or lack, be it health and vibrancy or illness, be it youth or old age.

To develop an efficient, practical approach to life, honor yourself by designing your thoughts around your desires. Use the example of determined people like Abraham Lincoln, Henry Ford, and Thomas Edison. Focus with determination on what you want, be it health, abundance, loving relationships, you name it.

Money, gems, real estate, stocks, and bonds are simply mediums of exchange. For example, I provide you my services; you recompense me with money. The exchange is impersonal. When you honor the abilities that you offer the world, you command abundance. It is efficient to gratefully receive payment for services rendered.

We all crave harmony and love. It corresponds to our inner divine blueprint.

Face yourself by listening to your words and thoughts. Catch any negative thoughts like jealousy, greed, resentment, bitterness, lack of forgiveness, or fear. Then, make mental corrections. With this practice, you prepare for peace.

The bottom line: when you are finished with suffering and you don't want to put up with the negative repercussions and limitations anymore, it is time to get ready, strengthen your desire, and go to work. You pick up your mat and walk.

You may be ready to seek employment. Think of Edwin Barnes and his determination to get a foot in the door to prove his worthiness to his employer, Thomas Edison. There are always positions available for people with internal drive.

In Matthew 9:22, a woman who suffered from hemorrhages fell into this category. After twelve years of losing blood, she approached Jesus. Her attempt was to touch the hem of his garment so that she might be healed. This woman's desire was strong. Through her faith, she knew that even an indirect contact with the Christ would end her suffering. Symbolically, losing blood signifies losing the life force. By touching the hem of Jesus' garment, she wanted to experience in the slightest way, his essence.

As the story goes, Jesus, representing Christ Consciousness, felt energy flow from his essence. *But Jesus turning and seeing her said, 'Daughter, be of good cheer; thy faith hath made thee whole.' And the woman was made whole from that hour.*

In this example, when the woman's desire was strong, she took corrective action. Through her faculty of faith, she was healed. This story illustrates that even a momentary glimpse of divinity manifests healing.

I knew a woman named Betty, who was extremely obese. For years, she felt humiliated, rejected, and degraded. Despite being told often that her problem was hopeless because it stemmed from endocrine and hormonal dysfunction, Betty reached a point where she decided differently. She made up her mind to change her condition, no longer accepting excuses. Her desire turned into determination. For three months, she fasted on juices and ate little. She sought an extreme solution, but accomplished the seemingly impossible. At the end of that period, she'd lost fifty pounds and looked fantastic.

Her faith restored her to health in the same manner as the woman who suffered hemorrhages. Her readiness factor was high. She had come to a point where she was unwilling to accept that she couldn't have what she wanted. Her single-minded focus paved the way to success. When Betty was ready, her inner voice guided her. And in following that guidance, she became a new person with a new lease on life.

This is true for everyone. When desire is great, follow up action is also dynamic, relentless, and ultimately successful. I often wonder if the memory of her accomplishment helped Betty surmount other challenges as her life progressed.

There is a right time to be enlightened! But as with Betty, a person must be in readiness, desire change, and then act on the intuitive promptings that stem from the desire.

Unconscious Fear

Conscious and unconscious fear produces many negative results, including bad attitudes, self-denial, and dis-ease. Fear, self-doubt, and indecisiveness have hampered many creative ventures. When fear consumes your mind, there is no space for love. Fear and love resonate different vibratory patterns. That is why they cannot house the same space. You have one or the other. To move to a high vibratory space and experience the fullness of Christ Consciousness, fear has to go. Love must dominate your mind to make this connection. That is why we must face our fears. Fear has to be set aside without compromise. The New Testament reiterated repeatedly, *Do not be afraid.*

When the angel came to Mary, the mother of Jesus, he said to her:

'Hail, thou that art highly favored, the Lord is with thee.' But she was greatly troubled at the saying, and cast in her mind what manner of salutation this might be. And the angel said unto her, 'Fear not, Mary: for thou hast found favor with God.' Luke 1:28-30

To the shepherds, the angel said to them, 'Be not afraid; for behold, I bring you good tidings of great joy which shall be to all the people.' Luke 2:10

When the fishermen's boat, which was previously empty, and was now filled with fish: Simon Peter, when he saw it, fell down at Jesus' knees, saying, 'Depart from me; for I am a sinful man, O Lord.' For he was amazed, and all that were with him, at the draught of the fishes which they had taken; and so were also James and John, sons of Zebedee, who were partners with Simon. And Jesus said unto Simon, 'Fear not; from henceforth thou shalt catch men.' Luke 5:8-10

When a man approached Jesus to heal his daughter, who was pronounced dead, Jesus responded: *Fear not: only believe, and she shall be made whole.* Luke 8:50

> *But the very hairs of your head are all numbered. Fear not: ye are of more value than many sparrows.* Luke 12:7

> *Fear not, little flock; for it is your Father's good pleasure to give you the kingdom.* Luke 12:32

Check out the fears below and identify yours. The work is to identify the fear present in your mind and remove your attention from it. It is the same thing as having an unwelcome visitor to your home. You ignore the person and the person ultimately goes away. Identification comes first, then release.

The *fear of being unlovable* creates hopelessness, despair, dependency, and continual compromises to placate others' needs. This person:

+ evades doing what is right
+ avoids voicing an opposing opinion
+ does not make waves
+ avoids *making* others angry
+ is emotionally dependent (co-dependent)
+ seeks others' acceptance (other-oriented)
+ lacks self-acceptance

The person who is *afraid of being alone* will:

+ create co-dependent relationships
+ tolerate offensive behavior
+ make excuses for people's bad behavior
+ lacks mental discipline
+ be unable to quiet the mind
+ lacks confidence and self-love

Typical behavior of someone *afraid of being unloved and insignificant*:

+ self-doubt and self-discounting
+ takes the back seat to others
+ becomes other people's rug
+ inability to receive compliments

The *fear of being wrong* keeps you:

+ stuck in indecisiveness
+ second-guessing and living in self-doubt
+ believing you are wrong and always holding back
+ A person who is *fearful of not being in control*:
+ becomes overly controlling
+ develops paranoia
+ limits potential; stays small
+ manipulates through guilt
+ tends to be angry if things don't go that person's way
+ develops obsessive-compulsive tendencies
+ focuses entirely on the external world

Someone who has *fear of being responsible*:

+ lacks self confidence
+ avoids responsibility at all costs
+ blames the world for everything (other-oriented)
+ has irresolvable issues because the cause is *out there*
+ feels small and insignificant
+ cannot acknowledge a personal place in the world
+ does not register or respect personal talents and gifts
+ is mentally handicapped
+ lacks personal power and vision
+ has a victim mentality

Not taking action to dissolve fear disables the most creative being. I know a talented artist who sculpts and paints beautifully, yet she avoids showing her work and offering it for sale. Her self-doubt keeps her talent small and contained. Her conflict is that she wants to express herself, but she hasn't dealt with the fear that holds her back. She will continue in this dilemma until her courage is stronger than her fear.

Gary Renard, author of the New York Times Bestseller, *The Disappearance of the Universe*, was paralyzed with fear when it came time to start telling his story of having two ascended masters materialize on his couch. They arrived in response to his desire to learn directly from Jesus. They told him that Jesus taught them, and they would teach him. Thus, the adventure began.

His book outlines the story of their visits and ensuing instructions. To make their wisdom known to the world, he had to talk to people. He approached the challenge to speak in public slowly with small conversational-type groups. He ultimately overcame his fear. Now, years later, he travels all over the world to share his story and his teachers' insights.

It is important to let your Light shine and your wisdom flow. In other words, give in to your art and let Spirit be your guide. When you block your creative flow and intuition, you block the energy of higher consciousness. The result is being trapped in the ego and world of illusion and error.

You get the idea. We have been taught the roles of pleaser and victim. Recognize when you are acting out of them because that is when your inner Light is dimmed. It is obscured by erroneous beliefs and judgments. I'll talk more about fear in a later chapter.

This is what Jesus said about being true to yourself:

No man, when he hath lighted a lamp, put it in a cellar, neither under the bushel, but on the stand, that they which enter in may see the light.

The lamp of thy body is thine eye: when thine eye is single, thy whole body also is full of light; but when it is evil, thy body also is full of darkness. Look therefore whether the light that is in thee be not darkness.

If therefore thy whole body be full of light, having no part dark, it shall be wholly full of light, as when the lamp with its bright shining doth give thee light. Luke 11:33-36

Shine your Light. Be your brilliant self. Focus your attention on goodness and let go of fear.

We were created in the likeness and image of God. We are Light. The *eye* refers to the third-eye chakra, which relates to vision. When we are focused intuitively on our inner Light, we radiate. The whole body is lighted up. As you accept and love yourself as a Spiritual Being, your Light shines. This inner Light is what I saw as a child and what I continue to recognize as my true essence. You can recognize this Light in you, too.

The Law of Attraction

When you establish a strong desire to be cleansed of fear and negativity, you set a law into motion. This law is called the Law of Attraction. It works by attracting to you the persons, means, information, and opportunities by which you can be healed or transformed. Strong, clear yearning creates a magnetic pull that draws in everything you need to manifest your desire.

Attraction works through the energy of the subconscious mind. By mentally stating the possibility you desire, you begin the process of attracting it. Within your vast subconscious reservoir resides every possibility. The mind matches up the necessary resources to serve your need, and these resources are made known to you. They come in the form of ideas, inspiration, serendipitous meetings, and opportunities of every variety. As you follow these leads and take action, you are guided to your goal.

For instance, you may remember the name of an influential person who can help, or be informed of a class in meditation or yoga, or hear a radio broadcast that connects you with a particular group or organization. I am sure you found this book through the Law of Attraction.

As I mentioned earlier, there is scientific evidence backing up the existence of a vast, subconscious reservoir of energy. In 1993, scientists verified this field of energy, which is everywhere present. This is the field of energy I spoke of in the last chapter. This energy has intelligence and is affected by what we think and feel. Quantum physicists call this field the Holographic Field, or more currently the Divine Holographic Field. Renowned scientist Albert Einstein referred to it as the Unified Field. It could also be called God, the Universe, or Spirit. The name doesn't matter. What is relevant is that you know about this field because, understanding that you are in and of this field, helps you interact with it and impact it.

In one of his newsletters, self-improvement expert Dr. Wayne Dyer describes it this way:

> Everything is energy. Everything and everyone has a frequency. Those frequencies that are out of balance with our natural harmony can be identified and removed. This is real, it is transforming; it is true healing.

Jesus understood this law and used it to heal many people.

The Law of Attraction is available to everyone. When you think in negative terms, you attract unpleasant outcomes, and when you hold positive expansive ideas, you attract pleasant opportunities. It is your choice. Whatever you choose, understand that using this law can open doors and create opportunities for you. It can also assist you in making conscious connection to God.

Cause and Effect

> And one of the Pharisees desired him that he would eat with him. And he entered into the Pharisee's house, and sat down to meat. And behold, a woman who was in the city, a sinner; and when she knew that he was sitting at meat in the Pharisee's house, she brought an alabaster cruse of ointment, and standing behind at his feet, weeping, she began to wet his feet with her tears, and wiped them with the hair of her head, and kissed his feet, and anointed them with the ointment.
>
> Now when the Pharisee that had bidden him saw it, he spake within himself, saying, 'This man, if he were a prophet, would have perceived who and what manner of woman this is that toucheth him, that she is a sinner.' And Jesus answering said

unto him, 'Simon, I have somewhat to say unto thee.' And he saith, 'Teacher, say on.'

'A certain lender had two debtors: the one owed five hundred shillings, and the other fifty. When they had not wherewith to pay, he forgave them both. Which of them therefore will love him most?'

Simon answered and said, 'He, I suppose, to whom he forgave the most.' And he said unto him, 'Thou hast rightly judged.' And turning to the woman, he said unto Simon, 'Seest thou this woman? I entered into thy house, thou gavest me no water for my feet: but she hath wetted my feet with her tears, and wiped them with her hair. Thou gavest me no kiss: but she, since the time I came in, hath not ceased to kiss my feet. My head with oil thou didst not anoint: but she hath anointed my feet with ointment. Wherefore I say unto thee, Her sins, which are many, are forgiven; for she loved much: but to whom little is forgiven, the same loveth little.' And he said unto her, 'Thy sins are forgiven.'

And they that sat at meat with him began to say within themselves, 'Who is this that even forgiveth sins?' And he said unto the woman, 'Thy faith hath saved thee; go in peace.'
Luke 7:36-50

This story illustrates the principle of Cause and Effect. The Pharisee with whom Jesus dined was judging on appearances. Jesus, on the other hand, looked at intent and action. In every situation, there is cause and there is effect. You drop a crumpled paper from your hand and it lands on the floor. Releasing the paper is cause; landing on the floor is effect. The principle is impersonal. The woman in the story performed the service of cleansing Jesus' feet with perfume and tears because she loved him. This established cause. Jesus acknowledged her devotion and service. The result or effect was forgiveness of sins.

Many people do not understand Cause and Effect because they believe that we live in a punishment-reward universe. If we are good, we are rewarded, and if bad, punished. Allowing that what is good or bad is left to interpretation, if we follow this line of thought, dis-ease of the physical body and poor attitudes of the mind might be considered punishment. Many people view it this way. If struck with illness, they lament a punishing God. However, life does not work this way.

Dis-ease, the disruption of physical-body ease, is the result of a cause set into motion. Dis-ease within the body or mind occurs by violating natural laws. When you hold a thought pattern in your mind, it registers in the field of energy in which you live, and it attracts a corresponding condition, a mirror effect. This process is called Cause and Effect. Understanding the workings of Cause and Effect can help you develop objectivity, perception, and intuition. It is never about punishment. There is no punishment. It is always about experiencing an effect from a cause.

A farmer sows corn in his field. That is the cause. The effect is a harvest of corn. If the same farmer chose to sow weeds, he would end up with a field of weeds. The field is neutral. It nourishes whatever is sown.

The mind works the same way. It is neutral and accepts whatever thoughts you plant. Sow thoughts of worry, limitation, and lack and that is what grows. On the other hand, thoughts of greatness, success, and possibility produce expansive results. If you want positive outcomes, you must weed out negative, limiting thoughts and ideas. It is necessary to discipline the mind toward the outcome you desire.

If disharmony is your experience, look for cross-purposes in your belief system. For example, you may want wealth, but believe that money is evil. The conflicting thoughts create the cause. The universe receives two diverse signals. Thus, the effect is confusion and chaos. That is what you attract.

Another example of Cause and Effect would be driving your car too fast, violating the speed limit, and getting a speeding ticket. You violated a man-made law by speeding: the cause. You got a ticket: the effect. You may not have known you were going too fast until a policeman informed you with a ticket, but it was an opportunity to learn. It was not a punishment. This example shows one way you learn how the principle of cause-effect works, and how you can change your actions to adjust the outcome in the future.

You may feel angry and unforgiving toward someone, filling your body with toxic, tight, restrictive energy. When restriction is present, energy cannot flow. It is stuck. Energy builds up and blocks organic functions, thus creating an adverse effect on your health. The cause in this case is anger, which creates a domino effect of negative outcomes in the body and results in inflammation, probably of the liver. The person toward whom you feel anger is fine.

Sometimes we turn on ourselves with criticism. If this continues, the body becomes inflamed. All dis-ease starts with inflammation.

Anger (inflammation) + lack of forgiveness = restriction.

Restriction (being stuck) + time = dis-ease.

How can you change the scenario? You can begin by recognizing your mental state and choosing to let go of anger while forgiving the person or yourself. In so doing, you release repressive energy in the body and are able to revert back to your natural state of health. The body knows how to be healthy when the blocks are removed.

Louise L. Hay in her renowned book, *Heal Your Life*, gives the example of forgiving the person who harmed her in her childhood. Through forgiveness, she was able to cure her cancer. Emotions are powerful. They can heal and they can harm. It is always your choice.

With honesty, vision, and perspective, you can learn how to harmonize with the universe of Cause and Effect, and your health can be restored. Health is ever available. You are free to change cause and adjust effects anytime you want.

Jesus made a powerful point in the story of the Pharisee and the girl who washed his feet. It is a point that is stated repeatedly in the gospels. Whatever has been done in the past or whatever debt is owed, it can be forgiven. When you set your mind to love and you live a life of love, sins, which are simply mistakes or errors of the past, are forgiven. Everything is adjusted according to the Law of Cause and Effect. You are always the one that sets up the causes. Therefore, you are the one responsible for the effects as well.

SECURITY or *security*

Lay not up for yourselves treasures upon the earth, where moth and rust consume, and where thieves break through and steal: but lay up for yourselves treasures in heaven, where neither moth nor rust doth consume, and where thieves do not break through nor steal: for where thy treasure is, there will thy heart be also. Matthew 6:19-21

In this verse, Jesus states clearly that it is important to take note of your values. What is your treasure and what does security mean to you? Material treasure can be corroded, destroyed, or stolen. Heavenly treasure, wisdom, cannot be destroyed.

Security is the subject here. The material world can never be secure because it is always moving and changing. Physical matter is unstable. Objects begin to deteriorate the second they are created. Nothing remains the same. Your inner Self, on the other hand, is stable, as it never changes. It is the same today as it was yesterday and will be tomorrow. It is based in love. Stability and security are the same thing. Your inner Self is secure because it is always stable and loving. As you go within, as in meditation, you will experience the same energy again and again. It is Light, soothing, and calm. It is never worried, frantic, or chaotic.

We have the option to focus on the wealth of the soul, which is wisdom, or attempt to create material opulence and hope that provides a sense of safety. The two are vastly different and the one does not exclude the other.

Inner security requires knowing who you are. You are a child of God, expansive, talented, strong, and responsive. No matter what challenge you face, you have the ability to determine a viable solution and live in peace, knowing you are loved, approved of, and provided for.

The other kind of security relates to protecting the ego. A fear-based person ever seeks options to be liked by others, make sure everyone is happy so as to avoid conflict, and build up a good monetary fund in an attempt to feel secure. The problem with this effort is that it is based on the instability of the ever-changing, material world, which shifts and modifies daily. Today, there is peace in the world; tomorrow there is not. Today the stock market is up and money flows; tomorrow it has crashed.

Insecure people are generally unable to see the bigger picture of where the universe is taking them. They try to control outcomes because they identify strongly with the status quo. Therefore, their effort to change is weak. They may reason out the need for change but are not fully invested because they lack vision and courage. Many simply want to remain invisible in their tribe of like-minded people. Thus, stepping out of the box or having a different point of view can be threatening. Fitting-in is their real goal. Personal and spiritual transformation would be a daunting exercise for them, as it requires letting go and rethinking every belief and behavior.

What produces a positive outcome and what produces a negative one? Observe and become objective. Learning how to step back and become observant is important because that is how objectivity is developed. For instance, if you are standing on the top of a building at the corner and you see a car driving down the street below on one side of the building and a different car driving along the road on the other side, you could calculate when these two cars would meet. Depending on their rate of travel, road conditions, and amount of light, you could predict what would happen when they meet. It would be a matter of observation. There is no emotion in observing.

When you have the ability to see *above* a situation, determining your next move is easy. If you get too involved in how you want things to turn out, instead of how they appear to be proceeding, you miss the point and the outcome. Therefore, if you are able you are to stand back and observe the workings of the universe without getting your opinions or jaded viewpoints in the way, you have a distinct advantage. You can cultivate security because you are not fighting the energy or flow of events as they occur. This is the stance of a wise person.

There is a story that further explains cultivating an objective view of life. It is about a horse that was tied outside a shop on a narrow street in a Chinese village. Whenever a man tried to walk past the horse, the horse would kick him. After a while, a crowd of people gathered and began debating how best to get by the hazardous horse.

Soon, someone came running, announcing, *The Old Master is coming. He'll know what to do.*

The crowd waited anxiously.

As the Old Master turned the corner, he saw the horse and immediately spun around to walk down another street. The Old Master had observed the situation and chose to avoid an unnecessary struggle. His attitude was one of ease. This is how a person cultivates inner security.

Creating a solid working relationship with your higher mind demands discipline. You must consistently adjust thought and behavioral patterns by addressing and releasing fear, then replacing it with love. The first step is to recognize fear-based thinking. Then you have the ability to course-correct.

Collapsing into old, comfortable roles may seem easier than disciplining your mind toward something better. The old ways are negative and limiting, but comfortable in their predictability. You know what to expect. When fearful, you make excuses that hide your resistance to change. You protect yourself and your ego so you can remain unchanged in your comfort zone. Being different, i.e., daring to walk to a different drumbeat, risks the loss of people with whom you have related. The truth is that comfort is your enemy. It will keep you from growing.

If your desire for wholeness is not great, it might be easy to let disharmony or illness take its course. Perhaps, preserving your place in the tribe, which could be your family, friends, ethic group, political alliance, or religious affiliations, is more important because it seems safe. In that instance, learning to identify with higher energy would be threatening.

I knew a young man names Bob who really wanted to be an evolved being. He read all the spiritual books and attended the latest seminars. He could verbalize all the concepts and principles of mastery with ease. He became a walking encyclopedia. It was as though someone could press a button and he would pour forth wisdom, but the wisdom was flat because he talked about it but did not live it.

Underneath it all, Bob possessed a hidden guilt that he had not been mature enough to help his father in his business during his father's last days on earth. Bob's guilt blocked his vision. He continually sought peace by seeking knowledge, but peace was not available because he did not have it in his heart. As he neglected to address his guilt and unconscious fear that he had failed his father, peace moved further away from him. In recompense, he lived in a bubble of make-believe and this is where he resided when he took over his dad's business after the funeral.

The business was not profitable as Bob continued to live in the shame of his immaturity and lack of preparedness in being unable to help his father. His difficulty in being successful was predictable because Bob's business involvement stemmed from guilt, not desire. His inability to make a profit affected his marriage and children, as well as his own self-worth. It took a long time for him to face the fact that he was letting guilt run his life.

Bob's example is not unusual for many people do the same thing. They deal with consequences but not causes. They make emotional decisions that are not logical.

In Bob's case, it would have served him well to admit that he had not been able to provide his father the assistance he needed during a critical time, then commit himself to be the kind of husband and father his family could rely upon. In other words, he could learn from the past and move forward with a commitment to grow in his circumstances.

The point here is that living in the fear of not having been good enough and the accompanying guilt, kept him small and operating in ego. He had neither inner security nor material wealth. Both would evade him until he could get honest, forgive himself, and start anew.

Simply reading holy books and studying under magnificent illumined masters without incorporating what you learn is useless. It will not effect change, nor will it help you feel secure. At best, you become an encyclopedia of New Age principles. And possibly create a lot of personal confusion.

Trial and error, falling down and getting up again, is an important way to learn. Failure does not exist because we are always learning. The act of trying again is a mark of success. The ego cannot win if you continue to challenge the status quo and push against the boundaries. In the process, you are building heavenly treasure: experience and wisdom.

By viewing every experience impersonally as coming from your inner teacher, the Universe, you will intuit the next step and action.

You are putting into play the Law of Cause and Effect. Through this process, you illuminate the breadth and depth of your capabilities. You expand into your rightful, exalted place in the universe.

To recap, desire motivates action. Action brings on personal transformation. Practical application of truth principles transforms personality and diminishes the ego. On-going spiritual practice produces a stable, secure, confident self.

Spiritual transformation is not an intellectual exercise. It is the result of lots of practice of listening intuitively, forgiving, and offering love.

With effort, you can accomplish anything. That includes inner security. Your relationship with God, the Universe, is what makes it all possible.

CHAPTER 3

THE ROLE OF FAITH

esire is important in affecting change, yet it is no more vital
than faith. Faith is the belief in something unseen. Everyone
has faith. We believe in a variety of things, and we may believe
differently about things than others, but we all believe.

You have faith that when you flick on the light switch, the room
is illuminated. Even though you have never seen electricity with your
physical eyes, you trust it is available in the wiring of the lamp, and that
the electricity will ignite the bulb when summoned. This simple act is
taken for granted; yet consider an aborigine flicking on the same switch.
He would be astounded and amazed. Electricity is not something he
assumes. He has no faith or belief in electricity.

You know electricity is a positive force because you have seen it
work and used it for useful purposes. The same force can be destructive.
People have been burned and even died from electrocution. In itself,
electricity is neither good nor bad. It is neutral. We can use it to our
betterment or to our demise.

This same thing is true of faith. We all have faith in something.
Perhaps you are using your faith productively, trusting that things will
turn out well, that people are essentially good, that you will always have
what you need. Or, you might be putting your faith in illness, money
problems, being over-weight, bad luck, futility, etcetera. No matter how
you focus it, positively or negatively, faith works. If your mind holds

a picture of your preferred outcome, the light goes on, your body is healthy, and there is money in the bank. Your faith produces the result you seek.

Faith is spoken of many times in the Bible. Here are a few quotes from Jesus:

> *And the Lord said, 'If ye had faith as a grain of mustard seed, ye would say unto this sycamine tree, Be thou rooted up, and be thou planted in the sea; and it would obey you.'* Luke 17:6
>
> *And Jesus answered and said unto them, Verily I say unto you, If ye have faith, and doubt not, ye shall not only do what is done to the fig tree, but even if ye shall say unto this mountain, Be thou taken up and cast into the sea, it shall be done. And all things, whatsoever ye shall ask in prayer, believing, ye shall receive.* Matthew 21:21-22

Mahatma Gandhi of India was a great example of the power of faith. Gandhi was a humble man without money, weapons, or any external symbols of power, yet he wielded more influence than any other man in his time. What Gandhi did have was faith in the unifying principle of fairness and equality. He held to this principle and transferred it to the minds of two million Indian people. Because of his belief and willingness to put himself on the line, he led his people in non-violent resistance and helped free India from British rule. His faith was powerful and true.

Talking Yourself Out of the Good Life

The way we get into trouble and create ego-attachment, pain, and struggle is by trying to live by irrational belief systems. Everyone has been exposed to these. They are based on the idea that we are separate from God, the Universe. Yet, we are *never* separated from our Source. As Jesus repeated, *I Am that I Am*, you are the *I AM* also. Anytime you choose to look within, you can experience the Light and feel Love, and that is the creative principle of I AM.

It is important to correct irrational, erroneous ideas because if we don't, we are basing our lives on lies that weigh heavy on the soul. Thinking rationally unchains the ego-drama and allows us to live in creative freedom.

Following are a few irrational ideas that most of us were taught. Of course, there are many more, but you will get the idea.

1) It is of dire necessity that I be loved and approved of.

This is a big one. People have given away their souls over this false idea.

Beverly, for instance, wanted her mother-in-law's approval, so she became a people-pleaser. She showed up at all the events, contributed food, and helped out. When she did this, she stole time from the things she really wanted to do and even the things she needed to do. Over time, she felt angry, resentful, and guilty because, inwardly, Beverly wanted her own life. To top it off, she didn't really like her mother-in-law, Shirley. She found her to be tedious, picky, and judgmental—not at all fun.

When I asked Beverly what would happen if Shirley did not like or approve of her, she had no answer. The idea of disapproval sent Beverly into a tizzy because it broke her rules of conduct. When she settled down, she realized that it was a lie to pretend to *like* Shirley and another lie to care what Shirley thought of her. Her deeper truth was that if she only attended the events she cared about and only contributed when she wanted to, she could become her authentic self. She not only did this with her in-laws but with everyone. Beverly eventually developed more confidence and self-trust. She began to experience more freedom and fun. She was happier.

2) It is awful, catastrophic, or terrible if things do not go or stay the way I want them to.

This is another common belief. Because the ego is so fragile, it wants to control everything. The way I *want* things to go is *the right way*. Think about the audaciousness and arrogance of this idea. Who is to say what is the *right* way? Is there a right way?

We all have preferences because we want to live joyful, prosperous, secure lives. But to believe that we have the only formula for everything to go perfectly all the time is ludicrous. Part of maturing is accepting that if things don't go exactly as we prescribe them, it is okay. In fact, it could be an amazing gift.

For example, Joe was a senior engineer at a manufacturing plant. At some point, there was a mistake in the production of a product. Since Joe was the top guy, the buck stopped at him. He lost his job. *Woe is me*, was his first response. Then he realized that he had always wanted to start his own business and now that he had been fired, he had time to do it. He followed this realization by creating an amazing, profitable technology-oriented business. It was not awful, catastrophic, or terrible that things went a different way than what Joe originally expected. It ended up being a huge blessing.

Everyone has a story like this whether it involves a job, a relationship, or some other endeavor. What's your story?

3) *The world, and especially other people, should be fair and justice should always triumph.*

Wow, what anguish stems from this irrational belief. Can you feel it? This belief is naive and suggests that we get to decide how *other* people should be.

Arella is a great example of putting her faith in the fairness of other people. She was divorced with children. Because of some legal issues that occurred years before and were consequently settled, Arella lost custody of her children. At the same time, she believed that her ex-husband, the father of her children, would be fair in allowing her sons time with their mother. The children clamored for their mom and calmed down considerably when they spent time with her.

Fairness, in her mind, amounted to him being a prince and putting the welfare of their children above all else. That translated to mean that, since their boys needed their mother's nurturing attention, he would graciously make sure they got it. Arella was putting her idea of fairness on her ex-husband without bothering to see if he held the same belief, which he didn't. Why didn't she know this, you ask? *Denial!*

In the end, Arella had to face the situation as it was and enter a court battle to get equal custody of her children. She also had to deal with the truth that everyone has their own idea of fairness and justice. Her belief did not rule the world. The Universe worked through cause and effect. She didn't get to redesign the system.

Ultimately Arella empowered herself and became the strong model of womanhood and motherhood she needed to be. That is when she got her kids back. Was there a powerful outcome? You bet! Did Arella learn and transform? Definitely!

4) Happiness and unhappiness are externally caused and I cannot control my emotions.

This is a beaut. The truth is that happiness is inside you. It is not external. You can most certainly manage your emotions. In fact, it is required that you manage and choose your emotions well if you want to have control over your life.

For example, when traffic is tied up for miles and you are running late, when your boss or spouse is in a bad mood, when the payment is overdue, you can still decide to be at peace. There is a reason behind these circumstances. You may not have caused them, but they pose an opportunity.

The traffic tie-ups offer you time to breathe and relax. Put on some music, call your friend, or take a break. You are not going to get there on time anyway, so chill.

Who knows why your boss is in a bad mood. Bosses do that sort of thing. Bless him. If you did something incorrectly, correct it. If not, do your work and let him be in a bad mood. Don't take it personally. Things may not be going well in his life. He has a right to his disposition.

So the bill payment is overdue? Pay what you can or call the company and tell them what's going on. Come up with a strategy. Figure it out. There is always a way. Melting down won't help and neither will self-pity.

5) There is a way to be and act that will please everyone.

All right, if there is a way to please everyone, would someone please tell us? The truth is, there is no way. In fact, people get to spend their entire lives being disgruntled and unhappy. It is a choice. Being rich, for instance, may please you, but be clear that it would not please everyone. Some folks actually believe that it is wrong to have wealth. Who would guess?

Bonnie is a great example of confusion between her desires and her beliefs. It would have pleased Bonnie greatly to have wealth, but her beliefs have kept her muddled, stuck, and unhappy. She actually had a fear of money.

Bonnie was frugal by nature. In her life, she had learned to put away money for emergencies and to make do with what little she had. Nonetheless, she always wished she could buy a big house with all the trimmings like some of her friends and acquaintances.

One day, a friend invited Bonnie to go with her to look at million-dollar homes that were on display for a grand opening. Bonnie was mesmerized by the houses and wished she could afford one. As they walked through the rooms, she talked about how she would decorate them. A little later, however, when they got in the car, Bonnie said with some venom, *People with money are all crooks.*

That is when Bonnie admitted her belief that having money would make her look like a crook. Her belief that people with money were evil translated to anger and kept her from manifesting her desire to own an expensive house and all its trappings. Despite the fact that Bonnie would like to have more money, as long as she holds to the idea that wealth equals dishonesty, she will keep money from appearing abundantly in her life.

Consider another aspect of having good things, like taking a fabulous vacation. This seems quite appealing to most people, yet some focus on how much it would cost, the amount of time it would take from work, or even the inconvenience of planning it, thus destroying the possibility of enjoying it.

If giving complements and being kind is your way of pleasing, understand that there are people who would immediately distrust and dislike you for those kinds of actions. Your intentions come across as incidental to your words and actions. Distrusting people look for negative motives.

Ultimately, people come from many different backgrounds, outlooks, and motivations on every topic imaginable. There is simply no way to act and be that will please everyone.

6) *Love should be earned. Therefore, I won't give love freely.*

Withholding love hurts *you*. It denies your connection to God, the Universe, which is love. Thus, the one that suffers is *you* because you are disconnected from your Source. Also, by holding this concept, you are accepting the idea that you must *earn* love. That creates a dire emptiness of love in your life.

If you choose to withhold love, you do not understand the nature of love. No one has to earn it. It is abundant at all times. The folks who hold this belief are seeking love externally, which is transient. They are not looking to a deeper source of love. To think that love must be earned buys into the idea of a punishing God. God *never* punishes.

It's easy to love. Just *see* the Light within each person and don't focus on behaviors. When you find yourself closed and withholding love, switch your mind to forgiveness. Start with yourself.

The bottom line is, when we live irrationally, we suffer. It is yet another distraction keeping us from the Light. In other words, we are to be about the Father's business and live as our authentic selves. Radiate the loving presence that you are.

Here are a couple of stories. See if you can spot the lies.

Ruth came to me for counseling at the behest of her doctor. He was frustrated and having a hard time helping her to improve her health.

Ruth was in her sixties. Her first question to me was, *Do you think I'm too old to be helped?* She reiterated her age often, informing me of her unwillingness to do the work to alter her physical condition. When I assured her that age was not a factor, she countered with lack of funds.

Even though, Ruth was depressed and in pain, she was not ready to change. On the contrary, she was armed with excuses. She clearly did not want to take responsibility for her condition or its remedy. Later, it came out that being ill was the only way she got attention from her husband. *Aha!* There was a benefit to her ill-health.

Ruth's story is not unusual. Many people do not want change. Most have invested a large part of their life in victimhood. Often with illness, they command attention and a bit of power. Letting go of poor-me attitudes divests them of power. Their problems serve them.

Ruth minimized herself because she did not have faith in her ability to be loved. She was dependent for love on her husband. In creating this contingency, she denied herself love. She lived in virtual spiritual poverty at the same time that love exists everywhere.

Her story reminds me of the fish who swims around the ocean looking for water. The fish is completely surrounded by water, yet cannot see it.

Mary is another story. When asked, *How are you?* she described a litany of illnesses and ailments that went on for several minutes. In a heartbeat, she could supply dates, locations, and all the details for each. She identified with disability, carrying it around like an ID card. Anyone could predict her future: more sickness and infirmity. It was her focus.

Nonetheless, Mary would be the first to evoke God for healing. She never saw the dichotomy between her prayers for healing and her focus being consumed with disabilities. Essentially, her prayers were answered efficiently. She was given plenty of disabilities. The law is neutral. It works like electricity, which depends on the way a person uses it. If Mary had focused her faith on health, joy, and abundance, that is what she would have received.

Ruth and Mary are great examples of using faith to keep themselves small and helpless. The power of faith is often taken for granted. It would benefit everyone to check himself on where he places his faith and make sure he is focused positively. In Ruth's case she could learn to love herself by providing herself with the loving attention she needs. That could be taking time to do the things she loves or developing positive self-talk.

In Mary's situation, she could adjust her focus to all the ways that she is a good, kind, and productive person. That would help her see how she might contribute to the wellbeing of others and the world.

This would not only empower her, but it would take her focus off her own dilemmas and, more than likely, reduce them significantly. She would also feel great because when you help others, you are helped as well.

In the earlier example, Bonnie's lack of monetary abundance started in her mind as the disempowering belief that money and dishonesty are somehow connected. If she were to examine that belief and recognize the irrationality of it, she could open herself to more abundance in her life. The truth is there are lots of wealthy people who build hospitals and fund charities.

A Course in Miracles, claiming to come from the channeled voice of Jesus, states: *The mind requires healing. All illness starts in the mind. Correct the mind and the illness disappears.*

All illness and all lack start as mental concepts. Change the mind and the results change. Remembering we are all abundant with many blessings helps us to live joy-filled lives.

The Power of Faith

And when he was entered into Capernaum, there came unto him a centurion, beseeching him, and saying, 'Lord, my servant lieth in the house sick of the palsy, grievously tormented.' And he saith unto him, 'I will come and heal him.' And the centurion answered and said, 'Lord, I am not worthy that thou shouldest come under my roof; but only say the word, and my servant shall be healed. For I also am a man under authority, having under myself soldiers: and I say to this one, Go, and he goeth; and to another, Come, and he cometh; and to my servant, Do this, and he doeth it.' And when Jesus heard it, he marveled, and said to them that followed, 'Verily I say unto you, I have not found so great faith, no, not in Israel. And I say unto you, that many shall come from the east and the west, and shall sit down with Abraham, and Isaac, and Jacob, in the kingdom of heaven: but the sons of the kingdom shall be cast forth into the outer darkness: there shall be the weeping and the gnashing of teeth.' And

Jesus said unto the centurion, 'Go thy way; as thou hast believed,
so be it done unto thee.' And the servant was healed in that hour.
Matthew 8:5-13

The significance of faith as demonstrated by the centurion is reiterated in Jesus' ministry. In the following case studies, it is helpful to identify with the victim. In this way, you internalize the experience. Remember, not all who came to Jesus were healed. There were those who left unchanged because of lack of faith.

Jesus asserted the necessity of faith in affecting healing. To the Canaanite woman with a sick daughter . . .

Jesus said unto her, 'O woman, great is thy faith: be it done unto
thee even as thou wilt.' And her daughter was healed from that
hour.' Matthew 15:28

And behold, they brought to him a man sick of the palsy, lying on
a bed: and Jesus seeing their faith said unto the sick of the palsy,
'Son, be of good cheer; thy sins are forgiven.'
And behold, certain of the scribes said within themselves,
'This man blasphemeth.' And Jesus knowing their thoughts said,
'Wherefore think ye evil in your hearts? For which is easier, to
say, Thy sins are forgiven; or to say, Arise, and walk? But that ye
may know that the Son of man hath authority on earth to forgive
sins.' (then saith he to the sick of the palsy), 'Arise, and take up
thy bed, and go up unto thy house.' Matthew 9:2-6

Faith and courage are coupled in each treatment. Faith requires courage. Have the courage of your convictions. Be courageous enough to act on your faith.

The metaphysical meaning of Capernaum is *village of consolation; shelter of comfort; covering of compassion; covering of repentance.* It refers to an inner conviction of the abiding compassion and restorative power of being. When one enters this state of consciousness, a healing virtually pours out of the soul and transforms all discord to harmony. It is this great soul compassion and yearning to help humanity out of its error that creates the so-called *natural healer.*

Capernaum is also defined as *covering of repentance*. This indicates a cleansing of the mind, both conscious and subconscious. In this repentant attitude, the individual is ready to alter his thinking.

Such a person, the paralyzed man, lived in the outer realms of consciousness where materiality reigned, but with Jesus' assistance, he had come to realize that there was another inner realm where he could know spiritual truth. In other words, the healed person has given up guilt, sin, or error and claimed wholeness. As a result, health is restored in the mind. A new mental picture reigns.

To reiterate, *A Course in Miracles* indicates that all illness is in the mind. It is pictured and held in the mind as an idea or possibility. The body follows the mental picture by precipitating it into form.

In our culture, positivity stands out because we are inundated with volumes of negativity, political drama, war, and general craziness. When someone declares positive possibilities, like health, prosperity, and freedom of expression, he is viewed as strange, weird, out of the norm, a silly Pollyanna. However, by focusing on the positive, you keep company with leaders such as Winston Churchill, John F. Kennedy, Mahatma Gandhi, Thomas A. Edison, and Jesus. Facing judgment by others is a small price to pay for enlightenment.

Remember also that negative judgments come from people who are afraid. Jesus addressed these folks thusly:

And Jesus said, 'Father, forgive them; for they know not what they do.' And parting his garments among them, they cast lots. Luke 23:34

Anyone who chooses to be negative, critical, and judgmental truly does not know what they are doing to themselves. Others' opinions cannot hurt you unless they agree with them. Negative opinions emanate from small minds and narrow viewpoints. You need not perpetuate them, fight them, or defend against them. Simply hold to your practice. The truth is Love and nothing is more powerful.

A Course in Miracles declares: *You cannot destroy anything that is real, and the only thing that is real is love.* That is to say the only thing that is on-going, consistent, and permanent is love.

Maintain your vision until it has formed or manifested in your life. There is nothing so outspoken as success. You can't argue with it.

It shall be done to you, as you believe. Your words speak your reward or punishment. Discipline your faith to outpour all the riches of life you deserve as a child of God. Let your power be in your faith.

CHAPTER 4

THE GOSPEL

Jesus proclaimed the gospel and cured all manner of disease. He admonished his disciples to do the same. Both dictates must be followed to speak the truth, to love, and to correct existing disharmony within yourself. Gospel is an Anglo Saxon word derived from God, good, and means *story, tidings.* Thus, proclaiming the gospel refers not only to speaking truth but living it according to the good news delivered by Jesus.

By following the guidelines laid down by Christ, we learn to live in harmony with ourselves, connect to our Inner Source, reach our potential, expand awareness and creativity, and express without limits. The teachings are good news because, through them, man takes command of himself.

The universe operates according to an orderly process of law. We call these Universal Laws or Principles. Webster defines law as a rule or principle stating something that always works in the same way under the same conditions. Thus, a law is regulated, dependable, and consistent. It always produces the same results under similar conditions.

We see law at work daily as we witness the sun rising or the ocean tides coming in and going out, all according to a predictable, calculated pattern. Law is also exemplified as we observe a person with fervent desire reach out for help and receive it, or see someone tenaciously seek an answer and find it. Desire, which is intention, is the foundation of law and acts as a catalyst for setting up appropriate responses.

Here is what Jesus taught about seeking and finding:

And I say unto you, Ask, and it shall be given you; seek, and ye shall find; knock, and it shall be opened unto you. For every one that asketh receiveth; and he that seeketh findeth; and to him that knocketh it shall be opened.

And of which of you that is a father shall his son ask a loaf, and he give him a stone? or a fish, and he for a fish give him a serpent? Or if he shall ask an egg, will he give him a scorpion?

If ye then, being evil, know how to give good gifts unto your children, how much more shall your heavenly Father give the Holy Spirit to them that ask him? Luke 11:9-13

The science of physics refers to Universal Law with the axiom: *For every action there is an opposite and equal reaction.* This law of action and reaction is also the Law of Cause and Effect. You can observe this cause-effect relationship everywhere. When a person acts with negative intention, to harm or steal from another, that person predictably reaps a similar consequence and may be harmed or robbed. Contrarily, when someone acts out of sincere concern, interest, and enthusiasm, the reward follows suit: opportunities open up, people are kind, and the way is made easier.

When we understand the workings of Universal Law, we recognize why people such as Helen Keller, with seemingly great adversities, were able to achieve so much.

In Helen's case, she was unable to see, hear, or talk; yet she became one of the most fulfilled positive people of the twentieth century. Helen passionately wanted to function like other people. On the advice of Alexander Graham Bell, her parents applied for a teacher to the Perkins Institute for the Blind in Boston. From that school, they were blessed with a magnificent teacher. Anne Mansfield Sullivan brought her extraordinary instruction to the girl and, ultimately, turned out to be the answer to her call for functionality. It was through Anne's amazing instruction that the little girl learned to understand and communicate. Helen went on to acquire an excellent education and became a world-renowned author, lecturer, and crusader for the blind and deaf.

The maxim is this: *Ask and you shall receive.* It is God's promise. When you ask, you are offered opportunities. By taking advantage of the opportunities, you achieve your goal, just as Helen Keller did.

Steven Spielberg, a skinny, shy, unknown mediocre high-school student is another example of this law at work. He was fixated on film. Even as a child, he created his own movies. Camera in hand, he turned his family home into a studio and followed people around, recording everything. He was determined to be in the film business. He boldly met people and persistently learned from them. He put no limits on his creativity and used it in broad, imaginative ways. Eventually, Spielberg went on to become involved with five of the top-ten grossing movies of all time. He knocked at the universal door and it opened for him.

These people used universal principles. They created a vision, sought appropriate education and opportunities, and persistently took steps until they reached their goals. They sought and they found. With each step, they graduated to the next. Their vision remained ever-present in their minds.

Look back at your own life and consider the changes you have made. Things you once hoped for are now in play in your life. Perhaps it is the type of work you are doing, your hobby, home, friends, travel, or the opportunities to express your talents.

You cannot think too big. The universe has no limits. Your only limit is your imagination.

What was once considered a disabling flaw or handicap can be navigated with innovation and imagination. Take this principle to heart. What is it that you want and previously considered pure fantasy?

In 1994, George Rickles lost both hands and most of his forearms in an accident that brought his carpentry career to a dramatic end. Rickles loved working with wood and was determined to return to carpentry. This led him to be fitted with prosthetic hooks. Volunteers for Medical Engineering designed tools and a special toolbox, just for him. Rickles is patiently building proficiency with his beloved power tools and learning a new way to do carpentry. Because he holds his vision strong, his future looks promising.

Jesus made the promise that, if you ask, you shall receive. That is how he described the workings of the Universal Laws. We see evidence of the mechanisms of these laws in the examples of Helen Keller, Steven Spielberg, and George Rickles.

You also use these laws. Every day, when you arise, your first thoughts predict your day. Your tone and expression, optimism or pessimism, willingness or resistance, set the pattern. Are your thoughts projecting what you really want?

You are constantly creating through your thoughts and actions. By consciously recognizing the power of this creative ability, you can observe and expand the possibilities. It is true that you can have or be anything you want. Remain true to your intention and learn to use the power of thought appropriately.

In physics, it is stated that we live within an energy field of possibilities. There are thousands of possibilities for how things can work out and the kind of life we can live. The possibilities we choose, think about, and act on are the ones that manifest.

Consider the various ways you can travel to work: walk, bike, run, skateboard, roller-skate, drive, fly, possibly swim, take a boat, or snow ski, depending on the terrain. Once you choose one of these possibilities, it becomes a reality for you. Why? Because you have registered it in your mind.

Just because you have chosen a particular possibility does not mean it is the only one that exists. Often a person thinks, *This is the only life I can live, based on my family of origin, religious training, amount of wealth in the family, and various other factors.* The truth is there are thousands of possibilities. At any time, you can change your mind and choose another possibility. Consider the stories of people like Keller, Spielberg, and Rickles. They expanded their possibilities. They did not let circumstances or serious physical or emotional limitations decide for them. They realized that the possibility they desired could be a reality. You are never stuck because the field of possibilities is limitless.

In the Gospel, we are instructed in the laws of love, expression, believing and knowing, cause and effect, attraction, service, and command. It is up to each of us, as evolved intelligence, to direct these laws. This is how we will come to know ourselves as God beings.

At each moment, you have the option to unleash your divine potential and achieve personal freedom. You have the choice to follow your intuitive knowing or man-made laws. One will lead you to higher levels of creativity and the other will guide you to tribal consciousness and captivity in a prison of rules and dogma. Negative focus creates mental bondage, attachment, and physical-world engrossment. It is all about choice.

Within the good tidings of the Gospel, there are many instructions on how to make the best use of your experiences and live as a God-being. In this chapter, we will explore these instructions.

Therefore I say unto you, All things whatsoever ye pray and ask for, believe that ye receive them, and ye shall have them.
Mark 11:24

Man's Potential

The good news of Christ put no limits on man's ability to be or do anything he desired. Nathan Stooke is a great example of a no-limit person.

Nathan Stooke, a St. Louis entrepreneur and the owner of Wisper ISP, was born in Grand Forks, North Dakota. Raised as an Air-Force brat, he lived all over the U.S. Although he grew up with a learning disability, dyslexia, which faced him with problems anew in every school he entered, he didn't let it stop him from developing his entrepreneurial skills. At the age of nine, he opened a lemonade stand in his neighborhood. In college, he went on to study programming and created a PC-building business, Stookeware, in his dorm room.

Stooke did not feel disabled because of his learning disorder. Instead, he claimed that living with dyslexia helped him discover innovative ways to turn learning into a catalyst for success. By 2003, he had put together plans for building a wireless network near St. Louis. After testing equipment and developing a dedicated team, Wisper Wireless Internet was born. His company mantra is: *Wireless is what we do. Service is our passion.*

Can you feel something ready to happen? Can you feel Stooke's fire?

Stooke spread his company across Illinois and into Missouri. In the process, Wisper Wireless has made thirteen strategic acquisitions and grown into a three-million-dollar company. Stooke has been featured as a *Top 30 under 30* by *St. Louis Business Journal*, a *Top 100 St. Louisans to Know*, one of *St. Louis' Top Small Companies* by the *St. Louis Small Business Monthly*, and featured in a story called *Getting his Employees to Financial Peace*.

Nathan Stooke established a no-limits philosophy early in life. Along the way, his commitment to service has helped cultivate loyal customers as well as a dedicated workforce. Most of his original team members are still with the organization and represent 150 years of experience in the industry.

His ongoing vision is to create standards in the wireless industry, establish Wisper as a household name, and serve customers everywhere with excellence. Today he teaches seminars on *The Formula for Business Growth—Hiring Rock-Star Employees*.

There are many stories of people like this who have succeeded despite disabilities, difficult childhoods, and various other issues and disorders. Because we are made of God Energy, we have the capacity and ability to rise above adversity and expand our talents and our success accordingly. Stooke is a great example of living the potential of the God-Self. He personifies the high standards, dedicated efforts, and excellent customer service that are possible for all of us.

We all have a vision. What is yours?

God is love. Therefore, everything created by God reflects love. Inherent within every particle of creation is love. If you were to gaze into a high-powered microscope and look past the quarks, atoms, molecules, and matter of any material substance, you would discover light. The primordial Light is the foundation and basis of all matter.

We live in a sea of light-energy. Our bodies are aglow. That is why when you love deeply the Light within intensifies. If you look closely, you will notice light emanating from people's faces. The greater the radiance, the happier and more loving that person tends to be. It is an interesting phenomenon.

Every part of humanity and particle of creation has within it an ideal of purity, goodness, and purpose. Each of us is a particle of God's creation, which is in the continuous process of expression. It is our inner drive to express outwardly in the world the ideal we hold within. This inner ideal of perfection is our guide and teacher. Our compulsion is to live a high-energy dynamic life of integrity. Jesus stated this motivational principle in these words: *Any man who desires to come to me will hear my words and put them into practice.* Luke 6:47

As we listen to our inner voice of intuition, we can feel the desire for growth and expansion. It is an inner drive and potential. It is from that place that we come to the Christ by putting truth into practice, by directing the Laws creatively and constructively.

> *The disciple is not above his teacher: but every one when he is perfected shall be as his teacher.* Luke 6:40

That is what the drive is about, to be on a par with our teacher, the Christ.

We have always known truth. As babies, we knew we were special. We laughed, sang, gurgled, and expressed as the spirit moved us. When we wanted something, we made our desire known. It did not occur to us to ask if it was convenient to feed us or to change our diapers. A baby expects to be loved and cared for and generously returns the love received. As babies, we are celebrated. Every gurgle, crawl, tooth, and step is met with applause and positive reinforcement. Babies are pure expressions of love. But what happens to this purity and innocence?

Because most people tend to identify with physical bodies and twenty-four-hour days, we have constructed the idea of limitation. Since the material world is often referred to as the real world, the unlimited nature of Spirit is lost.

Limitation is reiterated when good and bad is preached. We are told we are capable of doing this but not that: limitation. We are told that females must follow certain gender roles and rules while males must fulfill others: limitation. You are good if you do what you are told and bad if you don't: limitation. All these are self-diminishing and limiting beliefs.

Soon, the specialness we knew as babies is lost in the maze of programming. We adopt a new set of rules: man-made rules, dogma.

We are taught to believe what we see and ignore our feelings. Our eyes and senses become focused on the material world, and we turn away from our inner Light. We learn the rules and do what is expected of us. We follow the model of our earthly teachers. Soon, we are living in the darkness of the ego's need for acceptance and status.

As attention is turned from our universal Source of truth, the external standards of man are assumed and we become engrossed in the material aspects of life. Our goals become tangible and materialistic, identifying with position, status, houses, cars, ownership, a title, and money. With this identification, along with its entanglements and limitations, our possibilities become narrowed.

We accept strange ideas. For example, we believe we cannot succeed without a college education, and it must be from the right institution, and then we must add on a higher degree. We can't succeed without knowing the right people or living on the right side of the tracks.

We attempt to live according to these precepts and do what we are told and what is expected of us because we want to be *good* and *approved of*. Eventually, however, we burn out with frustration and insecurity.

How can we tell we have become domesticated? This is the sign: believing only what we see with our eyes. We lose touch with what we feel. And so it is that we perceive only a tiny spectrum of life. We ignore intuition and get in a lot of trouble. It does not work. It does not make us happy.

> *The lamp of the body is the eye: if therefore thine eye be single, thy whole body shall be full of light. But if thine eye be evil, thy whole body shall be full of darkness. If therefore the light that is in thee be darkness, how great is the darkness!*
> Matthew 6:22-23

This passage can be interpreted two different ways. If your eyes are good, your body will be filled with Light. If you see the Light in every person and situation, your body and whole being will be filled with Light. If your eyes are bad, your body will be in darkness. When you seek only the *maya*, illusion, of the physical world, your body will be darkness. In fact, your whole being is veiled with the illusion of duality: bad/good, judgment, guilt, shame, and sin.

With the second interpretation, the eye refers to our inner intuitive eye. When we look with our intuition, which is the direct line of communication and awareness of God, we are filled with Light and possibilities. If we disavow our inner Light, our life is truly dark, for again, we are making the world of duality real.

This external focus is what we must reverse to return to the love, trust, innocence, and openness of a child. In Luke 18:17, *Come into the Kingdom as a child*, refers to being open to truth and the gifts of Spirit.

Children are not intellectual. They don't possess huge vocabularies. They don't judge, but they do know how to feel. They listen to their intuition. They know how to trust and be vulnerable. They feel bad around mean-spirited people and good around loving ones. No one has to teach them this. The same innate knowing holds true of flowers and birds. Jesus speaks of this natural trust and openness.

And he said unto his disciples, 'Therefore I say unto you, 'Be not anxious for your life, what ye shall eat; nor yet for your body, what ye shall put on.

For life is more than the food, and the body than the raiment.

Consider the ravens, that they sow not, neither reap; which have no store-chamber nor barn; and God feedeth them: of how much more value are ye than the birds. And which of you by being anxious can add a cubit unto the measure of his life? If then ye are not able to do even that which is least, why are ye anxious concerning the rest?

Consider the lilies, how they grow: they toil not, neither do they spin; yet I say unto you, Even Solomon in all his glory was not arrayed like one of these. But if God doth so clothe the grass in the field, which to-day is, and to-morrow is cast into the oven; how much more shall he clothe you, O ye of little faith? And seek not ye what ye shall eat, and what ye shall drink, neither be ye of doubtful mind.

For all these things do the nations of the world seek after: but your Father knoweth that ye have need of these things. Yet seek ye his kingdom, and these things shall be added unto you. Fear not, little flock; for it is your Father's good pleasure to give you the kingdom. Luke 12:22:32

When you listen to the voice of intuition, you learn to trust. You become a believer because you feel the guidance of spirit. Just as you don't have to see electricity to know of its power, you don't have to see God to recognize God's guidance.

Jesus saith unto him, 'Because thou hast seen me, thou hast believed: blessed are they that have not seen, and yet have believed.' John 20:29

When we meditate, we close our eyes to the material world and move our attention to the quiet of our inner Self. As Jesus calmed the seas, we can tell ourselves: *Peace, be still!* Mark 4:39

By quieting the mind and focusing on the rhythm of the breath or on our inner Light, we turn our attention to our Source. We reacquaint ourselves with who we really are. The inner Light is stable, always the same, never changing. It is our stability. Light is open and expansive, never sorrowful. Pain and death do not exist. Spirit goes on forever.

Death, angst, sorrow, and pain become figments of the imagination of the mortal mind. They do not occur within the changeless immortal mind or soul of man. When we seek our inner Light, we are free.

Mental freedom offers the liberty to explore possibilities and ideas, to scout out truth, to consider the seemingly impossible, as many have done before you. Mental freedom lets go of silly ideas that bind the movement and flow of the mind. This is the way you open to the creative flow of the Universe: conceptual expanded possibilities. Imagine incredible solutions.

A little critter lived in the water near the bank of a river. It fed off elements within the river. Sometimes there was food to eat, and sometimes there wasn't. Either way, it clung tightly to the bank because it believed it would surely perish if swept away in the river's treacherous current. On the days when the current was particularly strong, the critter became exhausted from the effort of clinging, yet it would not let go because it was terrified by the idea that releasing the bank would insure its demise.

One day, overwhelmed with exhaustion, the critter could no longer hold to the bank. It released its grip. Tumbled and tossed by the tide, it was swept downstream. In a relatively short time, it landed in a beautiful pool of calm, pristine water. The critter looked around and saw that an abundance of food surrounded it, food that would require no struggle to obtain. It suddenly realized that, if it had trusted the river, it could have had this peaceful, abundant existence sooner.

Thus it is with each of us. We can let go and trust Spirit, allowing it to take us to a place of greater peace. Or, we can hold on, trying to control our circumstances with struggle and effort. Letting go requires courage and faith. Holding on keeps us small and in fear.

When you experience the freedom of Spirit, a corresponding physical effect occurs. Since the body always reflects the mind, tightness and tension are released when you let go. The body returns to its natural rhythm and function. When you shift your mental construct, a coordinating physical effect ensues. *A Course in Miracles* calls this shift in perception a *miracle*.

Health and vibrancy are man's natural state. The body knows instinctively how to be healthy. It doesn't know how to express health in a tight, restricted encasement. Like the water of a brook being dammed, it cannot flow until the obstruction is removed.

Hence, by turning your vision to the God within, sorrow, pain, and death cease to exist. These conditions, being figments of the imagination of the mortal, egoic mind, have no reality or substance in the immortal mind, the soul. Align your thoughts to truth; you are Spirit, and you are free.

Ye shall know the truth, and the truth shall make you free.
John 8:32

Truth refers to an inner understanding of the Laws of the Universe, which are constant, consistent, and never changing. They can be practically applied to one's circumstances. In other words, every time you explore a new concept, try a new approach, reach a new awareness, or draw a broader conclusion, you are utilizing the Universal Laws of expansion and experiencing truth. Each truth is like adding another puzzle piece to the picture. Once set in place, each piece, each truth unmasks the grand scheme of life. Truth liberates the truth-seeker. Each discovery sharpens clarity and vision.

An idea is felt intuitively first, then analyzed. Careful consideration opens possibilities. For instance, the idea that God is love, which is felt, reasoned with, and understood, changes the quality of the seeker's life. *You shall know it in your heart* means to measure truth intuitively in your heart.

The Wright brothers serve an example of listening with the heart, i.e., intuition, and following the guidance diligently. They did this in their quest to create a flying machine.

Wilbur and Orville Wright were two American inventors and aviation pioneers who are credited with inventing and building the first controlled, powered, and sustained heavier-than-air human flight machine on December 17, 1903. Orville had three years of high school and Wilbur had four years, but neither let their lack of formal education interfere with their dream of developing a flying machine. After having worked for years in their shop with printing presses, bicycles, motors, and other machinery, their mechanical engineering skills were honed.

Working on bicycles, particularly, influenced their belief that an unstable vehicle like a flying machine could be controlled and balanced with practice. They conducted numerous experiments and trials over years before they realized victory. Through that time, they never let the idea that they were simple bicycle mechanics interfere with their vision of flight or their determination. As a result, they lived to see airplanes flying all over the world. It was their development of aerodynamic controls that made it all possible.

When your mind is open and willing, amazing innovations are born. What has your intuition been saying to you?

The mind of man is pure potential. By opening your mind in the same unprejudiced manner of a child, you can connect with your divine potential. The child does not know limits. It operates from the drive to know, the curiosity to seek, and the courage to try. Nathan Stooke used his disability to innovate. The Wright brothers used their natural engineering skills to invent. We can use the circumstances of our lives in the same way. They can be the catalysts for success as well.

Unfolding the Blueprint

Every healing performed by Jesus holds a lesson of metaphysical truth. Peering beneath the surface reveals the true import of each so-called miracle.

Jesus, the archetypal man, symbolizes man's evolutionary movement as he educates himself to truth and releases concepts of mortality and limitation. Christ refers to the energy of perfect or fluid expression. Jesus, who incarnated into this world with a name that meant *God is With Us*, signifies an individual expression of God. This individualized expression is the Christ.

Everyone has an identical inner blueprint attempting, even pushing at times, to make its presence known. An acorn has the blueprint of a full-grown oak tree imprinted within it, just waiting for the right conditions to burst forth. Given those conditions, the acorn grows to its full potential, becoming a giant oak tree and duplicating the majesty of its parent.

We are like the acorn. Our circumstances, including our country, parents, friends, schooling, career, work, and everything else, are the soil, water, and sunshine we need to nurture our seed of divinity. These factors set up the conditions whereby we express the rhythm and harmony imprinted in our souls. Every thought we think, every attitude we express, every action we take, and every word we speak are part of the process. They create a potential vehicle for our demonstration. They also determine the rate and quality of growth. That puts us in charge.

When I was a child, I felt trapped within the fear-based concepts of my mother. Although she loved her children deeply, she was plagued with fear that expressed as anxiety. She was so distressed about everything that she was unable to sit still. I would became equally jittery just being near her. Even when she was attempting to relax, she would literally shift continuously with nervous energy.

Mom also readily expressed her concerns and complaints, which were many. It seemed that nothing anyone did was right or good enough. She had a hyper ability to find something wrong with everyone's actions and words. Even though she was a dedicated parent and would do anything for her children, I found it extremely taxing to be around her.

At some point, I came to understand that her anxiety and criticalness was based in fear. She was always afraid. For that reason, she was unable to control her nervousness. Her biggest concern stemmed from being out of control, which she was in many ways.

As a child, I had made a vow to do anything in my power to *not* be like my mother. Now, I am aware that was a negative, unproductive goal as it placed before me a negative image against which to measure myself. If instead, I had decided that I wanted to be peaceful, positive, motivated, and joyful, that would also be choosing to not be like my mother. And it would have offered a positive vision to work toward. But then, what did I know? I was a kid.

Later in life, I noticed I would annoyingly find a piece of lint that the vacuum didn't pick up or a spot of dust on the furniture after the house was cleaned. Or I would run a conversation through my mind repeatedly to find a better way to communicate my thoughts. It was tedious, like being with my mother. I had developed this patrolling aspect of myself that was ever on the lookout for what was wrong or incorrect. *Yikes!* I had become my mother.

I examined this quality of criticalness and recognized that, underneath it, I was always looking to make things perfect so my mother would be happy. That was actually a silly goal because Mom was never going to be happy. But there I was, a self-created critic. And I was good at it.

Now, I know that God does not give us anything that is not ultimately useful, so I decided to figure out what it was about criticalness that could be helpful. I already possessed the quality, so why not make positive use of it rather than tear down everyone's efforts, including my own?

Did you know that every quality we possess has both strength and weakness? It all depends on how your use it. That became the premise from which I operated. I found I could be a hard worker and I could work myself to death. I could be happy and, at the same time, ignore issues and never resolve anything. There has to be a balance. Thus, my mission was to figure out what to do with my natural ability to find the error, the flaw, or the thing that was out-of-whack. And I did it. Here's how.

Discrimination is a practical use for a critical mind. It means recognizing when things don't match up, when there is a piece missing to the puzzle, when something doesn't feel quite right. I cultivated discrimination. I chose to focus it by understanding situations, how people got stuck, when and how they made the wrong turn, and how to help them adjust their tracking systems to manifest their desires. I used it to dig deeply to find answers. It worked. As a result, I helped myself and many others because I have converted a detriment to an asset. I have honed the ability to find the flaws and correct them. It has became my gift.

Yes, there is a positive application for any quality. It is up to you to find it. What is the aspect of yourself that you find most annoying? How can you convert it and use it to your advantage?

This process is how we perfect our understanding and evolve. Through our external world experiences, we discover our errors and misperceptions. We learn how to love and forgive. We refine and self-correct. Our circumstances reflect our mental-feeling state. It is all cause and effect.

In time, we come to realize what love is and is not. It is expansive and unconditional. It is not judgmental and limited. The result is self-love. As we accomplish self-love, loving others becomes easier. It is then that we brilliantly reflect our Christ nature.

Jesus therefore said to those Jews that had believed him, 'If ye abide in my word, then are ye truly my disciples; and ye shall know the truth, and the truth shall make you free.' John 8:32

The truth is that we each have an internal blueprint that helps us develop as Christ-beings. Review your life and the circumstances and the people that continually show up. What are the challenges? How might you use them to grow and express in larger ways?

Your inner blueprint is your gift and your guide. Step back and observe what life is teaching you. Flow with the river and let it take you where it will. The outcome is greater joy and productivity. Try it! You'll like it!

CHAPTER 5

THE BODY AS A REFLECTION OF THE MIND

J esus employed a variety of techniques in his healing practices. He noted the patient's physical complaints and evaluated his mental and emotional states as well. This complete analysis revealed the underlying nature of their disorder. As mentioned earlier, my mother's disorder was fear; mine was self-criticism. These effects formed the circumstances of our lives. Individual choice played out with my mother and myself.

We all create our problems and we have a magnificent ability to resolve them as well. It is always a matter of choice.

All dis-ease begins in the mind, in the realm of thought. If inharmonious thought can cause body dis-ease, then love, harmonious thought, can create the opposite effect: health. Inner pressure, intensity, jealousy, guilt, anger, fear, hate, and lack of forgiveness create destructive energy patterns that eventually wear down the body's resources and result in inflammation and illness. Whereas calmness, peace, love, and forgiveness support a relaxed, healthy energy pattern that produces vibrancy and well-being.

My mother eventually died from cancer, which is an inflammatory disease and matches perfectly with her energy pattern of fear and worry. She was not able to achieve a peaceful state until the very end of her life, and she never understood how her thoughts contributed to her physical condition.

The physical world is our schoolroom and it provides a neutral instrument or mirror for us to objectively recognize the nature of our thoughts. In other words, every thought and reaction is reflective of beliefs and attitudes, which, in turn, show up in the physical body. The body and material world are the conclusive places for energy to express itself.

Your experiences unerringly mirror your state of mind. They are your teachers, a gift from the Universe. For example, if you are continually running into angry people, you might want to look at your own anger. Or, if you are connecting with failure, disappointment, and victimhood, check to see if this is your life's view.

You may not see any of this until you are willing to accept responsibility for your life. Often situations repeat before a person is ready to look within and make changes. People have blind spots. The ego loves to blame others. Yet, healing begins with self-responsibility.

I knew a man who wanted desperately to believe that others were responsible for his lack of ambition and success. He had parents who were uneducated and unsophisticated. Exhibiting industriousness, he went to work as a delivery boy when he was quite young. Not only did this job give him great experience but it supplied the money he needed for the things he wanted to buy. The experience could have taught him that he had the ability to make his own life better. Yet, his belief was that if he had different parents, he would have been availed of greater opportunity and a better life. That was his story and he was sticking to it.

The problem with his story is twofold. First, he did not give himself credit for what he had accomplished, which was a paid-for college education and a fine career in a hard-driving industry. Secondly, by not taking responsibility, he was focused on others being at blame for the lack he envisioned in his life. It gave him an easy out. By making others responsible for his predicament, he had given away his power to be more successful. The bottom line was that he was covering up a lot of resentment, which was killing his spirit and ambition.

These negative emotions of blame, resentment, and anger burst forth in an inflammatory disease that inhibited his physical movement. He had already blocked his emotional and spiritual progress with his critical thought process. The negative energy eventually took hold in his physical body and created disability. The truth is that he had always been disabled because he would not let go of blaming others for his shortcomings. He carried this behavior into his adult life by blaming his boss, his wife, his kids, and the neighbors for whatever he deemed to be wrong.

Negative emotions are expressed in a variety of ways. Anger may not be present externally, but it is still toxic and works against a person. Private pity-parties work the same way.

You may have someone in your life who is highly judgmental and on self-examination, you note that you are also judgmental, both of others and yourself. You have attracted this harsh person so that you can take ownership and change this aspect of yourself. Life reflects the positive and the negative energies you hold within.

I knew a kind, generous man named John. One day, he was driving behind his son Henry as they traveled through a small town where they knew no one. Henry's car broke down, so John followed his son to a local garage. The garage was about to close for the day, but the employees were willing to stay and look at Henry's car. Quickly, they ascertained the car needed an alternator. A swift call was made to an auto-parts store, which was also getting ready to close. The manager in the store obligingly stayed open past closing time so that the John and Henry could pick up the part. The alternator was quickly installed and Henry's car was humming with new life.

As John went to pay for the work, the owner told him, *I don't want any money. Your boy reminds me of my son. He is out and about fishing and hunting in various places. I want him to be able to get help from strangers when he needs it. So, I don't want your money.* The owner stuck adamantly to his words.

Confronted with the generosity of strangers, John and Henry were speechless. They found the kindness of the garage owner, his crew, and the manager of the parts store overwhelming.

This incident is a good example of cause and effect. This father and son experienced their own kindness reflected in the actions of strangers. This law is unerring in its execution. Whatever you put out, you get back in kind.

Occasionally, we make poor judgments. Perhaps we are rude to a sales clerk or steal the paper clips from the office. These actions do not mean that we are wrong or bad. They indicate only that we are inexperienced and must continue to learn. We are spiritual children.

When a baby sticks his finger in his ear and pulls it, he experiences pain. We do not call the baby bad or stupid. He is young and has not yet learned the parameters of his body. As the baby continues to learn, he will come to understand that pulling his ear hurts. The Universe never judges or censures. It just provides another opportunity to learn.

Man acquires knowledge from his decisions and actions. Progress is made by reviewing choices and deciding what works and what does not, deciding which situations serve and which do not. Consider the motivation and intention behind each action. As you understand the cause/effect associated with each manifestation in your life, you learn how to create desired effects at will.

Develop objective self-assessment, not chastisement. It is a tool for growth. There are no random experiences. Each experience represents a link in a never-ending chain of growth and possibility.

Is it not written in your law, I have said, 'You are gods.'
John 20:34

Can Illness be a Clue?

The body is a reflection of the mind. For example, if you discover that every Monday morning, following the regularly scheduled staff meeting, you have a migraine, you might deduce a connection between the pressure in your head and the meeting. On further reflection, you may remember your jaw tightening when your boss scrutinized the previous week's production figures because you felt responsible for these numbers. Reviewing the incident, you can deduce that your inner pressure resulted in the headache.

Perhaps on deeper analysis, you discover guilt. *I haven't done enough.* Or helplessness. *I can't do more.* Or over-responsibility. *It's all up to me.*

Now, you are enlightened regarding the cause. Your underlying beliefs create incredible mental-emotional tension that progressed to the body. Recognizing cause helps you make changes. You don't have to live with headaches, but you do have to face your beliefs and make appropriate adjustments.

Have you really not done enough? Are you really helpless and have no resources or ideas? Is it really up to you and no one else? What is the truth?

It might be time to lay your cards on the table with the boss, get clear about your responsibilities and what you can and cannot do. Unrealistic expectations, either yours or his, become barriers to a productive, joy-filled life. If the demands are too high, yours or his, or if your employer has overestimated your capabilities or under-estimated other contributing factors, let this be your fact-finding mission to make the necessary adjustments. Be unwilling to live with undo pressure. Confront the problem and correct it.

Other possibilities include such things as you being overly sensitive to pressure, too afraid to ask for help, or feeling guilty about factors outside your control. All of these elements can be dealt with successfully by recognizing them and making alterations. By objectively evaluating physical symptoms and uncovering their source, you can become aware of new options. There is no valid reason to live in pain.

The physical body is a symbol. Every organ and part represents a mental concept, a materialization of that concept. The eyes, for instance, symbolize the perception of truth. When visual problems are indicated, as in the example of the blind man of Bethsaida, we have consciously shut ourselves off from perceiving.

He called to him the multitude, and said unto them, 'Hear, and understand: Not that which enters into the mouth defiles the man; but that which proceeds out of the mouth, this defiled the man.' Matthew 15:10-11

Spiritual/Physical Blindness

And they come unto Bethsaida. And they bring to him a blind man, and beseech him to touch him. And he took hold of the blind man by the hand, and brought him out of the village; and when he had spit on his eyes, and laid his hands upon him, he asked him, 'Seest thou aught?' And he looked up, and said, 'I see men; for I behold them as trees, walking.'

Then again he laid his hands upon his eyes; and he looked steadfastly, and was restored, and saw all things clearly. And he sent him away to his home, saying, 'Do not even enter into the village.' Mark 8:22-26

Bethsaida is a Greek word taken from Hebrew and means *house of fishing*. Interpreting the story symbolically, house represents the mind or state of consciousness of the individual, and fish signifies spiritual substance or knowledge. This location, Bethsaida, indicates a place where the individual seeks spiritual knowledge. Thus, the theme of this healing indicates that new spiritual awareness, forming within the mind of the man, literally opens his eyes and understanding.

By identifying with the blind man, for we are all blind at times, we can examine the events of the story. Note that Jesus took the blind man's hand and led him outside the village. Village refers to a state of mind or belief. The village illustrates a thought system the man had grown used to. This old habitual pattern needed alteration. Hand represents purpose. Jesus took the man's hand and, with purpose, led him away from his old beliefs.

Remember, Jesus symbolizes our inner divinity. Jesus put spittle, Christ substance, on the man's eyes. Eyes represent perception. He laid hands on him. He touched the man with Christ-purpose, so that the blind man could let go of old ideas and illusion. With the increase of

Christ Consciousness and following two treatments, the man's sight was restored. The number two symbolizes decisiveness. Jesus sent him home with the admonition; *Do not even go into the village*, meaning that he was not to return to his old thought pattern. He was not to be around those who would question his recovery. He was not to doubt or challenge his new found sight.

As we reconnect to our natural condition of harmony, we are able to see with new eyes. Our purpose becomes clear. The illusion of blindness was corrected for the man Jesus healed, and it can be corrected for us as well.

Removing guilt and lack of forgiveness leads to seeing clearly who we are. We let go of the illusion of past hurts and negative emotions. We change our minds and we are healed.

When an inharmonious situation presents itself, you must lay hands on yourself. Take hold of your perception. Are you a material or spiritual being? Ask yourself, what is this situation trying to teach me? With persistence and decisiveness, your perception will clear and you will know your purpose. Then, you will not want to return to old, negative thought patterns. It is always appropriate to examine issues of guilt and lack of forgiveness. These patterns lie at the center of most disharmonies.

By treating the body as a symbolic instrument, new ideas open to you. For instance, ears symbolize receptivity—our ability to hear. Hearing problems stem from lack of receptivity—or possibly choosing to ignore your intuition. Many people hear but do not listen. Deafness indicates closing down, unwillingness to deal with life. You may notice this with stubborn, inflexible people. They focus on negative outcomes and refuse to see it any other way. That is their way of demonstrating lack of receptivity.

The story of Wilma Rudolph serves as an example of someone refusing to accept limitation. She was born prematurely; her survival was doubtful. At age four, she contracted double pneumonia and scarlet fever, which left her with a paralyzed left leg. She was told she would never walk again. She refused to accept this.

Wilma walked with the support of a metal brace until age nine, at which time she decided to play with the other children. She simply took off her brace. Walking was awkward at first, but by age thirteen, she had developed a rhythmic gait. It was considered a miracle.

That same year, Wilma decided to become a runner. With every race she entered, she came in last. Even though everyone told her to quit, she didn't. Eventually, she won one race and then another. Soon, she won every race she entered. She went on to win three Olympic gold medals.

She told the public, *My mother taught me very early to believe I could achieve anything I wanted. The first was to walk without braces.*

She also said, *I love the freedom in running, the fresh air, the feeling that the only person I'm competing with is me.* The freedom of running allowed her imagination to soar. She used the power of her mind to believe in herself, to keep going, and to use her imagination to define and solidify her goals. She refused to be blinded by what seemed to be a disability.

Wilma Rudolph chose her own destiny. She chose to live without limits.

As God-beings, we have the same power. The discipline to direct our mind is our power. Like Wilma, we can refuse limitation and focus on what we want, and then go after it.

Other Emotional-Physical Maladies

Teeth are tools for assimilating food. Food symbolizes knowledge. Life is constantly providing food for thought, allowing our knowledge to expand. How do we assimilate this knowledge? Difficulties with teeth or gums indicate a need for a closer scrutiny of our beliefs and reactions. What do we need to assimilate? Are we resisting a lesson? When we ask these questions, a wealth of information comes through,

Dis-eased skin conditions symbolize self-effacement or self-condemnation. Eczema, acne, rashes, or moles indicate over-criticalness, harshness with self. Consider relaxing and accepting yourself, warts and all.

Being hard on yourself creates many problems. Over-sensitivity may show up in the body as anxiety and insomnia. It may also manifest as hypertension. When you get hooked into others' opinions and become overly concerned with saying and doing the right thing, your perspective is lost. You are stuck in the world of form and directed away from your spiritual source. What others think of you or anything else is none of your business. Becoming distracted in the pettiness of the world keeps your attention in the world and keeps you from growing.

I know a woman named Louise who admits that she has a *tender heart*. That translates to feeling vulnerable and getting her feelings hurt easily. Because she has not gotten clear in her own mind that she is a beautiful, talented, worthwhile child of God, she has looked to others for this affirmation. Her *tender heart* could be remedied overnight by confirming her true identity. Recognizing her Christ Self would give her confidence and strength.

Learning to live in the truth of your exalted nature takes practice and discipline, but the results are tangible and definite. You get to live a glorious life of freedom. The Bible says that the *truth will set you free*. Remember who you are. You are God; you are Love. Let this truth elevate you. Then, if disgruntled people show up in your life, you will smile, knowing that their troubles are about themselves and have nothing to do with you. Your heart with be strong as it is filled with love.

Continuing on with physical-emotional maladies, problems with movement, crippled legs, or paralysis, can be taken literally: not moving forward or progressing in life. If this is your affliction, look for something you are holding on to that is stalemating growth. Often there is the misperception that, by staying put instead of moving on, you will be safe. That premise has proved illusory more times than not.

Wilma Rudolph overcame her crippled status when she decided to move forward and change her circumstances. Her story shows that a radical disability can be overcome by creating a different mental picture. She set goals and worked toward them step by step.

The feet symbolize your spiritual foundation, the underpinning of your ethics and values. Disturbance or loss of this foundation represents instability in your understanding. In other words, you are not acting on ethics or values as you know them. Perhaps you are treading the path of wrongdoing.

Body deformities symbolize feelings of guilt, not loving self, or even taking part in cruel practices, such as inflicting injury on another in this life or a past life. Deformities can also arise from ignoring or denying the needs of the physical body. Simply put, not honoring yourself or creating an internal state of deformity can be out-pictured into material reality.

Referring to past lives, we do bring into this lifetime the lessons that were unresolved in the past. Just as in a regular school, if you do not pass math, you get to take it again until you learn what is necessary. As spiritual beings, we do not get to by-pass lessons. That includes our treatment of others. If we have implemented cruel practices, we get to experience the consequences of our actions, which might be presented as a deformity.

Through the Law of Cause and Effect, we are held accountable for present and past practices. The bottom line is that there is an effect for every cause or intention, positive or negative.

There is also a solution. At any time, you can choose to change. Change comes from daily practice, discipline, and courage to live up to your ethics and spiritual precepts of kindness, unconditional love, and forgiveness. As you gain control of your thoughts and intentions, eliminating cruelty of any kind, the direction of your energy will be adjusted, as well as the outcome.

Here is a story of a former gang member that illustrates perfectly the fact that, at any time, a person can change direction.

When Dweisi Mfume was eleven, his step-dad abandoned the family. When he was sixteen, his mother died of cancer. At that point, his life spun out of control. He quit school and went to work to help support his sisters. He worked up to three jobs in a single week. He also began hanging out on street corners and drinking with friends.

I ran with the worst people and I became the leader, he said to *U.S. News and World Report*. *I was even locked up a couple of times on suspicion of theft because I happened to be young and black. And before I knew it, I was a teenage parent, not once but five times.*

However, Mfume's life changed on a July night in the late 1960's. He had been drinking with his friends when suddenly he began to feel strange. *People were standing around playing dice and everything else, and something just came over me*, he remembered. *I said, 'I can't live like this anymore.' And I walked away.* Mfume spent the rest of the night in prayer.

From there, he proceeded to earn his high school diploma and pursued a college degree. He went on to get his graduate degree from John Hopkins University, was elected to the Baltimore City Council, and then to Congress. As a congressman, Mfume became one of the most well known African-American politicians in Washington, DC. Believing he could achieve more to advance civil rights, he began working for the National Association for the Advancement of Colored People (NAACP). He eventually left congress to become president of the organization.

Mfume made a choice that he had to live from a higher reality than being a gang member. By taking matters into his own hands, he made broad, sweeping changes in his life, his intentions, and the imprint he placed on the community and the world. It all started with self-examination.

What are you holding in your mind as truth? People tend to believe that their thoughts do not have power, but they are incredibly powerful. Negativity can keep a person stuck inside a diseased or crippled body or in stifling, negative circumstances. Or we can use our thoughts to transform to a higher reality.

Adjusting our beliefs as we achieve deeper understanding is referred to as a *miracle* in *A Course in Miracles*. Shifting perception and belief is a miracle because, when we let go of stagnant ideas, we open to a mental freedom and that energy transfers to the body.

Do a survey on yourself. Do you hold grudges, resentment, anger? Do you have guilt? What can you do to let this go? Do it! Clear your mind of these toxins.

Living in the past will not help you in the present. It is an ego ploy to keep you from moving forward.

Paralysis is fear out-pictured. An intensely exaggerated fear or guilt can overwhelm the mind, paralyzing progress. The mind will be frozen. Thus, the body will be similarly frozen.

There was a man who endured horrific experiences as a prisoner of war. He was tortured, isolated, and starved. Upon his release, he struggled with walking. Enraged at his captors, he stayed in this condition until he was able to view his experience from a new perspective. It struck him one day that the prison guard with whom he was so angry, had tried, in his own way, to help him. This realization allowed the man to finally forgive his captors for their harsh treatment. Once he forgave and released his rage, his mind was set free. He regained his ability to walk. Anger was his personal prison. He was trapped until he let go. Forgiveness cleansed the mental paralysis and moved the man back to a natural state of freedom.

What is it that keeps you paralyzed? What is your fear? Who have you not forgiven? Clear your mental space of these negative energy patterns so that love can enter. Do it again and again until you feel complete. Then, with proper care and nurturing, you will move forward and your body will regain health.

Mary, a divorcee, wanted a loving marriage but she hated men. *They're all alike*, she'd say. *Men have caused all my problems. First husband: dishonest. Second husband: philanderer. Then a stingy boyfriend.* Mary continually saw these negative traits in every man she met.

The men, in turn, perceived an angry, resentful, prejudiced woman. They ran the other way.

Mary was stuck. She could not experience love until she 1) accepted responsibility for her part in her previous relationships, 2) learned to fulfill her own needs, and 3) forgave her partners and herself. Once she did that, Mary could recognize men as unique individuals. Eventually, with a lot of work with herself, she was able to develop a loving relationship.

The ego loves to place blame *out there*, but nothing changes until we look *inside* at ourselves and take responsibility for our situations.

We can create virtual prisons of our bodies.

Arthritis is a good example. Problems with joints reflect imprisoning thoughts and inhibitions. Inability to move and inflexibility are signs to look for in your thinking. There you will discover cause. Do you entertain limitations such as, *I can't do that. I shouldn't do this. I'm not capable of success. What would people think?* With these kinds of thoughts and words, your body will reflect a critical, unloving attitude that keeps you trapped.

Sinus conditions, colds, allergies, asthma, runny noses, stuffy heads, and watery eyes stem from another type of restriction: self-expression. Here, you let external situations aggravate and limit you.

Perhaps you take many things personally or feel the pain of rejection. These conditions reflect a desire to be loved and a need to cry.

Breathing difficulties are often relieved by crying because weeping releases the glue that holds sadness in place. With a good cry, this glue is dissipated and the individual achieves clarity.

On some level women, have known that crying is great therapy forever. If you won't allow tears to flow, the body handles this stuck energy with allergy and sinus issues. Instead of flowing, you remain stuffed up.

In this case, you should ask *who or what am I allergic to?* To feel better, act on what you know as truth. Make choices that free your personal expression, like singing, dancing, or taking a brisk walk. You might watch a sad movie to let the tears flow. Perhaps there is someone to whom you need to speak your truth or confront in some way. Do what feels best for you without making someone else the cause. In other words, don't ask someone else to change so that you can feel better. That never works. You have to take responsibility and change yourself if you want your life and your health to improve.

Disability or issues with arms or hands indicate problems surrounding purpose and activity. You have somehow contaminated your mind with negatives. *I can't do it. I don't have the right skills. I don't know the right people. People won't like me.* These are ego lies that keep you from your purpose. If you have an idea, you have the means to accomplish it. You can meet more people and develop greater skills. Anything is possible.

Decide what you want and take action to fulfill your purpose. Where is your heart? What does it speak to you? Where does your passion lie? Get busy. Find a way to express your heart's desire. Do it for you and no one else. If nothing else, let your purpose be happiness. It will make you feel great and your body will reflect it. Anytime you align your purpose and activities with love, you insure success.

Leprosy illustrates the mental conclusion that, *I am not good enough or I am sorely unable to deal with life.*

In the following story, Jesus healed a person with this problem. Note that, as he touched the man, he brought the man to higher consciousness and he willed the man to be cured. When we instate ourselves in higher energy and awareness, we have the ability to will our own transformation.

> *And there cometh to him a leper, beseeching him, and kneeling down to him, and saying unto him, 'If thou wilt, thou canst make me clean.' And being moved with compassion, he stretched forth his hand, and touched him, and saith unto him, 'I will; be thou made clean.' And straightway the leprosy departed from him, and he was made clean.* Mark 1:40-42

Jesus stretched out his hand, representing purpose, and touched the leper. This action indicates that this being was raised to a high vibrational frequency where wholeness exists and disease does not. This is how all healing occurs.

As the story of the leper unfolded, Jesus asked the man not to tell anyone. His admonition was that the man was to remain in the high consciousness of well-being. The ego, however, finds anonymity difficult, and the man went public with his healing. This action resulted in Jesus going out to the desert to seek solitude. We need quiet time to keep our connection to Higher Mind strong.

Our bodies reflect our mental image of who we are and what we believe. *What is my body telling me, and what do I want to do about it?*

In his seminars, scientist Greg Braden talks of laboratory tests that have indicated that happiness and joy de-stress the body, whereas anger and resentment create stress in the tissues that ultimately turn to inflammation. When we raise our energy to a higher vibratory rate, we are returning to our natural state of love. The body responds accordingly. Even science is recognizing the power of positive emotions.

We are divine beings made in the image of God. As such, we have the ability to exude health and vibrancy, as well as to live vast, expansive lives.

Jesus offers a path to wholeness. His example illustrates that when we bring people to the purity and wholeness of love, the illusion of disease dissolves. We all have this option. He showed us the way.

Verily, verily, I say unto you, he that believeth on me, the works that I do shall he do also; and greater works than these shall he do, because I go unto the Father. And whatsoever ye shall ask in my name, that will I do, that the Father may be glorified in the Son. John 14:12-13

You are the Son!

CHAPTER 6

DEPRESSION: A SIGN TO CHANGE DIRECTION

D epression is a common problem. As the result of self-doubt and loss of self-esteem, it is an epidemic illness plaguing mankind today. It is caused by and feeds upon condemning attitudes and unrealistic standards and expectations.

Most people react to everything: situations, people, events. A car cuts you off in traffic, your best friend is in a bad mood, it is raining, the company froze raises, the meeting ran late, etc. External factors become the controllers. Because these people judge conditions as bad or undesirable, they end up suffering. For example, a stranger's rudeness may be followed by feelings of self-rejection and failure. The situation may be taken personally along with the idea of being responsible for the problem. A double whammy!

Learning to respond and not react is an important skill. Otherwise, we exist as hapless victims, buffeted about by indecision, doubt, and self-pity. By using the external world as our measuring stick, we look *out there* instead of inside to our Light. In so doing, we lose value and find it hard to recognize our beauty and worthiness. In confusion, we construct virtual prisons of limiting beliefs that repress expression and create isolation. Thus, depression deepens until we take back control.

Author and scholar Eckhart Tolle was born in Germany and edu-cated at the Universities of London and Cambridge. Tolle went through a major depression early in life. By the time he was twenty-nine years old, he had come to a point of considering suicide, when suddenly, it occurred to him that *he* was not his depressive thoughts; he was the observer of them. This occurred with the idea, *I can't live with myself.*

He questioned, *Who is the I that can't live with myself?* This ques-tion radically changed the course of his life. He came to understand that he could go beyond his thoughts to the quiet place within and find peace. Once he did that, the depression disappeared.

For the next years, he devoted his life to integrating and deepen-ing the understanding of the mind and the transformational process. Later, he put pen to paper to author New York Times bestsellers, *The Power of Now* and *The New Earth.* In these books, he shares his new perspective.

When Tolle began to question his mental state, he was able to change it. He found new purpose.

You can pull yourself out of depression in a similar way. You are also the observer of your thoughts and you get to decide which thoughts you engage and which ones you don't. You do this with your thoughts in the same way as you would kick an unwanted visitor out of your house. Rather than engage each thought, choose the ones you want to entertain and let the others go, like wind sweeping across your body. Simply do not connect.

You are the creator of your thoughts. They follow your belief system. In that way, you have control. You can adjust your beliefs. Remember, a belief is just a thought that has been repeated many times. If you have a belief that you are unworthy, change it to recog-nize that you are of great value. It is your prerogative to reshape your thoughts as you see fit. Your self-esteem, productivity, health, and hap-piness depend on it. You choose the way you think and feel. So, make new choices based on higher consciousness.

The earth is our playground. The more we develop the attitude of adventure, the more fun we can have as we learn. They key is to lighten up. Our situations are meant to serve us. Their purpose is to assist in our growth. Every circumstance is neutral, that is, without feeling or intelligence. Each is subject to our interpretation and direction. We can take charge through choices. Just as I decided to play with my audiences as I learned to speak before groups, we all get to respond to circumstances in ways that benefit us.

Proper Perspective

People respond to circumstances through their self-view and belief systems. They are in charge of both of these whether they know it or not. To take control, first recognize that negative influences work on you through your subconscious mind, which has been programmed with many ineffective, impractical, even silly ideas. The idea that everyone must like you is frivolous. There have existed loving, compassionate masters walking the earth that were despised. It doesn't matter if you are a kind, considerate person, someone will decide that you are offensive. The masters were not encumbered with negative reactions. You don't have to be, either.

Acknowledge negative thoughts as they surface in your mind. Learn to observe them instead of react to them. This can be accomplished with practice. Make it a game you play with yourself.

A thought is a wave of energy. It can become an emotional storm, or it can pass over like a summer breeze. You are not your thoughts, even though you have created them. You are the one observing your thoughts. When you learn this distinction, you will have great power to achieve a non-reactive state.

We have all been handed unrealistic standards and perfectionist attitudes. Observe these when they show up and notice what triggers them. Then you can apply willpower to let them flow by. That means you *make a decision*. You don't react. You don't surrender your peace to anything. It is a discipline. You can develop it.

In the meantime, avoid people and situations who depress, discourage, or criticize. With practice, you can create a wall of immunity against negative, depressing thoughts. This will help you choose peace in each situation.

If you choose to observe life as an adventure, you will be able to spot the good in people, recognize blessings, and enjoy opportunities to learn. You will have more fun, discover new information, and learn to flow with it.

A pastor once told a story about two birds, a hummingbird and a vulture. Both birds went out into the desert to look for a specific object. The hummingbird wanted a beautiful flower from which to suck the nectar. The vulture sought a corpse to devour. They both found what they were looking for. Such it is with life. Whatever you are looking for, you will find. You decide what it is.

Recently, I spoke to a client who told me about her mean, demanding boss. How he required her to make decisions that were outside her authority and pay-grade. Even though the owner was frivolous with his company's financial accounts, she felt responsible for the its profitability. As a company financial officer, she believed, *I have to find the funds to pay the bills.*

I asked her why she saw it as her responsibility. *Isn't it the owner's obligation to make sure there are funds available to pay the bills, especially if he is making irresponsible choices (like buying lavish, expensive cars on the company's account)?*

Of course, this was true, but she had taken ownership of the problem, which let him off the hook. He used her habit of being over-responsible to his advantage. She had set herself up to be overwhelmed, overburdened, and stressed. So, what was her fear? It was that she would lose her job if she were not inventive in figuring out how to find the funds to pay the bills. Fear ruled her reactions. As a result, she moved funds around and robbed Peter to pay Paul. Everything was out of balance.

Consider the irrationality of this situation. She was losing her health and well being by trying to solve a problem that did not belong to her. She was also minimizing her value by believing she could be dismissed so easily and that future employment would not be available. That is certainly a way to fall into depression.

There appeared to be no way out as long as she accepted the situation from her ego-perception. Irrationality ruled her mind. Irrationality is a sign that ego is doing the thinking. When fear is present, creativity is not.

Have you ever seen a mountain stream? The water flows exuberantly around curves and over rocks, making its way down the mountain, never ceasing its movement. It is peaceful in its natural, uninhibited state. But if debris accumulates, the stream becomes blocked and the water ceases to flow.

The same is true with us. Our God-Energy flows out from our center naturally, like a mountain stream. However, if we focus our thoughts on helplessness, guilt, or unhappy memories, our inner Light becomes blocked and our natural flow of creativity and love is dammed up. We can unblock the energy flow by releasing the debris of ego-irrationality and self-delusion.

When faced with a problem, ask, *What is real in this situation?* Focus on what you can do and not what you cannot.

My client had to change her verbiage. Rather than, *How am I going to pay these bills*, it needed to be, *How are you planning to pay these bills?* By stepping back, she could take a position of power. In truth, the bills were not hers. From that perspective, she had options. One option was to look for another job where she could use her skills and feel valued. In the end, that is what she chose to do.

Breaking Out

There was a period when depression was part of my own story. It occurred at a time when I had a home, husband, and family. I realized that I had given all I had to the people in my life and there was nothing left for me. At the time, I thought that was the appropriate thing to do. Yet, I was emotionally depleted and empty, while feeling used and unappreciated.

By giving away everything I had, all my energy, love, devotion, and enthusiasm, I had created a group of people who expected as much. They saw me as their servant and nothing more.

The way I finally resolved my dilemma was through prayer. I knew that I did not have the answers I needed to make the changes that were necessary, and I knew that God did. Once I surrendered my life to my higher power, the solutions began to come.

I changed the way I dealt with my children. I required them to take responsibility for their actions and inactions. I set boundaries. I also took care of my need for nurturing by attending classes, learning to meditate, and pursuing personal growth. There followed a whole series of events that helped me climb out of my low-energy state. The great lesson I learned during that time was that, when a person is depressed, they are on the wrong path. I have found this to be true in every case. At such a time, awareness demands self-analysis, letting go of erroneous beliefs, and, in some ways, starting over.

As we let go of the fear-demons that keep us bound, we are able to return to lightness, vibrancy, and freedom. We let our Light radiate and live to our fullest potential as children of God.

All illness starts in the mind, grounded in worry, which is anxiety about the future, or in low self-esteem, feelings of helplessness, and guilt, which relate to the past. Making new choices and taking positive action can alter depressive thinking.

Many people believe that the biblical statement regarding being perfect as your Father in Heaven is perfect relates to intellectual and physical perfection. Therefore, because they know they are not perfect, they must be terribly flawed. This couldn't be further from the truth.

Perfection is raising your energy to love. Any lack, thereof, is due to adopting human ego values and dedication to sense-gratification in lieu of demonstrating kindness and compassion.

The reality is that you are no more defective than a baby is flawed. A baby cannot talk or walk, but it is still perfect. It has unlimited potential to do or be anything. You may do many things and not get it right, but that does not make you imperfect. It means only that you are learning.

Are your intentions honorable? Do you care about people? Do you do the best you can at any given time? Mistakes . . . whatever! You are perfect in essence and have the capability to be what you want. Quit judging by behaviors and look in your heart. Learn to see yourself as the perfect essence needing expression.

Experience is our teacher. That is how we discover what works for us. Experience offers lessons and opportunity. Our adventure through life helps us to mold and shape according to our divine plan.

Judge not, that ye be not judged. Matthew 7:1

This refers to the reality that your judgments are about you, and they limit your ability to be all that you can be.

Most of the time, people judge critically. Critical judgment limits expression and causes you to miss the point of the journey and, potentially, falter. You always become the victim of your judgments.

Don't waste any more time. Experience, learn, and radiate as a baby. Grasp opportunity with the infant's relish and enthusiasm. Compare yourself to the baby as he examines its hand and discovers the miracle of its body. The baby laughs and plays joyfully as it embraces the adventure of life. We can do the same.

CHAPTER 7

THE SUPREMACY
OF LOVE

One way we demonstrate love is through friendship. Buddhists have a term, *metta*, for the quality of boundless friendship toward oneself or others. *Metta* refers to being loving and kind. Practicing this principle, particularly toward people you don't know, expands your innate capacity for connecting. Through the quality of loving-kindness, you are able to break the habits of apathy and judgment that generate a feeling of separation from others. Separation fosters fear and prejudice.

Every person has the potential for friendship and kindness. It exists within everyone, no matter what dire experiences each have endured. This capacity cannot be destroyed, although it can be ignored or neglected.

The way you can rediscover your *metta* capability is to take a positive interest in people. We're often running through life so fast that we overlook or discount people. They don't even register. Yet relationships make up the fiber of our lives and constitute our greatest challenge and opportunity.

Practice being attentive. Start with someone you don't really know. As you pay attention, you will learn things about the person and yourself. Next, hold that person in your heart with a feeling of genuine warmth. At the same time, mentally wish that person well. In short order, you will no longer feel like a stranger. Your world will begin to change. Your life will suddenly feel freer.

The next step is to practice with someone you feel ambivalent toward. Aha! It gets easier. With success, you get bolder, which ultimately leads you to people with whom you're in conflict.

Choose someone you have injured or who has harmed you. With tenacity, you will get past the lightning bolts of anger. Your rage will dissipate over time and you will discover increased energy and deeper love, deeper than you had ever imagined. As your attention opens to the people you formerly dismissed, your world expands, along with your connection to yourself. Work on your ability to be kind and loving, and you will discover how truly unlimited and safe you are.

Why does this work? Because God is Love and we are individual sparks of God. Love is our inner essence, our core. When you remove the blocks of fear, shame, guilt, anger, and unforgiveness, which obstruct your true nature, love radiates from your center, illuminating the mind, body, and situations. At that point, practicing metta becomes a way of life. All things appear new in the Light of love. Jesus, our prototype, not only centered his teaching on love, he emanated it. His teaching demonstrates love's supremacy and overriding power.

Love, as our inner essence, purifies because love and disharmony cannot co-exist. The energies of love and disharmony are completely opposite. Therefore, they are incompatible and cannot exist at the same time.

All nature vibrates with love. It constitutes the natural, flowing state of all things. War, chaos, hatred, and jealousy do not exist in love. These qualities are restrictive, tight energies. Peace, wisdom, compassion, flow, and freedom are open, light, and expansive energy patterns. They resonate to love. This is why you feel safe when you are expressing love. The freedom you feel in your high-energy state equates to joyfulness. You cannot feel joyful and afraid at the same time.

Love is magnetic. It draws to us more of what we love. Whereas, fear, its opposite, repels everything: people, opportunities, fun. Practice living in gratitude, which is love, and you will observe wonderful things being magnetized to you. The edict is: "What you appreciate expands."

Appreciate everything you want more of in your life. Appreciate friends, family, work, abundance, beauty, nature, opportunity, everything.

Try an experiment. Think of someone you love or an event that was really fun. Notice how your body feels. Particularly observe your solar plexus, heart, and head. Now, let that thought go and think of a time of great difficulty, or a person that you find disturbing or mean. Again, notice the energy in your body.

If you do this a few times, you will recognize that there is an open, free energy that goes with joy and love; whereas the body feels tight and repressed when you contemplate stress or disturbance. This tells you a few things. First, your body and mind are connected. When one responds, so does the other. Secondly, you can shift your mind from fear and upset to love and joy at will.

When we express love mentally, emotionally, and physically, we automatically align to the Higher Self. Negative states dissolve because they exist in the ego, which is a lower energy.

With love, we see with new eyes. That is one of the reasons Jesus admonished to us to forgive people. *And Jesus said, 'Father, forgive them; for they know not what they do.'* Luke 23:34

It is the lower state of man, the ego, the wounded part that performs insidious acts. As we operate from love, we see with compassion and without judgment.

If you walked down a path and a small child kicked you for no apparent reason, you would not hate the child. You would understand that there is something amiss with the child. You would not lower yourself to the emotional angst of the child. This is how lower energies work in people. They don't know what they are doing. They are untrained children.

As you turn your attention from disharmony to love, you move back into your natural condition of balance, like a newborn child: open, receptive, tender and loving. Forgiveness is the way to accomplish this shift. With forgiveness, health and vibrancy return.

We are on the earth to be radiant beings, like the sun. The sun continually gives away its light and energy to everyone without conditions. We were all designed with the same potential, to radiate our inner sun/Son. When we give our Light generously because we want to, we are being our natural selves. We are at peace.

To radiate means to give. When the ego or small self comes into play and we focus on the outer world with the attitude of taking, we reverse the natural flow of energy. That is when we feel depressed and hopeless. So, instead of radiating outwardly, we try to pull energy in from the external world. This obstructs giving and generosity. Focus on taking from the world and you feel fearful and lacking. Why? Because you are going against the natural flow.

Many times, I have spoken to people about what they want their life to be like, what they want to receive from life. Often, they are clear and definitive about this, but they neglect to consider what they want to give. When you only wish to receive or take without giving, you create imbalance. The Universal Law does not operate that way. The Universe is the personification of balance. You are self-sabotaging if your focus is on taking without giving.

Recently, I saw a young girl on television who declared that, since she was pretty, she should not have to work. In fact, her plan was to marry a rich plastic surgeon so she could spend his money indulging her extravagant needs. Her vision was so far out of balance in me-me-me mode, I felt bad for her. The universe most assuredly will deliver her some interesting lessons so that she can learn balance. We are here to give. Receiving happens automatically when we give. Why is that? Because as we give, we create a void and nature abhors a void. It fills it with like energy. Therefore, you cannot give without receiving, and you get to determine the quality of energy that comes back to you as well.

Picture the sun radiating energy outward. You are a mini-sun. Your energy needs to flow out as well. Whatever you do—whether working, creating, performing tasks, or expressing yourself in any way— do it as an act of love. Make it your practice to radiate love in every situation and with every person. As you give your energy freely, more will pour in to you. Just like the sun, you can never run out of energy.

If there is a problem in your life, ask yourself how you have turned away from love and how you can demonstrate it in the conflicted area. When the answer comes, take steps to unconditionally accept and love each person, place, and situation in question. Your perspective will change. Your mind will relax and open to new possibilities and awareness. With practice, you maintain centeredness, clarity, and self-control.

There is an age-old story about bricklayers. When asked, *What are you doing?* one bricklayer said, *I'm earning a living.*

The next responded, *I'm laying brick.*

The third exclaimed, *I'm building a great cathedral.* The last bricklayer brought great pride, joy, and appreciation to his work. He went home fulfilled.

Which one are you?

We have it within us to have pride and joy in our work. You can build a great monument or work for a paycheck. The rewards are drastically different. You are the one who gets to decide what the reward will be.

Consider the homemaker who approaches meal preparation for her family with boredom and obligation. The meal might be nutritious, but the most important ingredient, love, has been left out. From appearances, her family fairs well enough, but how much better and more fun would it be she prepared her food with enthusiasm and love? This doesn't mean every dinner must be a feast, for there is much to be said for simplicity, especially after a long, active day, but it does not take extra effort to imbue love into what you do. This can be as easy as giving your work positive attention and having a loving intention for performing it.

In what activity, event, or work are you participating? Approach it with openness, appreciation, and as an opportunity to express your creativity and love. Then, step back and notice the results. First, did you enjoy it more? Did others appreciate it more? Which approach gives you the most satisfaction and fulfillment? Are you building a cathedral or just putting in your time?

There are many admonitions regarding love in the New Testament.

> *A new commandment I give unto you, that ye love one another;*
> *even as I have loved you, that ye also love one another. By this*
> *shall all men know that ye are my disciples, if ye have love one to*
> *another.* John 13:34-35

He that hath my commandments, and keepeth them, he it is that loveth me: and he that loveth me shall be loved of my Father, and I will love him, and will manifest myself unto him. John 14:21

But I say unto you that hear, Love your enemies, do good to them that hate you, bless them that curse you, pray for them that despitefully use you. Luke 6:27-28

And as ye would that men should do to you, do ye also to them likewise. And if ye love them that love you, what thank have ye; for even sinners love those that love them. And if ye do good to them that do good to you, what thank have ye; for even sinners do the same. Luke 6:31-33

Be ye therefore imitators of God, as beloved children. Ephesians 5:1

That Christ may dwell in your hearts through faith; to the end that ye, being rooted and grounded in love, may be strong to apprehend with all the saints what is the breadth and length and height and depth, and to know the love of Christ which passeth knowledge, that ye may be filled unto all the fullness of God. Ephesians 3:17-19

Beloved, let us love one another because love is of God; everyone who loves is begotten of God and has knowledge of God. The man without love has known nothing of God, for God is love. For love is of God. 1 John 4:7-8

And we know and have believed the love which God hath in us. God is love; and he that abideth in love abideth in God, and God abideth in him 1 John 4:16

To love him with all the heart, and with all the understanding, and with all the strength, and to love his neighbor as himself, is much more than all whole burnt-offerings and sacrifices. Mark 12:33

You are powerful when you love generously because love attracts the life you desire. You lose power when you are without love or in fear because that is when you repel the things you desire. You have the ability to choose which energy you want to express.

Pharisaical Attitudes Versus Compassion

Jesus offered love to all people, those considered good and bad alike. He sought to impress the Pharisees with the preeminence of love over the rigid, formal code of law they practiced. In doing this, he illustrated that the Christ Principle goes beyond man-made rules and the literally interpreted sabbatical laws.

Jesus, as the Christ, focused on the divinity within each person. By perceiving their perfection, he disavowed disharmonious patterns. He did not permit tradition or dogma to interfere with practicing the principle of love.

He taught that the healing power of love was to be demonstrated on the Sabbath and every other day. The Sabbath was established for man, as a time to rest, process his week, and refocus energies. Honoring this special time does not dictate ignoring the pain of others. The priority is to live in freedom and encourage others to do the same. This healing story of the infirm woman illustrates this teaching.

> And he was teaching in one of the synagogues on the Sabbath day. And behold, a woman that had a spirit of infirmity eighteen years; and she was bowed together, and could in no wise lift herself up. And when Jesus saw her, he called her, and said to her, 'Woman, thou art loosed from thine infirmity.' And he laid his hands upon her: and immediately she was made straight, and glorified God. Luke 13:10-13

Because it was negative, the spirit or thought possessing this woman drained her physical energy. Her guilt or fear became debilitating and burdensome. She was earthbound, as indicated by her stooped posture. She was unable to lift her vision to a higher reality. However, she responded to the call of Christ Consciousness. As she was affected, her malady dissipated. When we lift our focus, we are also freed.

Ye shall know the truth, and the truth shall make you free.
John 8:32

In other words, when you raise your consciousness to the purity of love, you are freed of limiting beliefs and can stand tall in truth.

Scribes represent *intellectualism*. They symbolize the part of self that forms opinions based on externally gleaned knowledge as opposed to intuitive knowing. Pharisees, on the other hand, indicate *adhering to the letter of the law* instead of to the spirit, essence, or purpose of the law. The Pharisees were hypocrites. Jesus regularly disavowed them.

We demonstrate pharisaical attitudes when we become intolerant, critical, and condemning, as well as when we run our lives according to rigid expectations and standards, the letter of the law, and thereby forego the bigger picture, our evolutionary purpose. When we negate mercy, compassion, understanding, and love, we are being Pharisees.

The point here is to live from your heart. Love is Universal power. It binds you to the Field of Universal Harmony. It magnetizes your desires to you and you to your desires. It heals the wounds and misunderstandings of life. It brings you back to the Light. As you radiate love, you connect with your divinity.

CHAPTER 8

TRADITION OR FREEDOM

Within our conscious, reasoning minds, there are two selves: the traditional person and the free-thinker.

The traditional self lives by rules and dogma. Its motto is: "You must see it before you believe it." The thinking is black-and-white and factual. The free-thinker, on the other hand, is the expanded self. It wants to break out, be free and authentic, do what feels right, and dare to test the new and untried. These two aspects, unless aligned through discipline and clear intention, war against each other. Often, we feel pressured to choose one over the other.

There is another option. That is to become traditional in your approach to freedom. That means to continue with your rituals as long as they do not override intuition. You let your intuition, your inner knowing, be your guide as you continue to live a traditional life.

Another possibility is to consider your traditions, the patterns and rules of your life, and create a way to make them purposeful. For instance, you might devise your own motivations for following the rules. This approach is what people refer to as "playing the game." It is learning the rules and winning with them. You play the game of life according to societal rules, but you have your own underlying reasons for doing what you do. You succeed because you are true to yourself while achieving your desired results.

An example would be conforming to the posted speed-limit as you drive down the road. Your intention may be to have sufficient reaction time as you navigate through traffic so that you arrive at your destination safely. You are following the rules for your own reasons and getting what you want.

This method works with your big picture or goal, too. It means being clear about your motives and actions in achieving your purpose. You don't have to become a societal maverick or be overly hooked into others' perceptions because you know what you are doing. There is nothing to explain or justify.

An example of combining traditional and free-thinking is to cooperate with the rules of government by paying your taxes while utilizing legal means to shelter your income. You achieve the results you want: the home, the vacation, the nest-egg and you use the laws of the land to make it possible.

You can also combine these elements by deciding the type of work you want and implementing a traditional approach to getting it. Basically, that means thinking outside the box. You can design a job description for which you are uniquely qualified. Then, present that position to a prospective employer. To do this, you would evaluate your accomplishments, skills, and experience, then state them, via a resume or application in a traditional format. In other words, you sculpt your resume around your credentials and desired position.

Pam Grouts is the New York Times best-selling author of *E-Squared* and *E-Cubed*, among other books. She started out as a single mother with no money. The traditional approach in her situation was to get a job and create a steady income. Yet, Pam had a passion to do what she loved, which was to write and travel. Most people would get a job first, save money, and then travel during vacations and breaks. Pam decided to have the best of both worlds. She used her skills to become a travel writer. She started with one assignment and built her desire into a full–time business.

After publishing a number of travel books, Pam got into her deepest love, metaphysics. That is when her books hit the New York Times' Best-Selling List. She had built her skills, experience, and confidence. Now, she does what she loves every day. She was traditional in that she built her profession from a single contract, but untraditional in that she followed her dream and did not let fear get in the way.

If your desire is not aligned with your soul purpose, it will be pharisaical and, most likely, not work. In other words, it may follow a traditional approach, but the purpose and spirit will be lacking. You may get the job, but there won't be joy and fulfillment. It is like dying a slow death. Assess the rules you live by and make sure they reflect your values.

Jesus made this point quite clear as he confronted the Pharisees regarding their hypocrisy. The Pharisees and some of the experts in law who had come from Jerusalem gathered around him. They had observed a few of the disciples eating meals without having purified themselves. That is to say, they did not wash their hands. The Pharisees, and in fact all Jews, cling to the custom of their ancestors and never eat without scrupulously washing their hands. Moreover, they do not eat anything from the market without sprinkling it. There were many other traditions they observed as well, such as the washing of cups and jugs and kettles. In this biblical story, the issue of washing their hands came into question.

> And there are gathered together unto him the Pharisees, and certain of the scribes, who had come from Jerusalem, and had seen that some of his disciples ate their bread with defiled, that is, unwashen, hands. (For the Pharisees, and all the Jews, except they wash their hands diligently, eat not, holding the tradition of the elders; and when they come from the market-place, except they bathe themselves, they eat not; and many other things there are, which they have received to hold, washings of cups, and pots, and brasen vessels.)
>
> And the Pharisees and the scribes ask him, 'Why walk not thy disciples according to the tradition of the elders, but eat their bread with defiled hands?' And he said unto them, 'Well did Isaiah prophesy of you hypocrites, as it is written, 'This people honoreth me with their lips, But their heart is far from me. But in vain do they worship me, Teaching as their doctrines the

precepts of men. Ye leave the commandment of God, and hold fast the tradition of men.' And he said unto them, 'Full well do ye reject the commandment of God, that ye may keep your tradition.' Mark 7:1-9

You can see from this text that our higher directing intelligence, Christ Consciousness, does not accept or approve of empty tradition that consists of rules that focus on the material world while ignoring the deeper connection to Spirit.

It is good to have standards, but not okay when these criterion busy us with meaningless activity that overrides higher focus. Many people don't find time to meditate because they do the laundry, clean the house, run errands. They will leave this lifetime no better than when they came in and wonder why. Meditation needs to be a priority.

An example of empty tradition is attending church because it is expected or obligatory, rather than acting out of love for God. Same thing goes for working for a paycheck without bringing love to the endeavor.

Maintaining Purpose

Spiritual freedom is most important when facing challenges. You always have a choice. The ego encourages fear, negativity, criticism, and blame. The higher way is to affirm your strength as you set about meeting the challenge. In other words, be about your Father's business. How can you bring your highest energy to this situation? Evaluate options and get moving. If a challenge is presented, you are ready for it. It is offered to teach you something. Rather than disdain it, move into it.

In 1966, Lou Holtz, the now famous football coach, was twenty-eight years old. He had lost his job when his wife Beth was expecting their third child. She wanted to lift his spirits, so encouraged him to read *The Magic of Thinking Big* by David J. Schwarz.

The book stated that there are many people who never do anything special with their lives. At the time, Holtz was totally lacking in motivation, so he related to that statement. He decided to write out one hundred and seven goals that he wanted to achieve before he died.

His list included having dinner at the White House, appearing on the Tonight Show, meeting the Pope, becoming head coach at Notre Dame, winning a national championship, being Coach of the Year, landing on an aircraft carrier, making a hole-in-one, and jumping out of an airplane. The goals seemed preposterous and impossible at the time because Holtz had no job or money.

Not long ago, however, Holtz had achieved eighty-one of those goals, including all those listed above. He dined with President Ronald Reagan at the White House, appeared with Johnny Carson on the Tonight Show, met the Pope, jumped from an airplane, and got two (not one) holes-in-one.

Perhaps you can follow Coach Holtz's example and give yourself permission to dream impossible dreams. Try being unrealistic for a change. The secret to this quest is not what you write down, but that you allow yourself to admit that you would like to climb Mount Kilimanjaro, endow a University, play the flute in Carnegie Hall, or be a better friend. Acknowledging your dream begins the process of magnetizing it.

There is a principle in Quantum Physics that states that a possibility becomes a reality when it is registered. Registering a possibility simply means to acknowledge or choose it. We all have potential to do amazing things. So register your dream, then let go of it. Put your written goals away. As time goes on, accept every opportunity to move in the direction of your objectives. As you take action, your goals will come into being.

Another principle in Quantum Physics is that, once you record your desire, the object and the subject change at the same time. In other words, once you claim your goal, or set your sights on what you want, *you* will change along with the goal. You will find yourself putting forth activity that will ultimately create your desired reality.

It worked for Lou Holtz, the award-winning coach of the Notre Dame football team. It will work for you as well. His turn of bad luck in losing his job led him to the fulfillment of his dreams. Perhaps something similar will happen for you as well.

What is your purpose? Every person and situation is offered to you in order to teach you something. What belief, energy, or emotion is being reflected to you? Address challenge objectively and without judgment as an opportunity so you can unlock the treasure. Positive attention expands options, increases vision. Negative focus reduces and restricts choices and closes down the possibilities. Growth requires openness.

CHAPTER 9

STAY TRUE TO
YOUR SELF

Since high school, Sue dreamed of being a singer. It was her only desire. As she grew, she sang with various groups and eventually joined a band. In each experience, she progressed to a certain point, then seemed to succumb to fear and give up. It was extremely frustrating for her because singing was the only thing she wanted to do.

Sue was like the man with the withered hand. She had potential, promise, talent, and purpose, but when she grew afraid, she ran. Her purpose withered because she would not confront her fear. Self-condemnation and unrealistic expectations not only created the fear, but stopped her progress. When she finally changed her mind, gave up perfectionism, and looked at progress differently, she overcame her problem.

Sue had a common issue in thinking she should be an instant success. She wanted a concert at Carnegie Hall to fall into her lap. When she stepped back and began to look at a singing career as a process, she was able to learn from past mistakes and use them to build future success. By processing her experience for its learning value, she built her career. She discovered what it takes to be a professional, how to read her audience, how to command attention, and how to sing from her heart. She fulfilled her purpose by facing her challenges and loving the process. Sue became a great performer.

We need courage to face challenges and fulfill our dreams. It takes practice to develop maturity and focus. Most *instant* successes happen to people who have been at their art for a long time.

We all have talents and gifts. Jesus told a parable to describe the need for developing our talents and skills.

> He said therefore, a certain nobleman went into a far country, to receive for himself a kingdom, and to return. And he called ten servants of his, and gave them ten pounds, and said unto them, 'Trade ye herewith till I come.'
>
> But his citizens hated him, and sent an ambassage after him, saying, 'We will not that this man reign over us.' And it came to pass, when he was come back again, having received the kingdom, that he commanded these servants, unto whom he had given the money, to be called to him, that he might know what they had gained by trading. And the first came before him, saying, 'Lord, thy pound hath made ten pounds more.'
>
> And he said unto him, 'Well done, thou good servant: because thou was found faithful in a very little, have thou authority over ten cities.' And the second came, saying, 'Thy pound, Lord, hath made five pounds.' And he said unto him also, 'Be thou also over five cities.'
>
> And another came, saying, 'Lord, behold, here is thy pound, which I kept laid up in a napkin: for I feared thee, because thou art an austere man: thou takest up that which thou layedst not down, and reapest that which thou didst not sow.'
>
> He saith unto him, 'Out of thine own mouth will I judge thee, thou wicked servant. Thou knewest that I am an austere man, taking up that which I laid not down, and reaping that which I did not sow; then wherefore gave thou not my money into the bank, and I at my coming should have required it with interest?'
>
> And he said unto them that stood by, 'Take away from him the pound, and give it unto him that hath the ten pounds.' And they said unto him, 'Lord, he hath ten pounds.' I say unto you, 'that unto every one that hath shall be given; but from him that

hath not, even that which he hath shall be taken away from him. But these mine enemies, that would not that I should reign over them, bring hither, and slay them before me.' Luke 19:12-27

The parable is stating that when we open to opportunities to be and have more, more comes to us. On the other hand, if we hide our talents and live in fear, what little we have is taken from us. In that case, we live in the poverty and despair of passivity and lack of creativity.

We are in the earth as creative beings. We are here to expand our creativity and talents.

Elbert Hubbard, the American author and editor, once said, *There is no failure except in no longer trying. There is no defeat except from within; no really insurmountable barrier, save our own inherent weakness of purpose.*

Look at your purpose. Are you fulfilling it by growing daily, or are you demanding instant gratification like Sue and many others, thus setting yourself up for failure?

Misdirection and Misinterpretation

Misdirection of purpose often instigates loss. This could be the misuse of one's own resources or encouraging others to do the same.

And he said unto his disciples, It is impossible but that occasions of stumbling should come; but woe unto him, through whom they come. It were well for him if a millstone were hanged about his neck, and he were thrown into the sea, rather than that he should cause one of these little ones to stumble. Luke 17:1-2

Intentionally misleading another results in a significant penalty. Being *thrown into the sea* indicates being thrown into life. With *a millstone around his neck* illustrates a burden or weight restricting the will (indicated by the neck). This could mean various things, but assuredly this person's future will be difficult. Some possibilities are being born with a paralyzing condition or with a diminished capacity.

What this is saying is that we have a responsibility to present truth as we understand it, not leaving out one word or adding a word to change its meaning. We do not have the right to change or protect another from the truth.

Understanding truth varies according to individual evolution and awareness. It is nevertheless necessary that truth be served. The depth of understanding is not as important as the willingness to offer truth without judgment or prejudice.

There is a story about an eleven-year-old boy who learned an important lesson regarding the interpretation of right action and values. Jeff played Little League Baseball on the Phoenix team. It was the last game of the season, the most important game because it would determine the championship.

It was the bottom of the sixth. Jeff's team, the Phoenix, was ahead 2–1. But the opposing team, the Pegasus, had the bases loaded with two outs and their best hitter at bat.

The batter hit an easy fly ball to Phoenix's right fielder, Bobby, who circled under it, his glove ready. It looked like an easy out as the crowd was still with anticipation. The ball fell into Bobby's glove, and then bounced out. Bobby scrambled after it, but by the time he retrieved the ball and decided where to throw it, the Pegasus team won the game 3–2. The defeated Phoenix team slunk off the field.

Suddenly, the manager of the Phoenix started screaming at Bobby. *You lost us the game. It is your fault we lost the championship.*

Shocked and devastated, Bobby ran off the field and into the woods.

After the gathering his things, Jeff went to meet his parents for the drive home. His dad wasn't there. His mom said, *Your dad has something to take care of.*

Jeff felt dejected. Then, in the distance, he saw his father walking down the road with an arm around Bobby. Bobby was the one who felt he didn't have a friend in the world. Jeff's dad had reached out to him in kindness and support.

Jeff never forgot the kindness his father extended that day. In a matter of one hour, Jeff's value system made a radical shift. The importance of kindness went to the top, while winning at all costs fell off the list.

Bobby never forgot the kindness, either. Whenever he saw Jeff's dad, he broke into a big smile and greeted him warmly.

Some people really believe that winning is everything. The team manager did not recognize the feelings of a vulnerable eleven-year-old Little League Baseball player when he set his priorities. He was misdirected in his belief about winning, and he misled his players when he yelled at Bobby for losing the championship. In sports, it should be understood by everyone that the team wins or loses together.

Real winners don't necessarily hit home runs or make spectacular plays and catch every ball. Real winners, like Jeff's dad, know how to be kind. He was clear in his direction and taught by example. Kindness is everything.

CHAPTER 10

TURNING AWAY FROM TRUTH

And a woman, who had an issue of blood twelve years, and had suffered many things of many physicians, and had spent all that she had, and was nothing bettered, but rather grew worse, having heard the things concerning Jesus, came in the crowd behind, and touched his garment. For she said, 'If I touch but his garments, I shall be made whole.' And straightway the fountain of her blood was dried up; and she felt in her body that she was healed of her plague.

And straightway Jesus, perceiving in himself that the power proceeding from him had gone forth, turned him about in the crowd, and said, 'Who touched my garments?' And his disciples said unto him, 'Thou seest the multitude thronging thee, and sayest thou, Who touched me?'

And he looked round about to see her that had done this thing. But the woman fearing and trembling, knowing what had been done to her, came and fell down before him, and told him all the truth. And he said unto her, 'Daughter, thy faith hath made thee whole; go in peace, and be whole of thy plague.'
Mark 5:25-34

In the Bible, blood is a symbol for life force or life essence. The story describes a woman who has been distracted from truth for a major portion of her life. The woman symbolizes the feminine principle, the receptive, intuitive aspect of man. The woman had been afflicted with an issue of blood, or loss of life force, for twelve years.

This woman's energy loss indicates she had been receptive to ideas that were limiting and draining. Since every story can be internalized, this might indicate that the woman was receptive to adopting senseless rules, letting others' make her decisions, focusing on other people's needs, while ignoring her own, letting fear run her. These beliefs and behaviors would certainly drain energy and enthusiasm.

Do any of these behaviors sound like your own?

The woman's initial attempts at being cured were external. She went to many doctors. They dealt with symptoms, not causes. For this reason, their solutions were ineffective. Treating symptoms such as illness or poverty with external measures, without addressing the inner cause, does not lead to permanent solutions. Healing takes place when the patient releases the indwelling cause.

The hemorrhaging woman had exhausted her savings. Money symbolizes self-worth, which was diminished. She found no relief as she was looking to the wrong source. Living by external values and order, rather than evoking love, is another way to manifest loss of life force.

This woman's cure occurred when she focused on Christ Consciousness, when she put her hand to Jesus' cloak. At that point, she reconnected to a higher energy, allowing her to rise above the problem. Her faith had restored her. She woke up to the truth. Touching Jesus' cloak is a metaphor for coming back to the reality of Spirit as whole and complete.

There is a law in physics that says when two particles are side by side, one can be influenced by the other. Some would call this *entrainment*. This means that, if you are with someone who has a high vibratory frequency, the second person can be temporarily lifted into a higher frequency. This often happens when you hear a good speaker, read an uplifting book, or attend an inspirational sermon. You walk away feeling good, happy, and experiencing high energy. When this occurs, it's important to do whatever is necessary to maintain the inspired state. Otherwise, you may revert back to the lower energy.

As we examine the healings performed by Jesus, each time he interacted or touched someone and they were lifted to a state of health, he admonished them to not return to the village. In other words, do not go back to your old energy patterns or the tribal belief system out of which you have been healed. Many times, the person is so excited with the transformation that the person does exactly the opposite, announcing the healing to everyone. In so doing, this person risks losing the exalted state and may revert back to the former state.

Understanding this law of physics helps you appreciate how instantaneous healing can occur. It makes it possible for you to achieve it. Your effort is to give up judgment, victimhood, guilt, and negativity and to raise and keep your energy in an exalted state of love.

It takes courage and insight to evaluate the circumstances of your life and commit to releasing distractions that keep you from love. Actions, beliefs, and obligations that are trite and meaningless must go. Freeing your attention from the minutia of life makes it possible to focus on Spirit. Purifying your intention so that you are working for the good of all, and focusing on your Christ Center, energizes your mind and body. Anything that could potentially be energy draining will no longer be part of your life. Negativity and blocks to energy flow are removed. With heightened energy, you radiate Light. You become the Light of the world.

Bondage or Freedom

In Luke 8:26-37, the Demoniac, one of my favorite stories, encompasses many lessons. It portrays another healing incident and illustrates how one can become trapped by tradition and ritual. This healing is of special interest because it involves possession by many demons, whose name is legion, indicating that the man or demoniac had many demons, i.e., many fear-based beliefs.

Why would you call fear-based beliefs demons? Because fear demonizes the person who entertains it. When you are afraid, you clench up, resist, hide, avoid, and keep your focus on the material world. All of these actions keep you from the Light. When Light passes through the body structure, it illuminates consciousness. It fills the outer self or mind with the inspiration to do something constructive. That is how man can be purified. This is what happens in the following story.

> And they arrived at the country of the Gerasenes, which is over against Galilee. And when he was come forth upon the land, there met him a certain man out of the city, who had demons; and for a long time he had worn no clothes, and abode not in any house, but in the tombs.
>
> And when he saw Jesus, he cried out, and fell down before him, and with a loud voice said, 'What have I to do with thee, Jesus, thou Son of the Most High God? I beseech thee, torment me not.'
>
> For he was commanding the unclean spirit to come out from the man. For oftentimes it had seized him: and he was kept under guard, and bound with chains and fetters; and breaking the bands asunder, he was driven of the demon into the deserts.
>
> And Jesus asked him, 'What is thy name?' And he said, 'Legion;' for many demons were entered into him. And they entreated him that he would not command them to depart into the abyss.
>
> Now there was there a herd of many swine feeding on the mountain: and they entreated him that he would give them leave to enter into them. And he gave them leave. And the demons came out from the man, and entered into the swine: and the herd rushed down the steep into the lake and were drowned.
>
> And when they that fed them saw what had come to pass, they fled, and told it in the city and in the country. And they went out to see what had come to pass; and they came to Jesus, and found the man, from whom the demons were gone out, sitting, clothed and in his right mind, at the feet of Jesus: and they were afraid. And they that saw it told them how he that was possessed with demons was made whole.

And all the people of the country of the Gerasenes round about asked him to depart from them, for they were holden with great fear: and he entered into a boat, and returned. Luke 8:26-37

Gerasene is a Hebrew word meaning *walled-about; fortified*. Since the subject of the healing came from the country of Gerasene, this story deals with someone holding a group of thoughts that are strongly organized, hold great energy, and are closed. Fortified would indicate that the man held plenty of rationales and excuses for maintaining these thoughts, traditions, or beliefs. Think of how a person might justify prejudice, anger, or lack of forgiveness.

This story reminds me of the way people hold uninformed opinions. *We've always done it this way,* they say. *Our authority figures say we must do this or believe that. My family has always been* _____. Fill in the blank: *Catholic, Jewish, Hindu, libertarians, freethinkers, diabetics, blue-color workers, underdogs, entrepreneurs,* etc. In other words, there is no other way.

In a contemporary setting, this would sound something like, *Certain religions or political parties or practices are wicked. Gays should not be married. Abortions are evil. You should hate minorities. Once a person goes bad, they can never be better. If you had a bad relationship, from then on, all men/women are evil/selfish/mean.* And so on . . . walled-off, fortified, immovable.

This walled-off area is across from Galilee. Galilee is associated with a mountain, which symbolizes a high state of consciousness. It literally means *rolling energy, turning, a circle, a circuit.* This is interpreted as a high state of moving energy. When we are living in the Light, there is fluidity of expression. New ideas and inspiration come readily. It is definitely not stagnant. Thus, Galilee, which symbolizes elevated, fluid consciousness, is the polar opposite of walled-off and fortified Gerasene.

Once a person is freed from walled-off, closed, fortified, disrupting tendencies, personal power can be directed to a higher purpose. In an unredeemed or error-possessed state, thoughts are violent and destructive. We can relate these thoughts to fear, hate, shame, guilt, jealousy, and prejudice. All these are violent and destructive. These emotional states keep a person imprisoned within animalistic, human desires. The legion of demons repeatedly generated destructive conditions for the possessed man.

Starting from the beginning of the story, think of this tale as describing an experience in life. When Jesus, the Christ or I AM Consciousness, enters into this closed mental state, the man is confronted with a part of self that is possessed by demons: negative thoughts. This aspect of self is naked, meaning vulnerable and without defenses. The man lives among the tombstones, which signifies the past. Thus, he is controlled by memories. Does this sound familiar?

This crazed aspect freaks out when confronted with I AM Consciousness. The man expresses thoughts of unworthiness. Representing the higher consciousness, Jesus takes no notice of this self-denial and proceeds to order the unclean spirits, the negative memories, out. Again, we see that, as with other healings, the presence of the Christ completely changes the energy of the person.

These demonic memories have taken hold many times, in the same way that unprocessed experiences have done. When they show up, they brutalize part of the self, literally imprisoning it. They trigger self-criticism and self-denegation. Nevertheless, this part of self has the ability to break free from the bonds, and when it does, it seeks solitude. This is what we do when we need time to regroup and process experiences. Thus, the story indicates that the man, or individual consciousness, has the ability to break through the torturing thoughts.

I AM demands that the negative thoughts identify themselves. The answer is given by describing their number: *legion* or *we are many*. In truth, it doesn't matter what we call these beliefs. The point is, they are dark energy and must go.

Once the I AM understands the issue, the dark energy is sent away and transformation takes place. Connecting with the I AM, Christ energy, instigates healing. The darkness is overcome with the Light.

What are your destructive behaviors? Self-hatred, prejudice, anger? These are a few possibilities. When you allow behaviors to have their way with you, you become crazed or out of control.

In the story of the demons, it happened that a large herd of swine was feeding nearby on the hillside. Swine represent compulsive animalistic tendencies and self-gratification. These animals do not reason. They function robotically. That is also what people do when they adopt beliefs simply because others hold those beliefs. They are not rational, following someone else's lead blindly. We see this compulsiveness in gangs and dysfunctional families.

When discord from these compulsions has been generated over a long period of time, it crowds back heart-desire for love so that only the animal desires of the outer-self are gratified. These desires include gluttony, self-indulging habits, or addictions, self-abuse, and self-hatred. These outer compulsions destroy self-respect, along with any opportunity to connect with higher truth.

When the human creation of ego is consumed or hits rock bottom, the I AM Presence has an opening or opportunity to expand the through the heart. That Light passes through the body structure and illuminates consciousness. It fills the outer self with the feeling that it wants to do something constructive. That is how we are transformed and purified. That is what the story of the Gerasene Demoniac relays.

Many people don't want to let go of their human sense desires to move to a higher energy. When the ego fears losing gratification of the outer self, it isn't concerned about the Light. Until the time the individual lets the heart-desire expand through the body and circumstances, the outer-self or ego, goes on creating the shadows of its own darkness by being stuck in the gratification of animal desires. This is to say that, once we can see and understand the nature of our imprisonment in sensory gratification, we have the ability to let go and be free. We evolve by making conscious, reasoned choices.

What makes sense? What is of highest value? Through productive choices, we are able to recover well-being. Spiritual wholeness returns as we replace our outer focus with inner connection: love versus fear.

After the swine appeared in the story, the negative spirits asked permission to enter the swine. With the request being granted, the dark energy left the man and entered the swine, meaning it went into the lower energy of animal desire and outer self-gratification. With that, the swine charged over the bluff and into the lake to drown. Low energy was eliminated, destroyed. The oppression had ended.

The transformation of the man from Gerasene was instantaneous and complete. From a demented, depressed, animalistic being, someone who was shunned by everyone, he became stable and calm. He sat at the feet or the foundation of his I AM, Christ.

This healing is a metaphor, representing the process of transmutation. It is meant for each of us. The lower, human thoughts of separation are transformed into higher realizations of love and harmony.

Following the cure of the man, the people from the territory asked Jesus to leave. When the populace of the territory faced the potential of this transformation and acknowledged the full recovery of the man, they were terrified. Radical change is frightening to many, as it was with this group. They were unwilling to bring change into their midst. This is a metaphor for those aspects of ourselves that are terrified of change, even if we know it is beneficial.

It is threatening when openness and love enter into the territory of closed-mindedness. This change is not welcomed. This is what people feel when they have invested a lifetime believing something, then suddenly discover it was phony or fake. It's mind-blowing. The reaction is, *Please go away. I don't want you. I can't handle this.*

Imagine living in a dark cave your whole life and then one day, you see a light. You crawl toward it, but you find you must move slowly because it blinds you if you go too quickly. You must let your eyes adjust gradually. As inviting as it may seem, running toward the light would be overwhelming. That is what happens with people as they change. They grow in increments as their psyches can handle it.

As we change, our neurology adjusts to accept expanded awareness. That is why, as you learn to meditate, you practice for a few minutes and extend your practice gradually so that your nervous system can manage the adjustments you are making.

Negativity works within the desire-body of man and keeps attention tied to the earth. In order to support an adverse belief, one must continually seek substantiating evidence. Validation comes through viewing facts alone. An example would be a person who thinks that physical beauty creates personal value. This concept may be pleasant for a while, but will ultimately lead to disappointment and disillusionment. There will come a time when wisdom and depth are required to manage the challenges of life. That is when the shallowness of appearances will be found lacking. That could be the rock-bottom catalyst that leads to change. Or the person may continue to live in misery and commiseration.

Another person may attempt to find security solely in money. He will invest energy and time to acquire wealth, while ignoring opportunities to become inwardly secure. Physical wealth can be lost or stolen. The stock market can go belly-up and real estate can lose value. Inner security, self-confidence, and truth cannot be lost. It is a heavenly treasure.

Narrow concepts are generally obsessive, and it is upsetting when a person realizes those concepts don't work and that change is in order. All destructive behaviors, like alcoholism, drug-abuse, sex, and shopping addiction, to name a few, fall into this category. Seeking the peace of I AM or Christ Consciousness will take us to enlightenment and peace.

When you begin to change your ideas and behaviors, it can be scary. You are walking into uncharted territory. Fear of the unknown keeps many from advancing. Unconscious fear and animal gratification has been held within the psyche for so long, it is like a familiar friend, albeit a destructive friend. You will be walking away from the familiar into the unfamiliar . . . *Yikes!*

We develop comfort zones by doing things certain ways. There is a reassuring kind of security in these habits, even when they bring unpleasant results. At least, you know what to expect. Despite the fact they may even be harmful, they are as comfortable as wearing old shoes.

Can you relate this comfort to a time when you attempted to give up a negative habit like smoking, drinking, eating sugar, criticizing, judging, or blaming others? Did you feel a perverse pleasure in sticking to the old way? Was there a natural resistance to letting go, even when you knew you were moving to something better?

Resistance indicates you are not ready to accept responsibility for a new path. It is like moving into sunlight too quickly after you have spent a long time in the darkness. Stop for a moment and realize it is okay to take your time to move to something new.

Perhaps you do not feel strong or deserving enough to make changes. Or, maybe you allow fear and self-doubt to distract you from your goal of peace. Of course, you have another choice. That is to recognize the pitfalls involved in remaining the same or living in the graveyard of the past. Use that recognition to fuel your determination.

When Jesus, the I AM or Christ Consciousness, left the territory, what remained was the rigidness of close-mindedness.

The last part of the story tells us that Jesus instructed the man from whom the devils had departed to return to his home and recount all that God had done for him. This clear, rational element could now bring others to the Light. As the story goes, the transformed man traveled to the surrounding territories and preached. He brought the miracle of healing to many others. We see this today. When drug addicts, alcoholics, or gang members reform and tell their story, it has the potential to help many others make similar changes.

Mental programming can blind and chain an individual. If you are repeatedly told that you never do anything right, that you are stupid, that you can't learn, that you always mess things up, you may accept these ideas as truth and, thus, fulfill their prophecy. That is very much like living in a graveyard. Your spirit is crushed and dead. You chain yourself with hopelessness. If you refuse to consider another way, it would be equivalent to turning away from the Light of your inner Self.

Challenge self-defeating ideas. Seek your perfected spiritual nature. Discover your new way. You will achieve success. The story about the Gerasene Demoniac is yours and mine. It is about transforming from bondage to freedom.

My intuition has always been strong and I have been dedicated to listening to it. In the late 1970's, I intuitively felt that I needed to be able to stand in front of an audience and speak. The idea scared the bejeebies out of me, but I would never back away from a gut feeling. I followed my usual tactic and attacked my fear head-on. I signed up to do talks to small groups. This was akin to learning to swim by jumping into the middle of the lake without a life vest. A more reasonable approach might have been to join Toastmasters or take a speech class.

Ah, but that was not my way. My strategy was to do lectures until I became acclimated to the scenario and relaxed. It was basically starting something new cold-turkey.

Thus, I traveled to the first talk, was introduced, and began my lecture. I was a mess. My knees shook behind a lectern. My voice quivered. No hiding that. I forgot my subject. This was not good. In my mind, I thanked my audience for coming out to be my guinea pigs so I could practice. I went through this practice several times.

With each event, I mentally reviewed the experience. When did I relax? When did I connect with the audience? All this was eye opening because I discovered that, when I was thinking about me, I was a mess. *Did they like me? Did they accept me? Did they understand me?* I eventually concluded that my focus had to be on giving to my audience. I would ask myself, *What am I here to give them?* I would answer the question and go into giving mode. Amazingly, as I kept my focus, I improved.

This was my Gerasene experience. I had to come out of the graveyard of believing that I didn't have anything to offer, that people would not get my message, and that they wouldn't want to participate. With each practice, I got better and, eventually, conquered my fear. Instead of wishing away the experience as the people of Gerasene did, I welcomed it, shaky knees and all, because I did not want fear to run my life.

This is a process that everyone has to endure. We've been handed false ideas that are based on what our cultures or our parents or families believed. It's time to change our neurology to accept a far greater truth. Whatever we want to do, we are capable of doing. As Jesus proclaimed, *Greater things than this, you, too, shall do.*

To this day, I thank what I called my guinea-pig audience for allowing me to practice on them. Thank you, guys! If it weren't for them, I never would have learned to speak before an audience. This has become an important skill for me.

To wrap up, consider your own bondage. I doubt that you would be reading this book if you were closed-minded, but you might possess narrow opinions and prejudices. Does ego-gratification override your desire for enlightenment? Is it time to leave the dark cave of self-denigration and fear? Are you ready to bring your consciousness out of the graveyard of past programming and into the expansive light of spirit? Freedom lies in knowing who you are as a spiritual being and, thereby, recognizing that you can confront your inhibitions and inner darkness. Whether this be standing before an audience to speak or changing a job or ending an abusive relationship, you are supported. You are a Christ Being. You are free!

Putting Fear in Proper Perspective

Fear reflects misunderstanding or false beliefs. Fear is generated from the ego, the result of not knowing who you are. Once it is firmly established in your mind that you are a divine being, blessed in every way, fear will begin to wane.

Jesus said, *And be not afraid of them that kill the body, but are not able to kill the soul: but rather fear him who is able to destroy both soul and body in hell.* Matthew 10:28

The soul cannot be destroyed because it is energy. Your essence is literally energy/soul/consciousness. You can lose contact or awareness with your inner essence, soul, by forgetting about it, by never seeking it, or by identifying completely with the physical body. Yet, it can never be lost. It is *you*. Seek the kingdom of heaven and all else shall be given unto you.

The moment you walk into a dark room and turn on the light, the darkness is gone. Love works the same way. Where there is love, which is Light, there is no fear, which is darkness, unawareness. When your awareness and understanding increase, darkness is gone. Thus, the key to unlock and release fear is to move into love.

Determine what your fear is and love its opposite. For instance, if you are afraid of poverty, love the money you have. Love the opportunities to make more money. Love the opportunity to balance your checkbook and pay your bills. Be grateful for all the services that have been provided that has made your life easier: electricity, gas, internet, telephone, laundry, dry-cleaning, grass-cutting, window-washing, handyman, to name a few. When you pay these bills, say, *Thank you,* and feel gratitude in your heart. This raises your energy to allow greater abundance to flow to you.

Love, the polar opposite of fear, is an attractive force. By directing your love to what you really want instead of to what you fear, you magnetize more of it into your life. I'll have more on how to use the power of love in the chapter called, *The Power and Potential of Love*.

For now, if you want more love, give more love. Smile at people, hold the door for them, let them have the parking spot. If you want better health, appreciate the health you have and love your body. Take care of it. Walk, dance, move, eat greens, drink water. Love can change your life and your relationship with everything around you.

CHAPTER 11

WHAT ARE YOUR DEMONS?

*B*y now, you have grasped the concept of innate perfection and your mission to radiate your Light. To move into this radiance, fear must be eliminated. Fear is the mechanism of the ego. It tries to convince you that you are not spirit, but a body, small and lacking. It tries to capture and distract attention to keep you centered on separation from God by introducing the idea that God is *out there*.

This chapter is to help you eradicate fear. In this discourse, we turn the spotlight on fear and the cause thereof, that we might remove it. In other words, you must know your enemy to defeat it.

> *But the fruit of the Spirit is love, joy, peace, longsuffering, kindness, goodness, faithfulness, meekness, self-control; against such there is no law.* Galatians 5:22-23

Anything opposing the above description must be cast out so that the Christ Light can shine through you in all its purity.

Fear is removed from our minds by realizing a higher truth. This is why it is important to identify personally with each of the miracles previously mentioned. This is how you open to a fuller realization of your divinity.

Demonstrating Christhood is a tall order, yet doable. You are equal to it because you are never asked to do more than you are capable of doing. Nonetheless, habitually entertained condemning, judgmental thoughts, interfere with growth and must be the first to go. Along with these, you must release ideas of inadequacy. In this chapter, you are to commit yourself to a new, perfected viewpoint that begins with self-love.

Since fear is the opposite of love, the two cannot be housed together. Fear and love resonate different energy patterns. That is why where there is fear, there is no love. Therefore, to unconditionally love ourselves and others, we must eliminate fear.

There are seven basic fears: fear of poverty, criticism, loss of love, ill-health, loss of freedom, old age, and fear of death or change, which is the same as the fear of the unknown. Not everyone has all of these fears, but most have some of them.

Now, it is time to spot these fears as they appear in your consciousness and begin the process of replacing them. Courageous action is the best approach. Education on the object of fear is another. Both work equally well. Additional clarification will help you spot fear as it attempts to limit your expression.

Most fears were framed during childhood, adolescence, and early adulthood, filed away in an unconscious section of your mind. You continually react to this stored data until you recognize, challenge, release, and replace the fears with new information and behavior.

Fear, in itself, implies a lack of knowledge, a void in understanding. Therefore, simple research and discovery of correct information regarding the area feared will do wonders in achieving freedom. Fill your voids with truth.

In the following pages, each of the seven fears will be examined.

Fear of Poverty

You will never be without substance to meet your needs as long as you are willing to work, i.e. express your energy. Work does not necessitate physical labor because mental exertion is a way to express creatively. Developing a consciousness of supply, which is the same as a consciousness of abundance, requires effort and devotion. Wealth is not a result of accumulating material goods. It is a state of mind that comes from comprehending your intrinsic value.

> *Fear not, little flock; for it is your Father's good pleasure to give you the kingdom. Sell that which ye have, and give alms; make for yourselves purses which wax not old, a treasure in the heavens that faileth not, where no thief draweth near, neither moth destroyeth. For where your treasure is, there will your heart be also.* Luke 12:32-34

Here, Jesus admonishes to have no fear because God, the Father, wants to give you the kingdom. In other words, it is a great pleasure for the Universe to supply your needs. Seeking the truth of your intrinsic value as Christ Beings opens your mind to accepting the gifts being continually offered.

Many people have a hard time receiving gifts. Because of that, they are not open to new opportunities or to people helping them.

We are in this world together as grains of sand on a beach. We need to assist one another. This can be in offering a complement, giving a gift, steering someone toward a job opportunity, or fixing someone's car.

Practice saying *Thank you*, when offered a gift. Even if is not something you care to have, receive the giver's intention. As you do this, you are signaling the Universe that you are open to receive. When you refuse gifts and offers of help, you are telling the Universe that you are closed and unwilling to receive. The field of energy we call the Universe will oblige you accordingly. As long as you are willing and responsive, you will find opportunities that will supply your needs.

Your greatest value is yourself. It is the one thing you can count on. If you are mature and creative, you will have security. Why is that? Because there are many others who are unwilling to show up and offer their hand in work. Those who are willing to bring their energy to work will never run dry of opportunities to learn, to express, and to make or receive money.

I recently read a story about a woman who was unemployed and seemingly could not find work. One might consider her in dire straits, but she had faith and was open to receiving. As it turned out, she won two raffles, each for $100,000. She did not give up on the idea that she was taken care of and the Universe came through for her. Faith the size of the mustard seed was all that was needed. She let the Universe do its work. The lesson: Have faith and do not be concerned how your desires will be fulfilled.

Your needs are not great, but your desires may be. By trimming your desires to match your needs, you can create a simplicity that will, in turn, produce a more relaxed attitude toward your situation.

Be aware of the Law of Abundance operating everywhere. A tree produces millions of leaves every season. It does this naturally, without any great effort. The tree does not consider producing leaves to be a struggle or an impossible task to accomplish. The tree's essence is Universal Consciousness. So is your essence. You are also capable of amazing acts.

Pay attention and you will notice evidence of abundance all over the place. There is water everywhere and every kind of food you can imagine. There are a myriad people of every shape, size, and color. There are more countries and cultures than you could ever hope to experience.

If you trust the flow of the Universe, you will never be without the things you need. Cultivate an awareness of this Law of Abundance by observing the wild flowers blooming along the roadside. Multiply them by the millions of miles of highways in the world. The number of wild flowers is incomprehensible. Consider the possibilities of meeting ten new people a day. Would you ever deplete the supply of people to meet? No, the supply is inexhaustible.

Therefore I say unto you, be not anxious for your life, what ye shall eat, or what ye shall drink; nor yet for your body, what ye shall put on. Is not the life more than the food, and the body than the raiment?

Behold the birds of the heaven, that they sow not, neither do they reap,, nor gather into barns; and your heavenly Father feeds them. Are not ye of much more value then they?

And which of you by being anxious can add one cubit unto the measure of his life?

And why are ye anxious concerning raiment? Consider the lilies of the field, how they grow; they toil not, neither do they spin: yet I say unto you, that even Solomon in all his glory was not arrayed like one of these.

But if God doth so clothe the grass of the field, which to-day is, and to-morrow is cast into the oven, shall he not much more clothe you, O ye of little faith? Be not therefore anxious, saying, 'What shall we eat? or, What shall we drink? or, Wherewithal shall we be clothed?' For after all these things do the Gentiles seek; for your Heavenly Father knows that ye have need of all these things.

But seek ye first his kingdom, and his righteousness; and all these things shall be added unto you. Be not therefore anxious for the morrow: for the morrow will be anxious for itself. Sufficient unto the day is the evil thereof. Matthew 6:25-34

Abundance is everywhere and in all forms. The more you want, expectantly command, and aggressively go after, the more you will have. Have faith in the universal flow of energy as it shows up in opportunities, ideas, intuition, people, and events. Stay open and you will never be without anything you need.

Don't let numbers bother you. Just know that whatever you want is available in unlimited supply. Hold the picture of your desire and don't let doubt or negative programming interfere with your belief that it is yours. Then, continue on your way, and soon you will realize, intuitively, a way to manifest the object of your desire.

Fear of Criticism or Rejection

Fear of criticism and rejection is rampant in an other-oriented society. In fact, the only person who can reject you is you. The way you do that is by focusing on what other people think instead of becoming self-oriented as your own authority. In other words, be the person that is right for you. You don't need anyone's approval.

Getting past the idea that everyone must love and approve of you and your actions is a giant step toward spiritual enlightenment.

Whatever the subject, there are a myriad opinions about it. You need only concern yourself with your own thoughts about yourself, for you are the one living your life. No one knows your path but you.

Many of the great visionaries and creative people in the world were considered crackpots for attempting to go beyond the norm of society. Christopher Columbus was relentless in challenging the idea of a flat world. He courageously sailed to the *end of the world* to find a new trade route.

The Wright brothers, bicycle mechanics, of all things, were audacious enough to believe in man's ability to fly. Thomas Edison stepped out of the box to develop the light bulb, Dictaphone, and record player, among other things. He was deaf but put no limits on his creative mind. Neither should you.

Ted Turner was crazy enough to believe that 24/7 news would be a big hit. You know what? He was right.

If these perceptive inventors and adventurers had waited for public opinion to catch up with them, nothing would have changed in the world. We would probably still believe the world was flat.

Imagine the rejection Jesus faced when he chose to preach a *New Way*. At that time, if a person spoke against the established religious practices, he could potentially be killed. So, Jesus courageously taught with parables for those who could hear and understand what he truly meant.

> And the disciples came, and said unto him, 'Why speakest thou unto them in parables?' And he answered and said unto them, 'Unto you it is given to know the mysteries of the kingdom of heaven, but to them it is not given. For whosoever hath, to him shall be given, and he shall have abundance: but whosoever hath not, from him shall be taken away even that which he hath. Therefore speak I to them in parables; because seeing they see not, and hearing they hear not, neither do they understand.
>
> And unto them is fulfilled the prophecy of Isaiah, which saith, By hearing ye shall hear, and shall in no wise understand; And seeing ye shall see, and shall in no wise perceive: For this people's heart is waxed gross, And their ears are dull of hearing,

And their eyes they have closed; Lest haply they should perceive with their eyes, And hear with their ears, And understand with their heart, And should turn again, And I should heal them.'
Matthew 13:10-15

When Jesus said to those that *have, more will be given,* he meant that when we gain spiritual truth and understanding of Universal Law, we are free and open for even greater blessings because fear no longer dominates our thinking. For the man or person who has no awareness or understanding of his divinity and Christ Spirit, he has nothing. He has no Heavenly Treasure; he has no comfort in knowing the truth of his relationship with God. All he has is ego identification, which brings no comfort. To live without Spirit is true poverty.

Jesus presented radical changes: forgiveness, loving your enemy, giving up false images. He could do this because he was not afraid of criticism or rejection. In fact, he expected it. Most people resist change.

Think not that I came to send peace on the earth: I came not to send peace, but a sword. For I came to set a man at variance against his father, and the daughter against her mother, and the daughter in law against her mother in law: and a man's foes shall be they of his own household.

He that loveth father or mother more than me is not worthy of me; and he that loveth son or daughter more than me is not worthy of me. And he that doth not take his cross and follow after me is not worthy of me.

He that findeth his life shall lose it; and he that loseth his life for my sake shall find it. He that receiveth you receiveth me, and he that receiveth me receiveth him that sent me. Matthew 10:34-40

The mission for all of us is to challenge old beliefs and customs. We are to rise up to our challenges, our crosses, and live from a place of love. If you seek only worldly goods, without attention to your spiritual growth, you are unworthy of experiencing the inner Christ Spirit.

But woe unto you, scribes and Pharisees, hypocrites! Because
ye shut the kingdom of heaven against men: for ye enter not in
yourselves, neither suffer ye them that are entering in to enter.
        Woe unto you, scribes and Pharisees, hypocrites! For
ye devour widows' houses, even while for a pretense ye make
long prayers: therefore ye shall receive greater condemnation.
Matthew 23:13-14

Throughout his ministry, Jesus, representing the Christ
Consciousness, admonishes the scribes and Pharisees, who symbolize
those elements in self that want to look good, but not do good, those
components of the personality that speak the right words, but don't
put the truth into action in their lives. We have these elements in the
personality. That is what this purge is all about: dissolving the ego.

Ye serpents, ye offspring of vipers, how shall ye escape the judg-
ment of hell? Matthew 23: 33

Behold, your house is left unto you desolate. Matthew 23:38

Here again, Jesus or Christ Consciousness condemns the scribes
and Pharisees for lack of ethical behavior and authenticity. He suggests
that they will be desolate in the end. When we are radical in expanding
our Light and following his example, we will run into rejection as well.
    The opposite of fear is love. Each moment, we get to choose love.

There is no fear in love: but perfect love castes out fear, because
fear hath punishment; and he that feareth is not made perfect in
love. I John 4:18

Again, let your mind be filled with gratitude, joy, thanksgiving, and
forgiveness, all aspects of love, and there will be no room for fear. Keep
perfecting your ability to love.
    The greatest reason a person feels rejection is that he believes he
is to be perfect and his model of perfection is external: sculpting a perfect body-type, looking a certain way, status, position, expensive house,

right college degree, everything just right. On the contrary, the manifest world holds no perfection. The idea that no improvement is possible is ludicrous because the ego will not accept the concept that everything is all right as it is.

Plus, your creative mind wants to play with expression and expansion. This is true in all areas. The automobile industry comes up with new models yearly: improved motors, sleeker lines, more buttons, and gadgets. Telephone systems are ever changing, along with sound systems, appliances, cosmetics, and even mattresses. New intuitive awareness brings sweeping engineering, advanced designs, and technological improvements. This process of improvement is on-going because the nature of the Universe is increase, expansion, and abundance. The physical world adjusts because the nature of matter is unstable and constantly in motion.

When you set aside your limited concepts of material perfection and accept who you are as a perfect being, you experience peace. The Light of God is within and it is stable and unchangeable.

Perfection as a spiritual principle refers to the purity of the soul. In your natural state, you are without guile, and you are loving and beautiful.

A baby is perfect as a spiritual being and soul, yet the baby lacks motor skills and vocabulary. Think of yourself as perfect in the same way. We have perfect potential, purity, and love, yet lack specific knowledge of earthly and spiritual things. Thus, criticism, as it relates to who we are, is of no importance. It is irrelevant. As souls, we are perfect and that is the only perfection that exists.

Another way to deal with criticism is to discern its beneficial essence, if there is any, and at the same time, remove the sting. If you are hurt by criticism, you are seeing yourself as ego, not as spirit. As a spiritual being, you are without flaw.

Enjoy exploring and learning new things and you will not lose your perspective. Ego-consciousness is putting your attention on the outer world and dismissing spiritual growth. The ego acts as a spoiled child, demanding what it wants, ignoring the bigger picture, thriving on praise from the world. Identifying with your soul essence frees you from the sting of the ego.

Admit mistakes and make appropriate decisions to alter circumstances. Aim for new strategies and new actions. Don't attach to criticism. Just keep it honest.

If criticism costs your sense of humor, the price is too high!

Dismiss it?

No, laugh at the ego.

Fear of Loss of Love

Fear of loss of love amounts to facing your imperfections. The reason most people are afraid another won't love them is because they don't love themselves. They focus too much on neediness so are not able to give love freely to another. They have too many requirements before giving love. *You must be this, that, or the other for me to love you.* When they accept and love themselves as imperfect earthly beings and perfect spiritual beings, they will be able to take the limits off the love they express to others.

As a material being, I am *imperfect.* I need eight hours of sleep at night. I get cranky when I'm tired. I have not developed all the skills I desire. I regularly misspell words or drop phone calls. Nonetheless, in the spiritual realm, I am perfect, just as you are.

People will say to me, *"Jean, in the real world . . ."* They are inferring that the physical world is the real world. Yet, I say, if this is true, why is it unstable and constantly changing? Can you even remember what you did last year or last month? Identifying with your physical circumstances and the body keeps you trapped and unable to feel love. Love is your Divine Nature. Get in touch with it and you will be a fountain of love.

Reality, from an earthly being's viewpoint, amounts to facing those things that we have yet to develop. It is okay if I am not a perfect writer and you are not a perfect gymnast, piano player, or soccer star. In an other-oriented world, perfectionism is a major handicap. We want to appear perfect to be judged well. When we honor ourselves with approval, other-oriented judgment is no longer a problem. We are here to evolve. We are still in process. Otherwise, we wouldn't still be here.

Your work is to learn *how* to love, *how* to lift your minds to a greater love than you have heretofore experienced. Jesus spoke readily that greater things than what he did you can do. You just might have to give up perfectionism to do these greater works. Why? Because perfectionism is based in the ego.

In his farewell discourse, Jesus, as the Christ Consciousness, addressed the disciples, those who represent the faculties of the personality:

> *Believe me that I am in the Father, and the Father in me: or else believe me for the very works' sake.*
>
> *Verily, verily, I say unto you, he that believeth on me, the works that I do shall he do also; and greater works than these shall he do; because I go unto the Father. And whatsoever ye shall ask in my name, that will I do, that the Father may be glorified in the Son. If ye shall ask anything in my name, that will I do.* John 14: 11-14

Jesus is saying that, as we accept and believe in our inner Christ, it will stream through us in the form of great works, like designing a building, penning a poem, healing the sick, teaching, creating, parenting. The Light of Christ's presence flows through all people.

When you affirm and identify with Spirit/Christ, it performs for you. Hold your consciousness in High Energy, in Love, and anything is possible: airplanes, movies, sound systems, recorders, 24/7 news, you name it.

Fear of Ill-Health

The individual harboring the fear of ill-health is repressed and restricted because of identification with form. As a result of placing attention in the world of materiality, this person places value on the rules of that world. Distractions keep the person from seeing the Light of God within.

I am come a light into the world, that whosoever believeth on me may not abide in the darkness. And if any man hear my sayings, and keep them not, I judge him not: for I came not to judge the world, but to save the world.

He that rejects me, and receives not my sayings, hath one that judges him: the word that I spake, the same shall judge him in the last day. John 12:46-48

These words tell us to turn to the Light within, allowing the mind, which has identified with form, to accept the spiritual Self. By taking this action, Spirit is freed. This shift in perspective promotes healing. However, if we do not turn to the inner Light, continuous identification with the material world will condemn us to the ills of that world.

Fear of ill health relates to a lack of control, to dependency, and to a feeling of being inadequate. The belief is that, if or when your body breaks down or loses its beauty, you cannot revert back to health or have the good life. You feel tied to physicality alone.

Your body, however, is under your control. This means that, as you alter your thinking, the body is adjusted as well. Because the physical body is composed of spiritual energy, it is a perfect display of your thoughts. Body, mind, spirit: all part of the same energy continuum.

Your thoughts and the accompanying beliefs set the tone for your body's condition. At all times, you get to choose your thoughts. Holding high, loving, kind, compassionate, positive thoughts lifts the body energy to a high vibrancy and health. Fill your mind with fear-based thoughts like resentment, anger, guilt, and shame, and the energy flow to the body is heavy and tight. Thus, blockages occur. Dis-ease is the result. Open your mind to peaceful thoughts and for-giveness and you free your energy along with your body's condition. The body has the ability to revert to its original state of vibrancy. Imagine what it would feel like if your body expressed vibrancy. Start by establishing peace.

Remove stress from your life. You don't have to be perfect. Tension drains energy, destroys the body, and shortens your life. Start by restructuring expectations. Slow down and simplify. Perfectionism limits the soul and is a barrier to health. Eliminate it by enjoying your imperfections while nurturing patience and love. As you shift to a more optimistic stance, your *vision* of wholeness will return, for you are designed in the image and likeness of God: whole and complete.

Discipline means becoming alert to interferences in the form of negativity: emotions, beliefs, and behaviors. These are heavy, dark energies. They impede life force and creativity. They must be removed and replaced.

> *But the unclean spirit, when he is gone out of the man, passed through waterless places, seeking rest, and findeth it not. Then he saith, 'I will return into my house whence I came out;' and when he is come, he finds it empty, swept, and garnished.*
>
> *Then goeth he, and taketh with himself seven other spirits more evil than himself, and they enter in and dwell there: and the last state of that man becomes worse than the first. Even so shall it be also unto this evil generation.* Matthew 12:43-45

This parable states that when you release negative, limiting thoughts but do not replace them with positive, affirming ones, you create a space for greater negativity to come into the mind. This could include self-degradation, self-hatred, or any kind of lower energy. Spiritual enlightenment is a process that requires discipline and alertness to keep the faith, operate in the energy of love and do good works.

You were designed whole. Claim your rightful state by cooperating with the body, respecting its right to function without stress. Direct your destiny through freedom of choice, not rote programs that keep you earth-bound. That means to look to yourself and not others for approval. Look to yourself to discover *your* path.

When your body ceases to function, you will continue on as a soul within the realm of mind. Your body does not control your destiny. Your thoughts do. Purify your thinking and you will cleanse your body as well.

People often fear dis-ease and loss of control because they have never done what they wanted. They are concerned with running out of time. Putting plans in place to do what you want can change that. If you wait, you will run out of time. The joy that results from having the freedom to do what you desire will keep your body running at a high pitch of health.

Fear of Loss of Freedom

People relate commitment to loss of freedom. It is true that we need to be cognizant of our commitments. Frivolous commitment wastes time and energy. However, never making a commitment does not bring freedom. The opposite is true. When we commit to a job, relationship, family, or spiritual practice, we begin to discover our ability and strength. Avoiding commitment does not make us free because we have not discovered the strength or the tools to provide service. The error that freedom equates to never making a commitment reflects loss of value.

In the Garden of Gethsemane Jesus prayed in these words: *Father, if thou be willing, remove this cup from me: nevertheless not my will, but thine be done.* Luke 22:42

In this passage, the inner Christ is committed to God's plan above all else.

It is what we are to do. Recognize there is a Greater Energy at work in our lives and submit to it. It is evermore gracious and abundant than what our egoic mind can imagine.

In this vein, it is important to evaluate the meaning of freedom. Commitment to self-discovery and bliss requires discipline. Discipline is the path to freedom. Commitment to a life of discipline results in expansiveness and freedom. The freedom to live a life of non-reaction, non-judgment, and non-resistance gives your life meaning. It opens the door to expression as a compassionate being of love.

The key to overcoming this fear is to *know who you are*. You are a child of God, pure and perfect. There is no title that can surpass this as your identity. It is only in this *knowing*, that you are truly free.

Margaret Mead, the famous anthropologist, was an inventive, free-thinker. When faced with the choice of motherhood or a professional career, she chose both. This determination took place many years before the women's liberation movement. Because her career demanded weeks and months away from home, she hired a family to live with her daughter so that the child would have her needs for home and family met while her mother was away. She created a most unorthodox solution to her dilemma.

When she returned from her long trips, the entire family remained in tack. Few adjustments had to be made. Stability reined.

Margaret Mead was a free person. She was willing to be unconventional, to march to the tune of a different drummer as she fulfilled her needs and met the demands and responsibilities of life. She listened to her inner voice to come up with this solution. She trusted her inner guide to fulfill her mission as an anthropologist and a mom.

Take charge of your freedom by making your own decisions. If you want control of your life, you must stop looking to others for decisions. You must give yourself approval and discontinue looking to others.

Generally, people who fear loss of freedom don't have it. Do you make your own decisions? Do you practice the profession you want? Are you expressing your authentic self? You are free when you express yourself as a free being, no longer living according to someone else's beliefs and values.

Often, people relate freedom to not having to work. But work is sacred and a privilege. True freedom comes when you express your energy through work.

Freedom is independence, being able to depend on yourself to fulfill your needs. If you think you must have a certain job, or be married, or live in a certain place or manner to feel free, you have limited yourself through dependence on things. Learn how to use people and situations as resources. Then, you will always be free because your resources are unlimited.

Of course, we all need people. But we do not have to place our dependence on a particular person. If that individual is incapacitated or dies, we have lost our freedom. Dependency of this type is not fair to either person.

Many people depend on their children for happiness, or on their job for fulfillment, or on money for security. These are delusional states. Anytime we make the transitory world our source of joy and exclude Spirit, we are building our house on sand and not rock. The fact that things change can be a source of excitement and joy rather than invoke fear or insecurity.

He is like a man building a house, who dug and went deep, and laid a foundation upon the rock: and when a flood arose, the stream broke against that house, and could not shake it, because it had been well built.

But he that hears, and doeth not, is like a man that built a house upon the earth without a foundation; against which the stream broke, and straightway it fell in; and the ruin of that house was great. Luke 6:48-49

Create your own happiness. Fulfill yourself in everything you do. Express your passion. You will be free and secure in who you are.

Your nature is free. You have choices. You are unlimited in your choices. You can walk out of your prison whenever you make the choice to be free.

Fear of Old Age

This fear relates to loss of control and self-esteem. Many people judge age by the number of years someone has inhabited this earth. Yet, there are those who are old at twenty and others young at eighty. Age is an attitude and disposition.

More and more information is coming out these days about the subconscious programming that goes with aging. Dr. Christianne Northrup has written a book called *Goddesses Don't Age*. It offers valuable information on this subject.

You can decide how old you want to be—then be that. Age, just like health, is a mental state. As long as you are as open as a child, you will stay young.

In recent times, researchers like Dr. Deepak Chopra have revealed that every cell in the body is replaced within a seven-year period. Thus, our material bodies are only seven years old. So why do people age? They age because they hold mental constructs regarding age. "At twenty, we are to look and be like this. At thirty, forty, fifty, sixty, seventy, eighty, ninety, etcetera, we are to look and act like that."

There are uncultivated places in the world where people don't place these narrow views on the body. Their residents are strong, flexible, healthy, and happy for many years. They don't keep track of their numbers.

The moment we put a number on anything, we have an opinion about it. We have limited it. Pay attention to how people talk about age and you will notice the stigmas.

The soul has no age. Perhaps as souls we have been around for eons, if indeed, there is such a thing as time.

General Douglas MacArthur stated,

People grow old by deserting their ideals. Years may wrinkle the skin, but to give up interest wrinkles the soul. You are as young as your faith, as old as your doubt; as young as your self confidence, as old as your fear; as young as your hope, as old as your despair.

As far as disability goes, there is no reason to identify age with incapacitation. You can keep your body free from disease and disharmony by being at peace with yourself and following the dictates of good judgment, proper care, diet, exercise, and sleep.

You are the creator of your destiny. Keep your mind stimulated by exploring new concepts, experimenting with life, and being adventuresome. You will never exhaust the possibilities to learn and grow and you need never be old.

Getting old is optional. As chronological years build, let your experience be beautiful, a time of maturity and wisdom. Let them reflect the expansion of your truth and freedom. As you progress in the spiritual principles of non-attachment, non-judgment, and non-resistance, you will become ageless because you will see with spiritual eyes.

Fear of Death or Change

The fear of death or change amounts to fear of the unknown. Most people do not know what to expect from death. Thus, they fear it. Death is nothing more than *change*. It signifies altering one's point of reference from the outer physical world to the inner soul realm.

At our core, we are Christ Consciousness. With the release of the body, we will no longer have the distractions of earthly life. We will be free to fully embrace the Light of our True Self.

Death is transformation. In our physical life, every change we make, whether a new job, a marriage, a new baby, a relocation, or an altering of an attitude, we are adjusting our frame of reference. We can learn to be at ease with this process. As you are at peace with each transition in your physical life, you will accept death of the physical body at its right time.

If you want to become comfortable with change, practice taking risks by giving yourself new experiences: new foods, travel to exotic places, connecting with interesting people, opening to new concepts. By doing this, you come to know that there is more to life than what you see with the body's eyes. If you meditate, you will discover that there is nothing to be afraid of that is beyond the physical world.

Make a point to be open to new ideas and consciously adjust your point of view from time to time. The more changes you make, the more you will learn to trust yourself in unknown territory. Also, be quiet and listen to the still small voice within. You will be guided through your changes with vision and hope. You will never feel alone and always be renewed.

Meditation is a tool for understanding your inner world. Become accustomed to this practice and you will develop comfort with the intangible world of Spirit. Then, death of the physical body will hold no threat, for you will have acclimated yourself to the other side.

Meditation, as a course of action, is comparable to preparing for a journey, providing yourself with information and road maps prior to departing. The more information you have prior to leaving, the more secure you will feel about the journey.

Knowing that, at some point, you will step away from your earthly body, you can use the practice of meditation to become familiar with your new territory. Death, which is simply transitioning your mind, will be peaceful, because you have already practiced living in Spirit on a daily basis. You might even approach death like an old friend, waiting up ahead and reaching out in welcome.

Don't let any fear control you. Decide what kind of information you will need for further progress. Educate yourself and gift yourself with opportunities to investigate the areas that need improvement. You will continue to be bound by fear until you conscientiously take action to eliminate it. There is nothing that man cannot learn. His nature is vast and unlimited. Your only boundary is a lack of imagination. Thus, use your imagination to free yourself to walk through change unfettered.

We are each the controller of our own destiny. Through our conscious decisions to learn, grow, and appreciate each experience, we choose happiness. Through the decision to repress expression, deny experience, and run from choices, we choose lack of fulfillment and unhappiness. Our thoughts produce our characters and our personalities. Our desires produce our opportunities. Our actions determine our environments and circumstances. Choice is everything.

This is Jesus' instruction for living life:

Ye are the light of the world. A city set on a hill cannot be hid. Neither do men light a lamp and put it under the bushel but on the stand; and it shines unto all that are in the house. Even so let your light shine before men; that they may see your good works, and glorify your Father who is in heaven. Matthew: 5:14-16

CHAPTER 12

TOOLS FOR FREEING YOURSELF

*E*veryone has worth, which includes the inherent right to express yourself in your unique way. Your value was established at the time of creation and can neither be added to nor taken from. You have the choice to recognize or ignore personal worth, but it cannot be changed or lost.

There are methods available to clarify and re-establish awareness of your inherent value, tools to help you free yourself from ego entrapment, move to a higher realization of truth, and live in the peace of Christ Consciousness. Some of these tools, which are covered in this chapter, include affirmations, non-reaction, non-judgment, and non-resistance. Unconditional love and forgiveness are also necessary to reach higher awareness. They will be explored later in the book.

Jesus said,

Not that which enters into the mouth defiles the man; but that which proceeded out of the mouth, this defiles the man. Matthew 15: 11

Perceive ye not, that whatsoever goes into the mouth passes into the belly, and is cast out into the draught? But the things which proceed out of the mouth come forth out of the heart; and they defile the man. Matthew 15:17-18

A man's words are reflections of his thoughts. He is defined by the nature of his thoughts. Author and teacher Dr. Wayne Dyer describes it this way:

> *When you squeeze a lemon, what comes out of the lemon is lemon juice because that is what is inside the lemon. When you squeeze a person, whether through stress or things not going as planned, what comes out is what is inside the person. Thus, if anger is the default emotion when tension builds, that is what is expressed because that is what is inside. If cooperation and patience are expressed, that is what is inside the person. We get to choose what is inside of us.*

Following this logic, negativity is generally coupled with stressed emotions or emotional wounds. Disturbed emotions and subsequent loss of objectivity complicate perception. If you are angry or upset, you see situations and people through these distressed emotions

You put your own color on things. You read into people's motives and the meaning of events. Take note of your negative reactions because they represent your uncompleted lessons.

Quiet introspection and meditation can assist in achieving an objective, an honest evaluation. Nevertheless, you have the ability to instigate treatment or cure without fully comprehending the originating cause of the problem, but if you are able to identify the thought pattern causing the problem, it may help you move more quickly into a cure.

Ask yourself, *What have I misperceived that has thrown me into depression? What have I missed? What is the error? How have I excluded love?*

Ultimately we must look deeper than our emotional state. Otherwise, we tend to transfer our distress to others. *It's your fault. You did it to me.* For example, road rage is transferred to the person who changed lanes three times or drives too slowly. We make them the target of our anger. In the end, we are responsible for our reactions, and thus, we are also responsible for healing our wounds so that we can be fully effective in all situations.

Here are some tactics to get you started. When you are depressed or in stress, one way to shift your energy is to divert attention to someone in need. Assisting others lifts your spirit and self-esteem. It gives you space to become more objective.

Another option for moving away from depression is by focusing on beauty and calmness. Get into nature. Relax by the stream or in the woods. Nature holds healing energy. It is peace personified. It soothes the soul.

Further choices might be to visit an art gallery or museum. Watch a silly movie. Stop telling yourself the story that started the whole thing in the first place. Most of the time, the story is based on self-pity and it keeps your attention diverted to the material world.

As you stabilize your inner strength, you move gradually into peace and freedom. Identify with your inner Light. This shift helps you acknowledge your inborn value. This is your commitment.

Meditation, as a vehicle for higher awareness, is important. Seeking the quiet space within opens the door to your intuition. Intuition is the voice of God. You have to quiet the external noise so you can listen to your deeper wisdom.

And it came to pass in these days that he went out into the mountain to pray; and he continued all night in prayer to God.
Luke 6:12

We commune with our Christ Consciousness when we *go to the mountain*, a high place, and become quiet. Mountain is a metaphor for high energies, such as love, peace, and joy. This high place is our center, our Light. We can go there at will. We move our attention from the external world in order to enter our deeper space.

And on that day, when even was come, he saith unto them, Let us go over unto the other side. And leaving the multitude, they take him with them, even as he was, in the boat. And other boats were with him. And there ariseth a great storm of wind, and the waves beat into the boat, insomuch that the boat was now filling. And he himself was in the stern, asleep on the cushion: and they

awake him, and say unto him, 'Teacher, carest thou not that we
perish?' And he awoke, and rebuked the wind, and said unto the
sea, 'Peace, be still' And the wind ceased, and there was a great
calm. Mark 4:35-39

As you achieve awareness of your Christ Self, you recognize that
you are bigger than the situation. You can command it. As you bring
inner peace to your circumstances, you rise above your personal squall.
Remember the words, Peace, be still'

Now is the time to shift your identity to recognize that you are
not a body or a set of circumstances. You are not your possessions, your
position, your status, your wealth, your history, or your story. You are
bigger than all of that. You are a Christ Self. Your worthiness is set and
cannot be changed. When you accept your identity as a Christ, you
transform and expand. Your life changes for the better.

Mistakes and miscalculations are necessary as we navigate through
life. Forgive them and move on. You wouldn't hold a baby guilty for
spilling his milk, and thus, you are not guilty either. This radical change
requires diligence and discipline. You are making a paradigm shift of
major proportions.

When a rocket is shot into space, radar determines whether or not
it is on track to hit its mark. All along the way, adjustments are made to
insure that this happens. It might mean changing the rocket's path by
a micro degree, which could make a huge difference of many miles in
its course. This diligence in managing the rocket insures its safe delivery
to its projected landing site. If, for some reason, a rocket misses,
corrections are made in the calculations to insure the next one's proper
delivery. The goal and ultimate result is contact with the target. It is all
a learning experience, conducted according to the laws of science.

It is the same with you. You have one target: living in connection
to Higher Consciousness with the ability to stabilize your life accordingly.
Be willing to develop the techniques necessary to keep yourself
on the path.

To reinforce this new way, practice self-loving behaviors: walk,
work out, take time out, meditate, eat healthy foods, spend time
with positive friends, have fun, read a favorite book, go dancing, do

something you love. Be kind to yourself. Treat yourself as you would an exalted being because you are one.

The practice of positive thinking may seem hard at first because there is a psychological tendency to resist change. But, once you establish a firm start, you will find the new way as beguiling as the old, and a lot more fun, interesting, and rewarding.

Deny and Then Affirm

Many people affirm negative limiting ideas all day long. *If I eat that, I'll gain a pound. The traffic is always congested. I can't seem to get along with my co-worker. I'll never to able to get a raise.* If this sounds familiar, you will want to pay attention to *deny and then affirm* as a method that will work for you. When you catch yourself in a negative thought pattern such as those listed above, stop and affirm the opposite.

For instance, *If I eat that, I'll gain a pound,* will be followed by, *I have a great metabolism and my body is healthy and trim.*

The traffic is always congested will be followed by, *I move through traffic easily and I am always on time.*

I can't seem to get along with my co-worker, will be followed with, *I radiate love to everyone and stay centered in every situation.*

I'll never get a raise in pay, is changed with an affirmation of, *I am open to abundance and I am valued and rewarded in my work.* You get the idea.

Until you have converted your thinking to a higher vibrational level, practice affirming a more enlightened reality when you find yourself in an old negative thought pattern. With practice, you will discover that being positive comes naturally, and it definitely feels better than beating yourself up and restricting your growth.

You are forming a new viewpoint and lifestyle. Each time you think a positive thought, repeat an affirmation, or make a decision to look on the bright side, you get stronger and gain more control. Remember, you don't destroy a weed by violently pulling it from the ground, for its roots will remain and the weed will eventually return.

Instead, remove the weed of limited thinking by digging around its base in the same way you remove a weed from the ground. You must remove the entire root or belief system; then place in its stead a flower or a positive thought. If you don't replace the weed with something better, another weed will grow. When there is a healthy plant or thought thriving, there is no room for a weed or negative thought. This point is made clear in the previous parable (Luke 11:24-26) concerning the unclean spirit (negative thought) that goes out from the man and when he is faced with a similar condition, the negativity returns to the man's mental state. As it find the mind clear, the thought takes root and this time the negativity is multiplied and far worse. This mind that is clear and open has not rooted a positive affirmation in the place where there was once negativity (or fear). We must ever be prepared to raise our mental energy to a place of blessing and reward. That can only be done with positivity.

We tend to be obsessive about behaviors and beliefs. Once an unpleasant habit has been established, such as gossiping, smoking, overeating, or being fearful, it requires mental, emotional, and physical discipline to cast it out and keep it out. Otherwise, we compulsively return to the old ways and they become more entrenched than before. This is the reason alcoholics, drug addicts, over-eaters, or gossipers find it difficult to reform.

Nature abhors a void and will fill it with something. More than likely, it will match what was previously there. This is similar to the woman who divorces her husband because he is an alcoholic and womanizer, then proceeds to marry another alcoholic womanizer.

Instead of allowing randomness to fill the void, you must make a choice as to what you want. Establish a new pattern by focusing on love, by staying open to intuition, and by lifting your energy as you practice positivity.

Changing strong repetitive patterns requires effort, attentiveness, and discipline. You are giving up lifelong learned actions. It is a big deal!

Affirmations: What They Are and How They Work

An affirmation is a statement of fact. We know that words have power because in Genesis 1:3, God spoke his word: *And God said, 'Let there be light: and there was light.'*

It is important that we learn to use our powerful words to facilitate our growth. When we affirm our desire as though it has already manifested, we are doing just that. Since the subconscious, or higher mind, does not know the difference between fantasy and reality, we state our desired condition as having already happened.

The subconscious mind is like a computer. It only knows the present moment. It does not relate to the past or the future. Neither exists as far as our higher mind is concerned. That is why affirmations are always stated in the present tense. We use the power of our words to establish the condition or circumstance that we choose to have right now.

Affirmations, therefore, are power tools for evoking change. Use them to assist in setting up your new positive state as a permanent part of yourself.

Start by clearly affirming your truth. As you do this, you will be triggering the subconscious mind to act accordingly. For instance, an affirmation such as "I am vibrantly healthy," ignites the subconscious mind to make the physical, chemical, and energetic changes required to establish the stated condition. The subconscious mind is like an obedient slave. It follows your guidance. It doesn't interfere or reason on its own. It simply fulfills an order given with passion and conviction. Think of it like a computer, which carries out your commands without concern for whether they are correct or not.

Since the subconscious mind does not know the difference between fantasy and reality, if you are seeing and feeling your new healthy state, it obligingly follows through to materialize it. It cannot refuse or deviate. Therefore, correctly used affirmations are powerful.

Be aware, though, that they work equally well when used to affirm negative conditions, like, *I don't know how I will pay my bills. I shouldn't be eating this cake; it will make me fat. Nothing ever works out for me.* If you don't want these statements to be your material reality, don't affirm them.

To use affirmations effectively, they must be stated in the present tense and with strong emotion. They must be clear and specific without negatives. For instance, *I am not fat*, is a negative affirmation. The subconscious receives this instruction as, *I am fat*. The statement should be along the line of, *Each day my body becomes thinner and healthier*.

You can turn *I am not poor* into, *Prosperity flows to me in every way and every day*. I have a friend who is clear is her use of the affirmation *Money loves me*. And it does love her. She has a continuous flow of opportunity and money arriving in her life.

I am not doing well in my career can be changed to *I am brilliantly guided to greater expression and success at work*.

A great general affirmation is, *Life is awesome. Miracles show up daily*.

Many people think only of what they don't want. Therefore, focusing on what they don't want manifests the don't-wants into their lives with regularity. If you find yourself speaking in negatives, follow these statements with a corrective, positive declaration. For instance, *I don't want to be sick*, should be followed with, *I exude and radiate health. Every day I feel better and better*.

When you notice a negative declaration, follow it with a correction.

Sticking with positive statements is the easiest way to set the stage for a joyful life of well being. *Every day I feel stronger and energized. I flow with abundance. My life is filled with wonder and magic*.

By using affirmations for health, you might find yourself eating healthier foods, getting more sleep, taking supplemental vitamins, working out at the gym, giving up caffeine and sugar. Or you might develop a new discipline at work, stay away from dooms-day people, volunteer for extra work, or ask your boss what you can do to advance your career.

The point is, with positive affirmations, you evoke the cooperation of the subconscious mind and you start to reinforce a constructive change. Because affirmations are wonderful transforming tools, it is good to include them as a part of your daily routine. As you do this, you will find yourself demonstrating the qualities registered in the affirmation.

For where two or three are gathered together in my name, there am I in the midst of them. Matthew 18:20

And the apostles said unto the Lord, 'Increase our faith.' And the Lord said, 'If ye had faith as a grain of mustard seed, ye would say unto this sycamine tree, Be thou rooted up, and be thou planted in the sea; and it would obey you.' Luke 17:5-6

Using affirmations will help you build your faith. Soon you will see results and know that you have evoked the desired change. Affirmations are scientifically based. They are declarations of truth.

Judge Not

Judge not, that ye be not judged. For with what judgment ye judge, ye shall be judged: and with what measure ye mete, it shall be measured unto you. And why behold thou the mote that is in thy brother's eye, but consider not the beam that is in thine own eye? Or how wilt thou say to thy brother, Let me cast out the mote out of thine eye; and lo, the beam is in thine own eye?
Thou hypocrite, cast out first the beam out of thine own eye; and then shalt thou see clearly to cast out the mote out of thy brother's eye. Matthew 7:1-5

Be ye merciful, even as your Father is merciful. And judge not, and ye shall not be judged: and condemn not, and ye shall not be condemned: release, and ye shall be released. Luke 6:36-37

Finally, be ye all likeminded, compassionate, loving as brethren, tenderhearted, humble-minded: not rendering evil for evil, or reviling for reviling; but contrariwise blessing; for hereunto were ye called, that ye should inherit a blessing. For, He that would love life, And see good days, Let him refrain his tongue from evil, And his lips that they speak no guile: And let him turn away from evil, and do good; Let him seek peace, and pursue it. 1 Peter 3:8-11

You live with your own energy, whether positive or negative. If you perceive fault or virtue in another, it is also yours. What is true about another is also true about you. It is like looking in a mirror.

You control the results in your life. When you judge, you shrink your perception and you keep your outcomes small. Is that what you want?

There is a story of a Chinese farmer who had an old horse that he used to till his fields. One day, the horse escaped. When the villagers heard about it, they sympathized. *How terrible; what bad luck.*

The farmer responded, *Bad luck? Good luck? Who knows?*

The next week, the horse returned home with a herd of wild horses. The neighbors congratulated the farmer's great fortune. *Such good luck!*

Of course, the farmer replied, *Bad luck? Good luck? Who knows?*

The next day, while he was attempting to tame one of the horses, the farmer's son fell and broke his leg. The village people exclaimed, *Oh, dear, how terrible, such bad luck!*

Again, *Good luck, bad luck. Who knows?* answered the farmer.

Sometime later, the Chinese army marched into the town and conscripted all the able-bodied youth. Because of his broken leg, the farmer's son was left at home. *Good luck? Bad luck? Who knows?*

This story illustrates perfectly the harmful effects of making judgments. It describes the principle of non-attachment to events and one's expectations. The Chinese farmer chose not to make judgments or get hooked into how things should be. What appeared to be good one moment turned around in the next. Staying open to the flow of energy was a far better and healthier choice. It allowed him to remain peaceful.

Most people habitually get themselves wadded up in judgments. Often they do this with little valid information. As a result, their lives are filled with drama. Through their judgments, they attempt to control events to the point that many of life's gifts are overlooked. Often, their preoccupation with what everyone else *should* be doing causes them to ignore their own lessons and opportunities.

Every event and circumstance that occurs is rife with opportunity to learn, prosper, and expand in some way. If a person makes a commitment to put off judgment and cultivate openness, that person could get off an emotional roller coaster, learn to experience the natural rhythm and peaceful flow of life, and ultimately be receptive to the many gifts awaiting. At that point, the incredible, bountiful blessings that life offers would become more obvious.

For example, there was a woman who was used to having a robust relationship with her daughter. When her daughter planned to get married, the mother was upset and protested what appeared to be the loss of that relationship. The mother further registered her disapproval of the union by wearing black to the wedding ceremony. Over time, she made such a ruckus that her daughter finally quit calling her and quit spending time with her. Thus, the woman lost what was most valuable to her: the relationship with her daughter. She couldn't see that instead of losing a daughter, she might have gained a son. That is what judgment and attachment do. They separate us from reality and keep us small.

Judgment in itself isn't bad. For instance, we have to make a judgment to decide which class to take, what work to engage in, or which people to hang out with. Yet, judgment turns negative when you choose to use it to make others *bad* or *wrong* or to make yourself right all the time. Ask yourself if your judgments are helpful or hurtful? What are the intentions behind your judgments?

Jesus taught that when you make negative judgments, you live with the consequences. Thus, with every judgment, positive or negative, you are currently living with the consequences. That is why what you see in others is also in you. You constantly transfer your values on to others. Dislike something about another and you will find fault with that same element in yourself. Indeed, others reflect back to you the things you find most disturbing about yourself. *Yikes!*

Judge others; judge yourself. When you *see* it, you can change it in yourself. That is a gift from the Universe.

How do you stop critical judgment? Remember, negative judgment comes from fear-based thinking. You are operating from fear when you are judgmental. In other words, others have to be wrong so you can be right. What do you need to do to love that person and yourself? What do you need to do to see the goodness in others and yourself? Do you really desire to love unconditionally?

An observation is different from a judgment. You can observe a quality in another without it being a judgment. For instance, someone appears to be late. That is not a judgment. It becomes judgmental when you decide that the person is *bad* or *unworthy* because of being late.

Endeavor to seek higher understanding. Remember, it is not your job to change others. You are playing the *earth game* to learn to love and, thereby, develop your own creative potential.

Do your judgments have to do with fear? Of what are you afraid? What can you do to move into Love and walk away from fear?

Here is an activity that can help. When you find yourself judging others or yourself, stop, take a breath, and move into the stillness within. Connect with your heart. Feel the love that is there. Breathe into your heart. Send love to the person with whom you find yourself out of harmony, even if it is you. Mentally say to the person, *I bless you and I forgive you for anything real or imagined you have done. I now relax into the Love of the Universe and let go.* Feel yourself letting go like a clenched fist that has opened. Ah! Freedom!

Another activity that will help you become less judgmental is to take note of the areas or topics where you find yourself in judgment. Is it with tardiness, weight, looks, rudeness, traffic, efficiency, professionalism? Make a conscious decision to let go of judgment on one of those topics. Then move to the next one and keep releasing. This could take over a period of days or months, but soon your mind will be free and open. You will observe a more beautiful world.

The more you do these exercises, the easier they become. You are always choosing your experience. Peace is far more rewarding than discord.

With affirmations and exercises to lift your consciousness to a higher awareness, you are working your mind like you would work a racehorse. You require obedience from the horse and the mind. The racehorse loves being worked, and so does the mind. You demand and command that it follow your directive. As you use these tools, your mind obligingly adjusts and gets stronger. Soon, you are able to find goodness and love where you never found it before.

The Power of Non-Attachment

Jesus' instructions to his disciples in conducting their ministries were:

And into whatsoever city or village ye shall enter, search out who in it is worthy; and there abide till ye go forth. And as ye enter into the house, salute it. And if the house be worthy, let your peace come upon it: but if it be not worthy, let your peace return to you. And whosoever shall not receive you, nor hear your words, as ye go forth out of that house or that city, shake off the dust of your feet. Matthew 10:11-14

In his instructions, Jesus teaches the principle of non-attachment. His disciples were to enter a town freely and, if it did not demonstrate its willingness to receive their message, they were to leave it. In other words, they were to accept the decision of the town and move on. This is a powerful principle and can save you lots of time and angst. Often, we try over and over to convince someone to be part of our world when it makes more sense to accept their initial decline. Bless them if they welcome you and move on if they don't.

What is non-attachment? It is the ability to enjoy things, people, and circumstances without needing to control them or hold on to them. Jack Schwarz, the founder of the Aletheia Foundation in Oregon, states that non-attachment is being fully involved in something but not being affected by it.

Here are some examples of non-attachment in nature:

The air moves freely.

Water flows freely to the river and ocean.

Waves flow freely to the beach.

The earth moves freely on its axis.

Letting things flow freely allows you to receive maximum benefits from each experience and relationship. The energy of the universe wants to flow freely through you and through your life. When you interfere with this natural energy flow, you block abundance, lower your energy, and create body discomfort.

Holding on to *the way things should be* blocks energy, money, and people from entering your life. This is why non-attachment, along with non-judgment and non-resistance, are three important aspects to enlightened living.

Gary Zukav, author of *Soul Stories*, relates an incident regarding a time when he was trapped in traffic behind an incredibly inept driver. His frustration built as it seemed he would never get from behind this bumbling fool who had tied up traffic in several lanes and was making him late for an important meeting. He honked at the guy, trying to get him to *Move!* He impatiently pounded the wheel and muttered expletives about this menace to driving safety.

Eventually, making his way around the impediment, he was agog to recognize the driver as an old friend he hadn't seen in years. In fact, this friend had been ill, frail, and disabled. Zukav was shocked that his friend was still alive because he had gone through incredibly difficult times.

Encumbered with guilt, Zukav felt horrible because he had made a judgment about this person without having sufficient information. The other driver, indeed, was doing the best that he could under the circumstances. Furthermore, the fact that Zukav's attitude, mood, and demeanor instantly changed from anger to compassion, once he determined the facts, was incredulous. He was stupefied to realize how quickly he jumped to a conclusion and let his ire get the better of him. Compassion was what was really needed.

On a similar note, Zukav relayed another saga concerning a man who showed up at this door to deliver firewood. A skinny young boy accompanied the man. Zukav ventured outside with them to show them where to deposit the firewood. The boy immediately jumped from the truck and started stacking firewood. The man just stood and watched him without making any attempt to help.

Zukav was fuming as he observed the inequity of the situation: this grown man lazily standing, doing nothing, while this skinny kid slaved away. It was obvious the man was taking advantage of the boy.

Finally, when the man got in his truck to fill out the papers, Zukav struck up a conversation with the boy. *How do you like delivering firewood?* he inquired.

Oh, I really like it. Mr. Smith really helped me out with this job. He pays me by the hour and, if it wasn't for him, I wouldn't be able to go to school. This job gives me the money I need to buy the things I need for school.

Again, Gary Zukav was humbled. He had judged too quickly. Things were not what they seemed to be.

Have you found yourself making judgments too quickly and without adequate information? It is easy to judge a shy person as being arrogant, when what is needed is compassion and encouragement.

How easy it is to indulge our egos and rationale, to believe we have all the facts to judge a situation when often we have none. It takes discipline to reserve judgment and check out our assumptions. It often goes to prove things are not always what they seem to be. The bottom line is that we can save ourselves embarrassment by going the extra mile to be kind, friendly, and helpful.

All judgments reflect attachment. All attachments result from irrational belief systems. One example would be, *It is of great importance to be liked and approved of by everyone.* Holding tight to this belief leads to judgment, anger, and criticism when and if it appears that someone doesn't approve of you.

Irrational belief = Attachment = Judgment and Criticism = Unhappiness

There are many such beliefs. Living in an irrational state wherein we believe that we have the answers and can control everything and everyone sets us up for constant turmoil. We are not moving freely as air, water, or ocean currents. We are resisting.

It is hard to achieve a non-attached state when we believe our personal identity is dependent on the object of attachment. This could be a particular job, a title, an amount of money, or any particular circumstance. For instance, the woman who did not want her daughter to marry was attached to her exclusive relationship with her daughter.

The only way to achieve peace and joy is to let go. In other words, we can enjoy the situation we are in, we can enjoy our home, car, position, airplane, or castle, but we must not let it define us. No matter who you love or where you work, no matter how much money you possess, you are still *you*, a being of Light. Moving to higher understanding allows you to let go in peace.

We don't know what others' lessons are. Most of the time, we aren't even sure of our own. Thus, it is foolish to judge what is going on with anyone else.

Generally, we make judgments of others so that we can avoid dealing with our own issues. Making them *wrong* so we can be *right* is a great ego trap. The Buddhists have a saying: *The finger pointing at the moon has four other fingers pointing back at self.* In other words, when we are criticizing others, we are really judging ourselves.

Attachment to a specific result causes judgment in the same way that holding to an irrational belief leads to judgment. Our world is full of attachments to special and particular results. We want things like achieving a certain status, living in a specific neighborhood, being good at golf, winning a gold medal, having our sports team win.

Result-orientation keeps us focused in the wrong place. We get hooked on a certain outcome and lose our vision of the evolutionary process. Paying attention to the process makes more sense.

Are you learning and growing right now? Are you developing skills and abilities? Are you learning to cope? Where are you in your process?

A golfer develops expertise by practicing his swing, his putt, and his assessment of the golf course. It requires lots of practice to develop expertise in these areas. If the golfer focuses on winning to the exclusion of learning his sport, he will become result-oriented and out of control. Why? Because every course is different. He cannot control the environment or his opponents, who may have been at this game a lot longer. Mistakes are part of the process and par for the course, if you will.

By focusing on the process rather than the result, progress is made. We are all in our own process of development. Time, practice, and patience can be our friends.

When we hold on to things that are no longer in use, we are governed by a belief that we know what we need better than the Universe knows. Holding on means we are denying the abundance and support of the Universe. As we stockpile items for some future use, which may or may not happen, we are not trusting the natural flow of the Universe to provide everything needed as it is required.

Again, bring your attention to nature. Note that the Universe functions perfectly. Birds seem quite small and vulnerable, yet they have been around for thousands of years. They know when to fly south, where to go for water and food, how to find trees for nesting. They are guided by a higher navigation system and allow it to work through them.

When we judge things as good or bad, we limit our experience because we are attached to our judgments. We enrich no one. For instance, we may judge death as bad: someone dies too young; someone waits too long; it's not the right time. How are we to know the rightness or wrongness of the time of death? We know nothing of another people's experience. Everyone is on an evolutionary journey. Each path has its own twists and turns and is completed at the right moment.

Think of a time when you received something with no effort on your part. You were open to receiving; you did not interfere with the Universe's ability to provide. Can you remember getting a check in the mail that you weren't expecting, a raise, a job opportunity, award, or a surprise gift? You allowed the bounty of the Universe to serve you. Develop the ability to expect and receive Universal bounty every day. It could be a smile from a stranger, someone buying your coffee, someone offering you a book or a complement or even money. Allow it to serve you.

Mastering the art of non-attachment requires willingness to believe that the Universe is a place of abundance. When we hold that belief, our circumstances reflect it. That's when we come to recognize that abundance is our natural state, the same way that trees produce millions of leaves each season without any great effort. Let go of any idea as to how things *should* be and observe the energy as it flows freely in your life.

In this way, you can love and appreciate your home, job, family, and possessions, yet have no attachment to them. When attached, if you lose your home, you lose a part of yourself. It's hard to recover because you are not operating in wholeness. When you are non-attached, you will find it easier to deal with the challenges that face you.

Relationships present a great opportunity to use this principle. When people hold on, they do it out of a belief in lack. You can enjoy your friends and family, but there is no guarantee for how long they will be with you. People move away, seek different employment opportunities, relocate for schooling, or even die. Non-attachment creates freedom for everyone, even your friends and family members. Your relationships flow because, in each moment, there is a commitment to that type of relationship. Each relationship adds value to all the other relationships.

Honoring the time you spend with another is a loving way to accept change. People grow at different rates and in different ways. Sometimes what starts out as a loving, tender relationship changes because the needs of the individuals alter. This doesn't have to mean failure or someone is at fault. Learning how to let go with love is a great statement of growth.

If you enjoy your home and it is inadvertently destroyed, you come to understand that there is another home for you. Who you are and your value as a person is not effected by a loss of this type. In your life, you will probably live in many different homes. None of them define who you really are.

Several years ago, a tornado came through my neighborhood and destroyed our condo. A huge oak tree fell on the roof and broke seven tresses. Water poured into the house and destroyed the wood flooring, walls, electrical system, and furniture. The house became uninhabitable.

We were instructed to move out, so we ventured to a hotel. Under normal circumstances, it would have taken a few months to rebuild our condo, but these conditions were not normal. Thus the reconstruction took ten months of hassling with the insurance and construction companies.

In the meantime, we lived in a hotel suite, much like a small apartment. It was overcrowded and extremely inconvenient. Since we'd had little time to remove items from our home, and since many of our belongings had been destroyed by the tornado damage, we had to manage with only a few things.

Despite all the turmoil going on around me, I was at peace. In my perception, a house is a thing that can be replaced. I have never identified with any of my houses, and I have moved often.

The end result of the tornado story is that our home was completely rebuilt with new electrical and plumbing systems, a new up-dated kitchen, new flooring, new fireplace, and a new guest bathroom. It was a *new* home. It was a great way to start over.

By staying in a space of non-judgment and non-attachment, I ended up with a newer house than the one I started with. Why? Because I kept my ego out of the situation and higher energy always gleans higher, better results.

The point is that no matter where you are or what your circumstances, you can choose peace.

Let Go of Resistance

Letting go is a challenge as well as an opportunity. Some consider letting go as a weakness, like fragility, failure, or loss. But the fact is, letting go results in freedom. It releases you to incredible new beginnings.

That which you resist has power over you. Why? Because resistance requires attention. Whatever you place your attention on controls you.

Healer Jack Schwarz, Founder of the Aletheia Foundation, stated this idea another way, *That which you identify with ultimately dominates you.* Thus, if you fight fear, you identify with fear and it dominates you. If you identify with loneliness, loneliness controls you because that is where you have placed your attention.

There are many ways we fight life. By avoiding illness, rather than maintaining health, we create a state of resistance. Attention on debt, rather than on the continuous flow of money and opportunity, is resistance. We resist life by concentrating on all the ways something won't work instead of finding ways it will, or by trying to change other people instead of ourselves.

Mother Theresa, the great saint who worked among the poor in India, was invited to attend a rally to oppose war. She refused and countered, *When you have a gathering on Creating Peace, I will be there.* She was willing to give her energy to promoting peace and not toward fighting anything.

There is a famous story of a man who was caught in a flood. As the water rose and lapped around his house, he sat on the roof praying to God to be saved. Soon a boat motored by and the captain called to the man, *Hop in and we will take you to safety.*

The man replied, *No, thank you.*

A little while later, a helicopter hovered overhead and the pilot yelled to the man, *Grab the rope and we will get you out of here.*

Again, the man called back, *No, thank you.*

Sometime later, the man admonished God, *Why have you not saved me?*

A voice came to the man. *I sent a boat and a helicopter to save you, and you refused to go with either of them. What do you want?*

Such is the nature of resistance.

Have you ever asked for something and then, when an opportunity showed up to have what you requested, you stepped back and said, *No, thank you.* This action of ignoring or avoiding the efforts of the Universe to respond to your desires is resistance. It blocks your connection to Spirit.

This is how it works: You ask for what you want, and the Universe supplies the opportunity for you to have it. In other words, you are part of the solution.

You lose power by resisting opportunity. Resistance blocks the free-flow of energy and movement. It keeps you stuck, denies pleasure, and most importantly, keeps you focused in the ego and not on Spirit. Resistance keeps you small and locked in fear.

Posture yourself in resistance and you avoid learning. You keep yourself from understanding the underlying purpose and meaning of the events and relationships you draw to yourself. Each person attracts the perfect circumstances and people to heal past wounds and grow in divinity. Stubbornness causes you to do it the way *you* deem perfect. This blinds you to new opportunities.

I know a fellow who asked God if he should leave his wife because they weren't getting along. That night, a storm brewed and a large tree fell on his car. He was unable to move the tree or his car. He understood the message: he was not going anywhere. And he didn't.

From his point of view, this incident was a true gift because it taught him to deal with the circumstances of his marriage along with his judgments and resistance. He let go of his concept of a perfect marriage. He became non-resistant and learned to listen more. He found the good in the union he had. In other words, the man worked on himself and he grew in understanding and patience, and the couple stayed together, had more fun, and improved their marriage.

During the span of your life, you have formed false perceptions about who you are. In order to heal these, you magnetize people and circumstances that resemble the past in order to become aware of what is happening, change your view, and discover a higher meaning. These are gifts, even though they may appear negative. By paying attention and receiving the gifts, you evolve.

Life flows easily as does energy. There are only two ways to deal with energy. You either flow with it or resist it. Resisting wastes energy and creates struggle, pain, and negativity. Flowing opens the way to newness and freedom.

Remember the story of the old master who happened on a ruckus in his village because there was a horse tied in front of a store kicking people and no one could pass without getting injured.

The master saw the problem and chose to take a different street to his destination. The master chose ease and non-resistance. He continued on his way in peace.

You can give up resistance by learning from the effortless movement of nature. Instead of struggling against the wind, trees bend with it. Water trickles effortlessly down the mountain, flowing around obstacles, letting gravity guide the way. Animals instinctively know, without trying, when to store food for the winter, or when to fly south, or when to step into and out of hibernation. Spring yields to fall and fall to winter with complete ease. We can live the same way.

Effortless ease requires listening to our bodies, to our inner voice, to what feels right. We block out listening when we push forward relentlessly without concern for stress and strain.

Listening can be as simple as sleeping until you're ready to rise, eating what you really want, working until you are tired, letting go of a goal that requires more from you than it gives, or releasing relationships that are toxic and unproductive. Each moment you give up resistance to life, you increase your health, energy, and personal resourcefulness. When you let go of everything that doesn't work or doesn't benefit you, you make room for all that can and will bless you. What do you need to let go of first?

When you practice non-resistance, you look for opportunities to grow and to seek expansion.

When you are in resistance, you bar Spirit from entering your life. You basically declare, "I, as the ego, want to be in control, and I am unwilling to be open to a Greater Intelligence." Of course, that doesn't keep God out of your life; it just keeps you trapped in your life.

There is deeper meaning in every event and circumstance. Many people deal with the ending of a relationship as a time of blame and recrimination. *He/she wasn't right for me anyway. My spouse or partner didn't appreciate me or treat me right. It is his/her fault.* When blame is your reaction, you are looking at appearances and reacting from ego.

Behind the outer expression, something else is happening. The Universe is literally moving you to a greater lesson and opportunity. Perhaps it is teaching you how to love, how to share, how to forgive, how to be a good partner, or possibly how to get out of your own way.

Often, the *real* lesson is missed because the person is protecting his ego. This indicates fear of looking bad or *being* the *bad* guy. An egoic reaction when a relationship has ended might be, *I guess I am no good at relationships, so I'll avoid them in the future.* This, like throwing the baby out with the bath water, is tossing the whole relationship experience aside and ignoring the wealth of knowledge that comes with relationship lessons. The choice is not to learn. Relationships are the chief mechanism we use to learn about ourselves. Avoiding them equates to avoiding growth.

The stream flows downhill, around tree stumps, and over rocks. Life flows in this way also. The brook trickles down the mountain, the wind blows where it will, waves roll freely to shore, the seasons flow one to the other, and so it is with life. This free-flow of energy exemplifies our natural state. It is Spirit! It carries change easily, subtly, and effortlessly. Change is the only constant in life. As we honor and trust this flow, we can be at peace.

CHAPTER 13

PROCESS OF CHANGE: ELEVEN STEPS TO A NEW YOU

Are you ready to change? If you are committed to become the person you want to be, the steps outlined in this chapter will be invaluable to you. By following these eleven steps, you will be guided in strengthening your determination and creating the changes you want in your life.

Here they are:

1. Make a decision as to what kind of person you want to be.
2. Strengthen your desire by contemplating the achievement of your goal.
3. Expand your faith through use of affirmations.
4. Visualize what you want.
5. Be honest and responsible.
6. Experiment and take risks to develop new techniques.
7. See the positive side of every situation.
8. Ask for guidance.
9. When you receive an answer or direction from your Higher Mind, follow it unquestioningly.

10. Forgive everyone who has ever wronged you, including yourself.

11. Love and appreciate everything.

Let me tell you a story of how I used these tools to make changes in my life. Many years ago, I used to work from my home. After a while, my home became Grand Central Station with all the comings and goings of counseling clients. Something had to be done. I decided to use my tools to create a new suite of offices.

It was 1982. I started by visualizing the kind of office I wanted in a commercial building. Since I had been using visualization as a tool for many years, I knew what to do. I imagined a suite with a private office for me, and one for my business partner, Joan, as well as a waiting area and a separate room where we could teach classes. Since I knew that I could have what I wanted as long as I accepted it as truth, I set my intention to acquire this suite for a maximum amount of $300 a month. I kept this ideal sacred; meaning private, because I knew that most people would think my requirement outrageous. And it was. But the Universe does outrageous things all the time—many of them way bigger than what I required.

Joan was aware of my plan, my visualization, and my determination to get our suite of offices in a good area at a reduced rate.

For about three weeks, I did five minutes of visualization every day, mentally walking through my new business suite, touching the walls, feeling the floor under my feet, and generally enjoying the feel of my new space.

At that point, my inner voice, my *intuition*, told me to go to a particular two-block section in the Clayton area of St. Louis, Missouri, and check out the rental signs. There, I discovered three posters indicating office space for rent. I recorded the numbers and followed up with phone calls, querying each property manager. On the third call, the person answering the phone said, *Yes, I can give you any amount of space and negotiate price.*

Bingo! I had found the space. I could feel it.

The following day, Joan and I went to check it out. I wasn't even sure which building it was, but we eventually found it. The office space was on the second floor of a large house, converted for commercial use.

We met the property manager at the building and discussed the cost of square footage, which actually meant nothing to me. The price he offered was over twice what I had planned on paying, but I was not deterred. When the fatal moment arrived and he asked me what I was willing to pay, I told him $300 a month. He almost choked as he laughed at my audacity and straightforwardness.

I did not laugh. I said, *Well, it isn't rented. Could you ask the owner if he would take our offer?*

The property manager walked away with a smile on his face, shaking his head. *I will check on it and get back to you in two days.* He left the keys to the suite with us. This was another sign I took to mean that we had our offices.

As he was walking out the door, I called to him. *The offices are dirty and need to be painted. Would you take care of that?*

He responded with another smile and nod. *I will see to it.* Then, he was gone.

Okay, we are in business, I told Joan. *We have just manifested our new suite of offices.*

Joan was as stunned as the property manager, but went along with me. The two of us went off to buy furniture. Both my partner and the property manager were amazed, but I knew that these were our offices.

Less than a month later, we moved in to our newly painted offices.

This story illustrates the power of the mind and the imagination. As I stated earlier, far greater demonstrations than getting an office suite at a low cost have been experienced by using these principles. Some people have overcome serious, even fatal illnesses, wars have ended, families have settled feuds, lives have been saved. You ignite your innate power when you focus your mind clearly, consciously, and with imagination.

Everything I have done, you can also do. Let's look closer at the process.

1. *Make a decision as to what kind of person you want to be.*

Decisions become goals. Being decisive is how you take control of your life. What kind of person do you want to be: peaceful, healthy, optimistic, appreciative, happy, funny, playful, secure, and prosperous?

Paint a picture in your imagination of this new you. Make this person as real as possible. Generate emotion as you visualize yourself in this perfected state. This new you is the goal. The fact that you have consciously made this choice means you are connected to your vision and it is already real. If this *new you* did not exist, you would not be able to imagine it. That is how imagination works.

As a part of your decision, consider all the reasons why it is right that you manifest this new self. For example, you will have more to give, be happier, and be more able to help others.

Continue by assessing your positive qualities, i.e., sensitivity, honesty, sincerity, caring, friendly, hard-working, good friend, loyal, and so forth.

Make a list of these good points and add to it daily. Being honest and keeping this list will help raise your energy and make your desired change easier to accomplish. As you acknowledge your good qualities, you will build a deserving attitude.

Goals are birthed as decisions. No one achieves anything without first deciding to do so. Goals give purpose and meaning to life, and they build confidence and strengthen positivity. Making a firm decision and working toward a specific outcome makes you strong. It is a powerful way to discover your capabilities.

If you are not making decisions and setting your own goals, someone else is. Following, rather than leading, is not an expression of self-love. Make your decisions and allow others to make theirs. Your life takes on significance when you take control by being decisive.

Follow up with action on your decisions, as I did when I drove to the Clayton area of St. Louis, collected phone numbers, and followed up with an appointment to check out the building. Each action you take will bring your closer to your desired result. Action also encourages a sense of fulfillment, which helps you to realize your full potential. It all starts with a decision.

2. *Strengthen your desire by contemplating the achievement of your goal.*

Consider how attaining your goal will benefit you, your family, your job, the world. Understand that the more you have personally, whether that is strength, a special ability, intelligence, or money, the more you have to offer others. Build enthusiasm and excitement. Let your imagination soar as to how you will share your resources. Get excited!

In my hometown of St. Louis, our baseball team is the Cardinals. Whenever they get close to achieving some sort of success, like when the bases are loaded and the next batter steps up to the plate, or when they are about to tie up the game and get their needed run, the billboards light up. *Make some noise! Get excited!* Why? Excitement builds magnetic energy. You can feel it in the ballpark.

So, I say to you, *Make some noise and get excited! You are on your way!*

Desire is a motivating force. If your desire is strong, you will be motivated. You have to know why you want to get busy and take action. *Why* is an important question. I wanted new offices because it was time to expand my counseling practice and reach out to more clients and students, and time to expand my service in the community. I also wanted my home to be a *home*, not a business. These were my motivating factors. What are yours?

Create a strong desire so that you will be *in action* and willing to do what it takes to achieve your result. There are many people who will say, *I really want this or that*, but that is all they do. They just *want* it. They don't put action behind their desire. And surprise: nothing happens. Make sure you are busy moving toward your goal.

3. *Expand your faith through use of affirmations.*

Affirm your desired objective as a statement of fact. Jesus taught us to ask for what we want as though we have already received it. That means to affirm the existence of our desires in the present moment.

The truth is that, if you want something, it already exists in your mind. Affirming the reality of your idea by *feeling* it, adds energy and density to its ultimate precipitation into the physical world. Also, your faith strengthens with the repeated use of affirmations.

Expectation is part of faith. You hold expectations according to your faith. Remember the light switch? You flick it on and the light illumines the room. Expect the result you want in the same manner. When you expect the best, you don't accept anything less than the best.

Cultivate an *I-know-it-is-going-to-happen* attitude. Have your hair stand on end with anticipation. Use faith and expectation together. Believe that what you want is yours while you keep your eyes open for opportunities to fulfill your desire. Remember, God is outrageous in fulfilling desires.

Jesus taught us that if we have faith the size of a mustard seed, which is quite tiny, we could move mountains. So, let's move some mountains.

4. Visualize what you want.

Can you imagine how joy feels? Create the feeling of exhilaration, excitement, pleasure, happiness, love, peace, and fulfillment. Constructing these sensations in your mind and body influences your emotional state. A corresponding physical response will ensue. Take control of your creative faculty, your imagination. Then, you will not only control your thoughts, but program your reactions as well. Visualization is a powerful tool. With proper use, you can uproot past negativity and create beautiful tomorrows.

Roger Crawford was an avid visualizer. He was born in October, 1960, with rare birth defects that included a thumb-like projection extending directly out of his right forearm and a thumb and one finger stuck out of his left forearm. He had no palms. His arms and legs were shortened. He had only three toes on his shrunken right foot and a withered left leg, which was later amputated. The doctor said that Roger would never walk or be able to take care of himself.

Fortunately, his parents did not accept this. They taught their son that he was only as handicapped as he wanted to be. Roger said, *they never allowed me to feel sorry for myself or take advantage of people because of my handicap.*

To complete his homework, Roger had to hold his pencil with both hands, writing very slowly. As a result, he regularly got into trouble because his school papers were late. To remedy the situation, Roger asked his dad to write a note to his teachers requesting a two-day extension. Instead, his dad made Roger start writing the papers two days earlier. As Roger puts it, *My parents always taught me that I was only as handicapped as I wanted to be.*

Roger's father encouraged him to get involved in sports. He taught him how to catch and throw a volleyball and play backyard football. At age twelve, Roger won a spot on the school football team. Before every game, Roger visualized his dream of scoring a touchdown.

One day, the ball landed in his arms. Off he ran as fast as he could on his artificial leg. Everyone cheered wildly.

At the ten-yard line, a fellow from the other team grabbed his left ankle. Roger tried to pull his artificial leg free, but instead he ended up having his leg pulled off. Can you imagine the surprise of the opposing player who was left holding a leg?

Roger, still standing, and without anything else to do, hopped across the goal line.

The referee threw his hands up in the air. *TOUCHDOWN!*

Roger puts it this way, *You know, even better than the six points was the look on the face of the other kid who was holding my artificial leg.*

With each experience, Roger's confidence grew. He loved sports so much that every obstacle dissolved with his determination to play. Along the way, he developed a philosophy. *You can't do everything. It's better to concentrate on what you can do.*

He could swing a tennis racket. Unfortunately, when he swung it too hard, his weak grip would launch it into space. As luck, or the Universe would have it, Roger stumbled on an odd-looking tennis racket in a sports shop. He could wedge his finger between its double-barred handle when he picked it up. The snug fit with the racket made it possible for Roger to swing, serve, and volley like an able-bodied tennis player. He practiced daily and soon was playing and losing matches.

Roger persisted. He practiced and practiced. Surgery on his left hand enabled him to grip his special racket better, thus greatly improving his game. He became obsessed with tennis and, in time, started to win. He went on to play college tennis, finishing his tennis career with twenty-two wins and eleven losses. He later became the first physically handicapped player to be certified as a teaching professional by the United States Professional Tennis Association.

Roger now tours the country, speaking to groups about what it takes to be a winner, no matter who you are. *The only difference between you and me is that you can see my handicap but I can't see yours. We all have them.*

When people ask me how I've been able to overcome my physical handicaps, I tell them that I haven't overcome anything. I simply learned what I can't do, such as play the piano or eat with chopsticks. But more importantly, I've learned what I can do. Then, I do it with all my heart and soul. That is the prescription for success.

Happiness, according to Webster's dictionary is *an agreeable sensation, which springs from the enjoyment of good; that state of being in which desires are gratified by the enjoyment of pleasure without pain.* Happiness is an attainable state because you can create through visualization agreeable sensations, pleasure, and good. You are good and you can choose to feel good.

You have the ability to place your attention and focus your mind on whatever you desire. Because you have free will, you can choose to create pleasant situations or horrible ones. We have a natural tendency to reflect upon the past. As you do this, you recreate the feelings and emotions of that memory. If these periods were enjoyable, your thoughts are pleasant. Conversely, when the past seemed unhappy, you respond by feeling sad.

You are free to think about happy or sad memories, just as you get to decide whether your present attitudes will focus on deserving, or not. By choosing to feel deserving, you arm yourself with optimism. Instead of acting as a spoiled child, your imagination is now under your control as you face life's challenges and opportunities. As an aside, did you know that the Chinese symbol for challenge is the same as the symbol for opportunity? Hmmm! Which would you prefer?

Instead of living in the past, practice being in the present moment. See the beauty it holds. Recognize the opportunities it offers. Appreciate and love it. If you do all these things, you will be happy.

Direct your imagination by visualizing what your goal looks like, feels like, smells, tastes, and sounds like. Get involved with the new you, your goal, as you imagine its completion. Have fun with it, but most of all, *become* your goal. With repeated practice, your goal assumes more realistic proportions. This is when you have trained your imagination.

Once your imagination is under your domain, you can decide your fate.

Visualization and emotion are magic twins. Combined, they increase the magnetic quality of your desire. After a while and with increased discipline, you will have a hard time imagining life without the object of your desire. When you have achieved this degree of comfort with your picture, you know you have succeeded. It is now just a matter of time, more than likely a short time, until you see your projected goal/condition in physical form.

In 1943, Thomas Watson, Chairman of IBM, said, *I think there is a world market for maybe five computers.*

In 1949, in forecasting scientific progress, *Popular Mechanics* stated, *Computers in the future may weigh no more than 1.5 tons.*

In 1957, the editor in charge of business books for Prentice Hall reported, *I have traveled the length and breadth of this country and talked with the best people, and I can assure you that data processing is a fad that won't last out the year.*

In 1977, Ken Olson, President, Chairman, and Founder of Digital Equipment Corporation stated, *There is no reason anyone would want a computer in their home.*

Then, Bill Gates, Founder of Apple Computers, came along and made it his mission to put a computer in everyone's home.

Which one had vision?

Use visualization as your magic genie. Anything you can imagine has the potential of becoming your reality.

5. *Be honest and responsible.*

If your new self seems slow to come, review your efforts and determine where you have been lacking in sincerity or belief. Honestly accept responsibility for doubts that have filtered in and blocked your manifestation.

On the other hand, if you have been successful in attaining your desire, but it seems blemished or not exactly as you wanted, realize what you will need to do to refine your future efforts. Consider the components as well as what interferes with success. Learn from your efforts so you can further develop your process.

The other part of being honest and responsible is that you cannot create for others. There are two reasons: 1) They are here to grow and do their own work, and 2) you could interfere with their lessons. Of course, that doesn't mean you can't support and applaud their efforts.

6. *Experiment and take risks to develop new techniques.*

There's a saying that goes like this: *What you don't know won't hurt you.* Consider, however, that inexperience and lack of knowledge can cost a lot because it encourages mistakes—sometimes costly mistakes. Mistakes can be great teachers, but repeating the same ones wastes time. Gain experience so that you have more information to draw upon when making future choices.

You can't grow if you don't take risks. Plus, the more you risk, the more you grow. With each new experiment, calculate the potential results and make your experiences count. Earth is a schoolroom. We are here to play and grow.

There is an inventive fifth-grade writing teacher in Michigan who helped his students, early in life, get over the hurdle of having courage to take risks. In one of his assignments, he has his students write to local businesses and make *outlandish* requests. The students are also to tell something personal about themselves and explain their project.

The teacher's primary intention in making this assignment is to encourage students to make letter-writing fun. Strangely enough, the kids usually get what they ask for, including such things as a month's supply of chocolate milk or a lifetime supply of french-fries.

Besides providing the students with an inventive, fun writing assignment, the teacher contributes hands-on experience to one of life's important lessons: no matter how outrageous you might perceive your wishes to be, you might as well ask. You just might receive the very thing you desire. It never hurts to ask.

Is there anything you need to ask for right now?

A person who always does the safe thing and never tries anything new places physical security ahead of growth. As a consequence, he ends up with neither physical nor spiritual security.

In the Bible, there are some great examples of people taking risks for a higher purpose. Moses, for one, did not think he had the ability and intelligence to meet with the Egyptian pharaoh to plead for the release of his people, but he did it. He kept stating his case to the pharaoh and steadfastly held to the belief that he deserved what he requested. Whenever he doubted himself, an inner knowing told him to press on. He persevered and, eventually, led the Israelites across the Red Sea.

Joshua is another example of steadfastness and willingness to put higher purpose ahead of personal comfort. He walked through the desert with the Israelites for forty years before reaching the Promised Land. He knew he could not stop until he reached his goal.

There was David, of course, a mere boy who killed a giant with a sling-fired missile. He was quite courageous in facing seemingly impossible odds, but he maintained his faith, commitment, and courage. And he succeeded.

Our nature is expansion. To stay small and *safe* in our comfort zone goes against our spiritual nature. Expansion means to keep learning, to push our limits, to try new things, to grow. Along the way, we can learn to laugh at ourselves so that we keep things in perspective. Being able to find humor also keeps the ego in check because the ego thinks it is awful to make a mistake or be the object of humor.

Never deny yourself an experience that you really want and need for your personal growth. You must test your limits or you will never be able to comprehend your vastness.

7. See the positive side of every situation.

Look for the pearl. It works like this: Oysters live inside hard shells, but inside the shell, they have soft, sensitive bodies. When a grain of sand pushes in to the shell, the oyster experiences great agony. If the oyster is unable to remove the irritant, it takes another approach and coats the sand with layers of soft iridescent mother of pearl. Thus, what was initially an annoyance is transformed, over time, to a beautiful object of great value.

We can do the same thing by refusing to accept an experience as negative. There will always be something in it to help you. Adversity builds strength and inventiveness. Diligently find your blessing. Here is an example:

The merchandiser J. C. Penney was challenged as the seventh of twelve children in a very poor family. He decided to use his abilities for enterprise to get what he wanted. Consequently, he raised and sold pigs to buy his school clothes. The undertaking that created a practical solution for purchasing school clothes eventually expanded into a lucrative business, J.C. Penney Department Stores. This man used his resourcefulness to fulfill his needs. We can all be resourceful in whatever situation we find ourselves.

There are pearls hidden in every situation, seeds of a new way in a career, a relationship, a business, a hobby, or a process. Your choice is to either be a victim of circumstances or be an opportunist. Recognizing opportunity requires vision, willingness, courage, and effort. Do you have what it takes? Are you willing to find the pearls in your situation?

Decide how to use, not misuse, an incidence to your advantage. Even the so-called dullest event or association can yield benefits if you take charge of it. I call this philosophy turning lemons into lemonade.

The lamp of the body is the eye: if therefore thine eye be single, thy whole body shall be full of light.3 But if thine eye be evil, thy whole body shall be full of darkness. If therefore the light that is in thee be darkness, how great is the darkness! Matthew 6:22-23

If you choose to see only the limitations or challenges, you place yourself in fear. Then, you are truly experiencing darkness. And, how deep the darkness will be!

By keeping your eyes, your perception, focused on the purpose and beneficial aspect of a situation, you allow yourself to live in the Light.

8. *Ask for guidance.*

Establish a daily quiet time and be steadfast about maintaining it. Everyone needs an hour a day to reflect on life, to make decisions, to make plans, and to determine options. Thinking on-the-run just doesn't work. After a while, your mind moves so fast, you block your creativity.

Quiet time helps you to slow down mentally. As you still your mind, you become more receptive and open. Your creativity expands. Your Christ-Self has much inspiration to offer, but cannot deliver it if you will not listen.

Meditation is a way to listen to your Higher Mind and is a further refinement of time to yourself. Meditation helps you build the connection between your inner and outer minds or the subconscious and conscious. With regular meditation practice, your right and left begin to work together and your neurology strengthens. The better the connection, the greater the inspiration and flow from within.

Jesus often went up to the mountain (translated as *high place*) to pray and meditate. He often did this after teaching large groups of people. This was how he rested and restored his energy. It worked for him, and it will work for you, too.

9. *When you receive an answer or direction from your Higher Mind, follow it unquestioningly.*

Do not waste time in doubt. Just do it. As you learn to act on this guidance with belief and faith, it will increase. Then, you will know that there is always an answer for every question, a solution for every problem. You will know the truth and the truth will have set you free. The power of prayer and meditation is spoken of in this passage:

> Ask, and it shall be given you; seek, and ye shall find; knock, and it shall be opened unto you: for every one that asks receives; and he that seeks find; and to him that knocks it shall be opened. Matthew 7:7-8

10. *Forgive everyone who has ever wronged you, including yourself.*

To forgive means to *let go of*. Let go of all hurts and injustices. Recognize that no one hurt you unless you were receptive to being hurt. Be responsible for your vulnerability and willingness. Forgive those that through their shortsightedness, fear, or ignorance, caused you pain. No one is sensitive or considerate all the time. Nor are we capable of perfectly reading each other's needs. It is very possible and probable that you have inadvertently been insensitive at a time when someone was in dire need.

These are human mistakes and we are all human. As you aspire to spiritual maturity, you will find it easier to forgive mistakes. By dwelling on them, your attention is stuck in the physical realm, *ego*, and your true mission is lost.

Rise above these minor occurrences. They are not important to the soul. The Christ-Self views them as opportunities to develop perspective. Letting go of resentment creates space for new life to flow in, and it will be of a higher quality.

Focus on love to fill your inner space. Love ensures meaningful, gratifying future experiences. The first step toward love is forgiveness.

11. *Love and appreciate everything.*

Most importantly, love and appreciate everything: your life, your family, job, employer, employees, friends, home, goals, past experiences—everything. What you love expands.

The basic essence of divinity is love. As you match your conscious thinking to your inner Core of divinity through love, its natural creativity flows unhampered. Then, everything you do will be a demonstration of your Christ. You will never come up short when you commit to love. Jesus made this clear. Refer back to the passage in Matthew 5:43-48, where he spoke of the cultural directive of loving your neighbor and hating your enemy. Contrarily, the master's teaching was that not only should you love your enemy, but also pray for him. This is how you evolve into Sons of your Heavenly Father.

God made the sun rise on evil and good and the rain to fall on the just and unjust. If you just love your brethren, you have achieved little as anyone can do that. In fact the question is, what more do you do than others? His instruction is to be spiritually perfect as is the Father.

The more familiar you become with these eleven steps, or *tools*, the more dependable they will become for you. Build your expertise through practice and repetition.

Replace the weed of negative thinking with goals, activity, and desire to become a fully functional individual. Replace former habits with the understanding that you are the most important person you know and you have the innate ability to be the person you want to be. Certainly, the things you do will have the greatest impact on yourself.

Develop a quiet, secure mind. Create positive situations in your mind and perceive your life the same way. Expect pleasantness. Look for it and *be* it. Refuse to be unhappy. Imagine yourself as joyous, effective, and complete. Become immersed in positive, helpful activities. Live in gratitude. When you are happy, your body, mind, soul, and relationships will be harmonious as well.

Earth school offers many opportunities to understand your potential. As you live life with a positive, appreciative attitude, you unleash your inner talent and potential. It is a matter of individual choice, which unfolds with every thought and action.

In *The Aquarian Gospel of Jesus the Christ* by Levi, Jesus states this truth: *If you will keep your mind fully occupied with good, the evil spirits cannot find a place to stay. They only come to empty heads and hearts. Go your way and sin no more.* Sin no more means error no more. Don't make the error of entertaining negativity.

Daily discipline in using these tools will glean incredible changes in your life. Discipline includes meditation, quiet time, positive affirmations, eating nutritiously, exercising, and looking for wonder in everything. With these practices, you lift your spirit. Discipline is therapy for the soul and provides a positive, constructive way to express your energy.

To manifest your desires, you must know that you deserve them. In God's eyes, there is no question of deserving. Only you can hold back on this.

No matter what steps you take to create your desires, perform them with love and you will magnetize abundance into your life. Remember, Jesus started out in life as an inconspicuous carpenter. Through discipline, training, facing temptations, and determination, he not only transformed himself but affected the entire world. You can do the same.

CHAPTER 14

THE POWER AND POTENTIAL OF LOVE

Beloved, let us love one another: for love is of God; and every one that loves is begotten of God, and knows God. He that loves not knows not God; for God is love. I John 4:7-8

Love is perhaps the most misunderstood and underestimated principle in the universe. We often think of love in egoic terms: emotional, possessive and conditional. *If you love me, you will do what I want.* Love is put on the line in this example as something with which to threaten or bargain, a manipulative ploy. But possessiveness is not love. It is, at best, a warped interpretation that serves the possessor only.

Pure love has no conditions. You either feel it or you don't. It is not dependent on payoffs.

Love, according to Webster is *strong affection; warm attachment; to cherish, show affection, devotion, and tenderness.* Even this definition is limited and does not express the expansiveness and freedom of love.

Paul describes love as follows:

Love suffers long, and is kind; love envies not; love vaunts not itself, is not puffed up, doth not behave itself unseemly, seeks not its own, is not provoked, takes not account of evil; rejoices not

in unrighteousness, but rejoices with the truth; bears all things,
believeth all things, hopes all things, endures all things.

Love never fails: but whether there be prophecies, they shall
be done away; whether there be tongues, they shall cease; whether
there be knowledge, it shall be done away. 1 Corinthians 13:4-8

As we learn the true meaning of love and begin offering it fully
and unconditionally, we begin to understand its power.

In the Bible, we are told: *God is love.* 1 John 4:16

We are also informed that:

In the beginning was the Word, and the Word was with God,
and the Word was God. The same was in the beginning with
God. All things were made through him; and without him was
not anything made that hath been made. In him was life; and
the life was the light of men. John 1:1-4

These passages explain that not only is God Love, but also the
Word, and God is Life and Light. In other words, God is the initiating,
active factor of creation and the faculty through which all things came
into being. Therefore, if God is Love as well as the underlying principle
of all creation, Love is also a contributing force in creation. God is love.
God is creation. Love is creation.

You begin to see that love is much more than a simple show of
affection. Through its deepest understanding, we start to comprehend
the nature of creation.

But now abide in faith, hope, love, these three; and the greatest
of these is love. 1 Corinthians 13:13

Love: An Attracting Force

Love is an attracting force. It is magnetic. Through the magnetic-
attracting power of love, the Universe is held together. Simply put, love
as a universal principle draws to you the object or situation of your
desire. Understand also that because love is the essence of the Universe,

love is present in every thought. So even if you are resentful, angry, or afraid, your thoughts are formed out of the same universal substance, which is love. Think of it as living in an ocean of magnetic energy and the energy of this ocean is Love. Everything that is created emerges from this ocean of energy.

Here is an example of how magnetism works. Around every magnet is an invisible magnetic field of attracting energy. If a nail comes into contact with the magnetic field, the nail will be pulled to it. It may seem magical on observation, but the nail has no choice. It cannot ignore the magnetic force field of the magnet.

Further, when the nail comes into contact with the permanent magnetism of the magnet, the nail becomes a temporary magnet itself. It acquires the power of attraction that it originally did not have. As long as the nail remains near the magnet, it retains this magnetism. The reason for this is that the atoms of the nail already possessed magnetic attributes. However, the attributes were disorganized because they pointed in numerous directions, canceling out one another's electro-magnetic charge.

In contrast, the atoms of the magnet are perfectly aligned. The north and south poles face the same direction. Therefore, when the magnet attracts a nail, the atoms of the nail begin to line up to match the atoms of the magnet. In other words, the nail mimics the magnet. The more aligned the atoms, the more the nail emulates the magnet.

Of course, the same thing is true with people. A strong, charismatic individual can magnetize a whole room of people to mimic that person's thoughts and beliefs. It happens all the time.

The point in all this is that *you* are a field of electromagnetic energy. You are a magnet. Each of the trillions of atoms in your body generates magnetic energy. This makes you a walking, talking, breathing magnet. You possess magnetic power and are constantly attracting the things you like or dislike.

Your dominating thoughts, lining up like the atoms of a magnet, attract people, forces, and circumstances that harmonize with the nature of your thoughts. In other words, through the power of love's magnetism, you are literally creating the circumstances of your life. Hold your mind in a high vibrational energy like compassion and appreciation, and you magnetize into your life, high-energy people and situations. This can be a lot of fun.

To increase your magnetic qualities, pour universal, unconditional love into your thoughts, behaviors, and actions, and you will become a charismatic magnet. By the same token, if you have doubts, if you vacillate and change your mind repeatedly, or if you lack clarity in your desires, you will find this confusion reflected in the things, events, and people that show up in your life.

What are your dominating thoughts? What are you magnetizing into your world?

Again, remember that there is only one substance/energy in the Universe, one quantum field of energy out of which everything is made. Einstein called it the Unified Field. Scientists also call it the Holographic Field and the Divine Holographic Field. This field is God, the Universe, and it is Love. Thus, every thought you think, even those that are molded in the shape of anger, fear, or resentment, is composed of this one essential energy.

The rule is: What you focus on increases. So if you fill your mind with negativity, negativity will have magnetic power. Again, because love is the essence of the Universe, and it lies behind every thought and manifestation, this law of magnetic attraction cannot be refused.

To extend this principle of magnetism a bit further, let's consider the universal Law of Circulation. It works like this: You radiate out your ideas, thoughts, creativity, tangible and intangible gifts, and this energy circles back to you the same quality of energy. The energy that comes back to you is called magnification. You radiate out and you magnetize back. That is a full circle. Remember the rule: What you focus on increases. You literally radiate and magnify that which you place attention on. Giving attention to something is the same as loving it. Attention = Love.

For instance, if you love making money, opportunities to create money circle back to you, so you can have more of what you love. Or, maybe you love sharing with people. You radiate the love of sharing and people with whom you can share show up in your life. They circle back to you. What you focus on or give attention to or love increases. It is a law.

You might say, *if what I love attracts its own kind, why am I poor and alone?* The answer is that your dominating thoughts pour love and energy into the concept of poverty and aloneness. Even something as innocent as, *Why am I always short on money? Will I ever find a partner?* originates from a thought system of fear and lack, which have magnetic energy. Thought patterns of fear draw you to that which you fear. Fear has the same universal, magnetic energy as every other emotion.

The law is impersonal and unequivocal. At any time, you can decide to change your dominating thought patterns and the Universe responds equally well to your new choice. Decide and then be firm in your desire. Change your thoughts and you change your attraction.

Let's speak of the purpose or the intention of love. Love, expressed, and given freely, has no conditions, restraints, or possessiveness. It is offered for the unconditional welfare of all.

As you think about the things and people you love, consider your intention. If you focus on what you want from them, your love is tainted. Your thoughts are focused in lack. This affects the magnetic quality of what comes back to you. People sense your neediness. You may find the people you love to be resistant, rebellious, or avoid you. Were you to love them unconditionally, your field of magnification would be expanded without limits and all your relationships would improve.

To create in a God-like manner, your aim must reflect a purity of purpose. There can be no malice, guilt, or harm intended. This is not to say that love's attracting power will not work if you have an evil or unenlightened purpose. On the contrary, love, as attraction, will draw, i.e., magnetize, to you, the object of your desire, along with the underlying intention of that desire, whether pure or blemished. This means that, if your desire has a malicious component, that will be reflected in its manifestation. For example, vindictiveness, radiating out, will flow back to you in negative, hateful energy, just as compassion will circle back to you in warm, loving circumstances and people. Even though vindictiveness, war, and bombs seem to be the polar opposite of love, within its form is the creative energy of love. Love is the basis of all things.

In our egoic mind, we believe that if someone hurts us, we will hurt that person back in a worse way, and that seems to make sense. But the ego is illogical and never makes sense. The more we engage in negative thought processes, the more separate we feel from the radiant love of God, which is our center.

Awakening to your thoughts and learning to direct them intentionally, with purpose, is how you discover your power. Look at the conditions of your life and you will see the quality of thought you emanate. There are no mistakes. Consciously live from the highest energy possible and you will discover the keys to the Kingdom. You can have what you want. You must have the mental discipline to magnetize it into your life. The clearer, more purposeful, and positive your intention, the more pleasant will be the result.

I know a beautiful lady named Angela who decided she wanted to materialize a loving relationship with a fun, caring man, one who also danced. She knew about the power of visualization, but wanted to go beyond that to make her dream lover real in her mind. In the evenings at home, she would dress up, play dance music on the stereo, and dance around the living room, imagining she was in the arms of her make-believe partner. While pretending, she thoroughly enjoyed his company and felt the love he had for her. This went on for several months during the evenings she was at home. In the process, she was creating a strong magnetic force. Six months later, while visiting a friend, she met Scott, a kind-hearted, fun-loving dancer. Bingo! It was a perfect match. They have been together ever since.

Imagination and love combined to bring these two people together. Through this combination, a magnetic-attractive energy was formed, bringing the objects of the visualization together. When you bring love into your picture, it glows with possibility. This is a law of nature and cannot be denied.

I am speaking here about cause and effect. You always reap what you sow. If you lovingly seek a partner, a loving partner shows up. If you seek an exalted position in the political, business, or social worlds for the purpose of having others applaud and revere you, your results will be less enjoyable and more stressful than if you pursued the position to offer unselfish service. Fulfilling ego needs of adulation and reverence tend to be taxing because you are forever at the mercy and dependence of others' opinions, and you have no control over other people. You could be a bright shining star today and tomorrow you are supplanted. As always, you receive what you seek, along with the energy with which you seek it.

Whether your intention is for your welfare alone or for the betterment of all, your desire cannot be refused. Whatever intention you set will show in the results. The purpose is always out-pictured, along with the definition of the desire.

Bottom line: You are working with unerring attractive energy. Your job is to make the most of it.

Love: The Connecting Link

Love is the basic essence of the Universe. Out of it, all things are made, including you. Love is the core of your being. It is the divine essence of God within you. The more you purify your conscious thoughts to match or equal the divine quality of love, the greater your conscious alignment is to God. You are literally raising your energy. Achieving this connection is man's greatest accomplishment. Through it, we demonstrate Sonship. Love is the vehicle you use to make the connection.

> Behold what manner of love the Father hath bestowed upon us, that we should be called children of God; and such we are. For this cause the world knows us not, because it knew him not.
> Beloved, now are we children of God, and it is not yet made manifest what we shall be. We know that, if he shall be manifested, we shall be like him; for we shall see him even as he is. And every one that hath this hope set on him purifieth himself, even as he is pure. 1 John 3:1-3

This goal of Sonship indicates the importance of being diligent in purifying your attitudes and thoughts. Each unloving thought, be it criticism or condemnation, which permeates your consciousness, becomes a dark area and interferes with your connection to the

God-Mind. Throw out judgmental ways so you may perceive the Light of Love within you. There is no person who is without love except those who have turned away from it.

In the New Testament, Jesus, the individualization of God within man, illustrates and gives direction to the pure expression of love.

> *Whosoever shall confess that Jesus is the Son of God, God abideth in him, and he in God. And we know and have believed the love, which God hath in us. God is love; and he that abideth in love abideth in God, and God abideth in him. Herein is love made perfect with us, that we may have boldness in the day of judgment; because as he is, even so are we in this world.*
>
>   *There is no fear in love: but perfect love casteth out fear, because fear hath punishment; and he that feareth is not made perfect in love.*
>
>   *We love, because he first loved us. If a man say, 'I love God, and hateth his brother,' he is a liar: for he that loveth not his brother whom he hath seen, cannot love God whom he hath not seen. And this commandment have we from him, that he who loveth God love his brother also.* 1 John 4:15-21

Brother should be considered both esoteric and exoteric. It refers both to another individual as your brother and to an internalized aspect of yourself. In this reference, to say, *I love God,* but condemn yourself or another, is to lie.

It is clear that the love referred to in these passages is impersonal love. It is based not on behaviors, but on Spirit. You dare to love the true essence of the individuals in your world. Jesus' commandment was simple:

> *And if ye love them that love you, what thank have ye? for even sinners love those that love them. And if ye do good to them that do good to you, what thank have ye? for even sinners do the same.* Luke 6:32-33

We may find a person's behaviors hurtful and negative, but we must look beyond to see the beauty of his soul. By doing this, we hold a higher vision for this person. In this way we offer energy that he may identify with his True Nature. We also keep ourselves open and free, continually aware that we are Spirit as well.

If you occupy your mind with faultfinding and criticism, you are not fixated on love. Your intention, instead, is focused on egoic concerns: appearances, behaviors, and words.

To have love, you must give love. What you give away comes back to you by the Law of Circulation. As you extend lighthearted feelings of love, joy, support, and acceptance, you naturally move toward those who offer the same. There is a saying: *By your actions you will be known.* It means, simply, that the energy you express through your actions speaks volumes about *you*. Next to your actions, your words are meaningless. The edict is this: *You shall know them by their works.*

For there is no good tree that brings forth corrupt fruit; nor again a corrupt tree that brings forth good fruit. For each tree is known by its own fruit. For of thorns men do not gather figs, nor of a bramble bush gather they grapes.

The good man out of the good treasure of his heart brings forth that which is good; and the evil man out of the evil treasure brings forth that which is evil: for out of the abundance of the heart his mouth speaks. Luke 6:43-45

How are you expressing your energy? Is it loving and supportive or angry and blaming? Are you congruent? Do your words and actions match, or are you saying one thing and doing another? Self-examination is key for seeing where you are and making appropriate changes for self-growth.

Anglican Bishop Desmond Tutu of South Africa demonstrates a prime example of living the ideal of love and fairness. In 1972, he was invited to London to serve as the vice-director of the Theological Education Fund of the World Council of Churches. He was denied his passport. He addressed the matter by going to the top. He wrote Prime Minister John Vorster, explaining that his position would be prestigious for his country as he would be in a capacity to direct educational funds to South Africa.

Vorster acquiesced and authorized the passport.

In 1975, when offered the status of Dean of Johannesburg Anglican Church, Tutu gave up the freedom of England to return to South Africa. At that time, he refused the luxury of the dean's quarters in a white section of town. He chose to live among his own people in Soweto. Early on, Tutu's choices revealed his deep commitment to his people, which precluded concern for his own comfort.

The bishop used his high-ranking position to speak out loudly and frequently, consistently advocating reconciliation between all parties involved in apartheid. He considered apartheid a moral issue. Thus, it came under the providence of the church. He stated to the press, "I want to declare, categorically, that I declare apartheid to be evil and immoral, and therefore, unchristian."

He firmly denounced South Africa's white-ruled government and was equally harsh in his criticism of violent tactics of anti-apartheid groups. He relentlessly preached against the evils of apartheid in lectures and writings.

In 1976, he wrote Prime Minister John Vorster, warning him of impending violence. He described the situation in South Africa as a *powder barrel that can explode at any time*. In his letter, Tutu sought accommodation, appealing to Vorster in *deep humility and courtesy*, noting that Vorster was a loving and caring father, husband, and a doting grandfather. His letter was never answered.

On two occasions, the government tried to silence Tuto by revoking his passport and forbidding newspapers to publish his remarks. He was even jailed briefly in 1980 after a protest march. It was thought that Tutu's expanding international reputation and his vigorous advocacy of non-violence protected him from harsher consequences.

Despite many obstacles, Tutu persevered. He never swayed from his ideal of freedom for all of South Africa. He considered his life a small price to pay for that freedom. The ending of apartheid and the bringing of democracy to South Africa is credited to his continual, vigorous, and unequivocal efforts.

This 1984 Nobel Peace Prize winner's conciliatory approach was the hallmark of his leadership. Bishop Desmond Tutu lived his talk and walked his walk. Through his unique mix of leadership, courage, diplomacy, and grace, he demonstrated his love for his people by pushing for democracy, fairness, and human rights.

Does Bishop Tutu's story sound familiar? He loved his people and put his safety aside to speak for freedom, fairness, and equality. To live for an ideal that is bigger than oneself is the true mark of a leader.

Do you know what your highest ideal is? Are you courageous enough to stand in the face of controversy?

Love connects all people. To live the high ideal of love exalts everyone.

Love: As Acceptance

The United States, and indeed the world, is going through a great transition. One of the most important elements of this change is the way we are learning to love. This adjustment is subtle, yet dramatic. It involves the way people express compassion and kindness.

In the past, folks mostly gave love by accepting and appreciating those who gave to them. That was easy. The challenge has always been to go beyond that tight circle. Loving those you don't know may appear chancy, but it isn't. If you're expressing a love that appreciates and accepts the *person* rather than approves of his behavior, you are coming from a place of spiritual strength.

Those who fear love perceive it as an external expression, perhaps a way to control or possess another. They are wrong. Love is an intrinsic part of self. It radiates from deep inside and flows out everywhere, much like the sun beaming light to the planets. The more you radiate to others, the greater your awareness of love.

As you give love unconditionally, you are able to receive it in the same manner. This is an act of being true to yourself and being your true Self. Loving is natural and easy. It has nothing to do with catering to ulterior motives.

If we think about babies or puppies, it is easy to smile. Expressing love to babies and puppies comes naturally. We know they are innocent. People are innocent, too, because they have naively taken on the programs and mental training of the folks around them. They act out of this training until they are ready to become aware. They are their own worst enemies, building up guilt and shame, which are totally created by the ego,. In Spirit, there is *no* guilt or shame.

It is our job to recognize the innocence of each person. *Forgive them, for they don't know what they are doing,* is the credo handed to us by Jesus.

Resentment, hatred, and criticism inhibit the experience of love. As we release these barriers, we are able to receive love as open vessels.

Self-love is not an ego trip. It is focusing on our positive qualities. Everyone has them. The more we love, appreciate, and accept ourselves as growing, well-intentioned beings who occasionally stumble, the easier it will be to love others in the same way.

You can practice loving yourself by doing those things you normally equate with receiving love from others. Be nice to you! Have fun—relax. Treat yourself to your favorite restaurant, movie, flowers, or ball game. Phone your best friend. You get the idea.

By making love the focus of your life, you will participate in the transformation that is currently taking place around the world, uniting all of us into a global family.

In Michael A. Singer's latest book, *The Surrender Experiment,* he tells a story about meditating outdoors alone near a secluded lake in Mexico. All of a sudden, he heard men and horses approach. He remained in meditation and fought to stay centered. His rational mind went into fear and worry about what was going to happen next. *Who are these men? What do they want with me?*

When he finally opened his eyes, he faced several men on horses who worked for the landowner and were patrolling the property for him. In broken Spanish, Michael communicated with the Mexicans. They invited him to their village to meet their families. He was afraid, but unwilling to give in to the fear.

As he entered the village with the men, everyone welcomed him warmly. The people graciously invited him to eat with them. They generously shared their meager food supplies. They seemed excited to meet an American.

Singer did his best to communicate his practice of meditation with the villagers. By the time he departed, they were fast friends. He felt humbled that his mind had gone into fear when confronted with a strange situation. Because he had determinedly stayed open to the new opportunity, everything turned out beautifully.

This incident clarified to Singer that practicing non-judgment and staying open to love was being reinforced in his life. He accepted the situation and, thus, he was in a state of openness and love. The Mexicans accepted him in the same way.

When fear enters the mind, reason is lost. The worst is assumed. In Singer's case, it became his goal to expunge fear from his thinking and to listen intently to his inner Voice in making decisions. That became his practice. It can become yours, as well.

Love, as a mental concern, is liberating. It causes you to recognize your eternal connection with Source. Through the attracting power of love, we draw a never-ending stream of wisdom and understanding that provides endless opportunities to learn valuable lessons.

To experience Christ Consciousness, it is necessary to see the good in all people, to love them as souls, whether you approve or disapprove of their behavior and beliefs. To be unconditional means you are to give up judgment and criticism and accept people as they are. Appreciate each person for whom that person is, not for what you want that person to be. Appreciate yourself in the same manner. Then use acceptance to step to higher awareness.

As stated earlier, fear is the opposite of love. If fear is your ruling thought-system, you are earth-bound. If fear is present, let it signal misinterpretation or error in your thinking. Strive to be objective so that you might recognize the possibilities in all situations. Place your trust in goodness, in good, which is God, instead of fear. That is how you will release all thoughts of guilt or punishment.

We have been taught that it is wrong to love ourselves, but that is the ego speaking. It is right and necessary to love yourself. If you are made of God substance, yet you do not love yourself, then you do not love God. To love and accept yourself is required in attaining peace and contentment. Furthermore, you cannot love others until you love yourself. You are God; God is you; you cannot love God without loving you. Stilling the ego voice of fear is an excellent way to love yourself. Do this by ignoring the ego voice. Hold love in your mind and stubbornly refuse to relinquish it as Michael Singer did with the villagers.

Love is consistent, stable, never-ending, everywhere present, and all-powerful. Love yourself, then reach out to love others. Without love, you have nothing to share.

Loving yourself starts with respecting your uniqueness. Respect is the act of holding something in high estimation, deference, or honor; according a feeling of esteem, regard. There are no two snowflakes alike and there are no two people alike. This is truly wonderful as it opens up limitless possibilities for learning.

Exercising respect is as simple as recognizing the positive ways you express your energy, knowing you are ever-improving, and acknowledging your positive intentions.

> *Beloved, let us love one another: for love is of God; and every one that loveth is begotten of God, and knoweth God. He that loveth not knoweth not God; for God is love.* I John 4:7-8

Jesus addressed his students with the term, *Beloved.* Beloved means one greatly loved. Our Creator loves each of us as a parent loves a child. We are greatly loved. Each of us is love, for God is love, and we are reflections of God. As a child of the Creator, we have all the qualities and potentialities of our Father. Therefore, we must emanate love to fulfill this potential and be like our Parent.

Because we are all made of divine energy and we are brothers, in the true sense of the word, we must accept one another. We are God-Beings on an earthly journey. Acceptance is how we will advance ourselves in our awakening as Children of God.

Forgiveness Leads to Release

Often, people do not create the life they desire because they are focused on the past or future instead of the present moment. The only thing you can control is the present. It is the only thing that exists because the past is gone and the future has not happened yet. It is your present conduct, thinking, and behavior that produces the circumstances you experience. Focus on the present moment and you will be able to use it fully. To do that, you must let go of the past and be unconcerned about the future.

Releasing the past requires breaking free of memories and grievances that haunt you. Even though these situations may be long gone, they will continually affect you because of judgments you have created about them. These judgments live as feelings, which are habitually aroused every time something similar occurs. They interfere with your ability to fully acknowledge the present moment. They form energy blocks that inhibit forward movement. You not only harbor anger, frustration, and judgment, they also affect you. Thus, you are also the primary beneficiary when you release these negative feelings.

To let go of the judgments attached to past incidents, practice forgiveness. Forgiveness releases energy that is held stagnant in our bodies and minds. Because forgiveness frees up energy, it liberates us. By forgiving and releasing the persons, groups, and situations of the past, you secure your ability to live completely in the moment. Freedom is illusive until you have separated yourself from the past.

Remember Mary, the divorcee who desired a loving marriage but hated men? She represents many men and women who experience a difficult relationship and decide all people of the opposite gender are bad. She crippled herself with anger and negativity and was therefore unable to create a happy partnership. Mary would never find the love she desired until she 1) accepted responsibility for her part in her previous relationships, 2) learned to fulfill her own needs, and 3) forgave her partners and herself. Once she was able to do that, she was able to recognize men as unique individuals. Eventually, this led her to a loving relationship. Forgiveness was her key.

Before we can love, we must forgive.

Jesus said to the paralytic: 'Have courage, son, your sins are forgiven.' Matthew 9:2

Sin represents error. Everyone has made misjudgments, critical judgments, and misinterpretations. These are mistakes. It is a common error to think of oneself in negative terms. When you do that, you also project your erroneous thoughts to others in your world.

A primary error is to withhold love based on what the other person is or isn't. Of course, we do the same thing with ourselves. I actually knew a woman who informed me that she did not like people with fat ankles. Wow, you say? So did I. If Jesus or Buddha had possessed thick ankles, would she have turned away from them?

Of course, I have heard people decide they don't like Italians, or Republicans, or redheads, or rich people. This is the irrationality of the ego. Withholding love is irrational and keeps you away from love.

What about withholding love from ourselves? Here is a story of a person who did that.

Marge was a perfectionist. She told me how she cleaned her house thoroughly, the right way. The right way included dusting every corner, the top of the cornices, all the woodwork and molding. Her description was quite excruciating. She also informed me that she had to get all her tasks completed before she had time to meditate, read a book, take a walk, nap, or do anything for herself. We've heard this a lot: *Work before play.*

Basically, Marge had a long list of items to complete and, of course, she never got far enough down her list to have time for herself. She was exhausted and burned out. She wanted to land a great new job, but her energy was depleted. Her issue was lack of balance. Everything came before her own needs.

My suggestion to her was to put something imperfect in every room so she could remind herself that it didn't have to be perfect, whatever she thought that was. She was to rearrange her to-do list with the items that would replenish herself at the top. And, finally, one day a week, throw the list away and go play. She got it!

Marge left my office an empowered woman. It was clear that her thoroughness was her cross to bear. In actuality, Marge had adopted cleaning the house as a child as a way to bring order to a chaotic household where Mom and Dad fought. If things were clean and in order, she thought maybe there would be peace at home. It was a child's way to problem-solve. Kids often try to take care of their parents' issues. Marge's solution involved self-love and self-care, giving herself time to relax and flow with the Universe. She was visibly relieved.

Many people withhold love from themselves by judging themselves cruelly. *I am ugly, stupid, incompetent.* We are not taught self-love in our culture, and it is important if we are to have a relationship with God because God is Love. We must elevate our energy to make the connection to Love.

Another common error in not attaining love is lack of forgiveness. Jesus' instructions were clear. We are to forgive because none of us knows what we are really doing.

Most people feel they cannot forgive another's actions. The error here is that, by holding on to resentment, you are not punishing the other person. You are punishing yourself. The one to whom you direct your anger does not feel the anger. You do. This is equivalent to drinking poison and expecting the other person to die. You become stuck with the negative repercussions of resentment and lack of forgiveness. If and when a difficult situation occurs, look closely to make sure that you are forgiving yourself. This is a continual process.

Again, sin is *error, misjudgment.* We commit error when we choose anything other than love. We keep ourselves from the Light when we choose the low energies of hate, fear, or anger. The question is always: *How can I love more?*

Let go of all the mistakes of the past so that you can establish a new order of thinking. By the same token, forgive those who you believe have wronged you. You don't want the dark blotch of resentment in your consciousness blocking out your inner Light. That is a high price to pay to hold a grudge.

Forgiving yourself and others sets the groundwork for healing on all levels. Because love is of God, love has healing qualities. If you are not at peace or have found it difficult to forgive your brother, let love help you correct the disharmony.

Here is a technique you can use to release disharmony toward yourself or another. Use your imagination and will to construct a mental picture. Begin by placing the person or situation in your mind.

Imagine a pink cloud surrounding the person and/or situation. Pink is the color of love. The cloud represents the desire to love, to understand, to release, and to forgive the situation or relationship.

Hold this picture until you feel love emanating in your mind. Let the pink cloud of love come alive with sensation and saturate everything in your mind: the person, circumstances, physical room, environment, everything.

Now, mentally speak to the person or circumstance saying, *I surround you with love. I release you in love. I know that the understanding I need is coming to me, and I now set you free to do what you must do as I proceed to do what I must do. I love you and forgive you and release you unconditionally.*

Following this mental monologue, imagine the person or situation fading away in the pink cloud of love.

After you have completed this visualization, go about your business. You have symbolically let go and made peace with yourself and the other person or circumstance. No need to think about it or carry it with you any longer.

Perform this releasing technique twice a day, morning and evening, until you feel a sense of peace. That is when you will know your work is done.

Two things happen when you practice this forgiveness technique. First, the person involved in the situation you wish to heal will experience your love and your monologue on an inner mental level. It eases that person's stress so that the person can begin to let go and transform. Second, you are opening your mind, through love, to allow greater vision and awareness to enter. This new energy replaces the unease of the past with greater understanding, compassion, and expansion.

This exercise triggers great changes in your life. As a result of using this technique, I have seen wayward children return home to their parents with a strong commitment to work things out. I have observed misunderstandings that have gone on for years be resolved quickly and without conflict. Personally, I have experienced floods of insight and inspiration pour into my mind as a consequence of releasing individuals in love. Through new perceptions, I have felt freedom and peace. Try it. See what happens for you.

A friend of mine, Anita, has used the pink cloud technique often over the years to learn to love people with whom she experienced conflict. In every case, the results created magic in her life.

In one situation, Anita was hired to take charge of a computer project for a large company. On her three-man team, she had a programmer named Linda who resented the fact that Anita was in charge of the project when Linda had seniority and *knew more*. In their little staff meetings, Linda would buck Anita at every turn. No matter what Anita suggested, Linda would not only disagree, but forcefully come up with complicated, unreasonable solutions. Anita didn't want to complain about Linda to her supervisor, who was busy with many other projects, but she was growing more and more frustrated with the situation and feared that Linda would hinder the project.

Anita decided to use the pink cloud on Linda. Several times daily at home, she surrounded Linda in pink, forgave her, sincerely wished her love, then sent her off into the ethers in the cloud. She knew it was working well when she held her staff meeting at the end of that week. Feeling relaxed and unthreatened, Anita sat back and smiled to herself as Linda explained her complicated formulas. Anita even consciously surrounded Linda in a pink cloud right there in the room. She felt no anger or animosity because she knew with confidence that Linda had no final say in how the project would operate or how the work would be divvied out. It was all okay.

Lo and behold, the next Monday morning, Anita's supervisor called her in and informed her that Linda would be taken off her project and she would be assigned another programmer. Wow, she could hardly contain her joy at this surprise. She felt like she had won the lottery, like she was *cashing in at the bank*. The pink cloud had been a fantastic tool to keep her in her own empowerment with a sense of peace. While she came to love and accept Linda for who she was, it taught Anita to love and forgive herself, as well.

If only you could love enough, you would be the happiest and most powerful being in the world. Start now by forgiving everyone who has ever wronged you, whether real or imagined. Be sure to include yourself.

CHAPTER 15

THE PURPOSE
OF SERVICE

Service has often been misunderstood. We tend to think of serving others as sacrifice, giving something up with no recompense. But this is not true. Serving others is, in its purest form, an act that rewards the server and the one being served.

From our time of birth, we have been served. Our parents supplied food, clothing, shelter, and love. The world offered air, natural resources, beauty, and opportunity. There have been friends, relatives, and companions with whom to share knowledge, encouragement, insight, and fun. God has given us life and free will.

It is because of this abundance flowing freely to us from many sources that we have matured. Responsibility increases with adulthood. At some point, it is necessary to offer back to the world, family, friends, and God that which we have received. It is through service that we balance the books. Service is a privilege and a blessing.

Service, then, provides the vehicle through which we demonstrate appreciation for the love and nurturing received. But service has another important aspect. And that is, when we unconditionally offer our talent, energy, time, and wealth to the world, a channel opens from within that leads directly to God. As we share our energy and wisdom, more flows to us.

Consider a vase that is filled with water. No more water can be added until some has been poured out. If no water is released, the vessel becomes stagnant and useless. To keep the water fresh, you must continually pour it out so that there is room for new water to be added. In the same way, you, as a being who is pouring out and being added to, refine and update your wisdom and skills. As you share value, you increase your supply.

> *Ye are the salt of the earth: but if the salt has lost its savor, where-with shall it be salted? It is thenceforth good for nothing, but to be cast out and trodden under foot of men.*
>
> *Ye are the light of the world. A city set on a hill cannot be hid. Neither do men light a lamp, and put it under the bushel, but on the stand; and it shine unto all that are in the house.*
>
> *Even so let your light shine before men, that they may see your good works, and glorify your Father who is in heaven.*
> Matthew 5:13-16

You are like the sun: brilliant and beautiful. It is your privilege to offer your radiance to the world. The sun gives abundantly without concern for receiving; you must do the same. You share your Light through your experiences, whether you grill hamburgers or build jet planes. You give as you are given to in the ways you are able. You are to offer the talents and skills you have. You are blessed as you bless others.

Jesus spoke and lived this truth. During his ministry, he laid it on the line by demonstrating and offering his abilities. He walked through temptation, ridicule, trial, and tribulation, as well as acknowledgment, acclaim, success, and fame. Through each of these phases, he learned and perfected himself. He reiterated often that he did nothing by himself. He performed his Father's work. These were his disclaimers, his way of giving credit where credit was due.

> *Now before the feast of the Passover, Jesus knowing that his hour was come that he should depart out of this world unto his Father, having loved his own that were in the world, he loved them unto the end. And during supper, the devil having already put into the heart of Judas Iscariot, Simon's son, to betray him,*

*Jesus, knowing that the Father had given all the things into
his hands, and that he came forth from God, and goes unto God,
rose from supper, and laid aside his garments; and he took a
towel, and girded himself. Then he poured water into the basin,
and began to wash the disciples' feet, and to wipe them with the
towel wherewith he was girded.*

*So, he cometh to Simon Peter. He said unto him, 'Lord, dost
thou wash my feet?' Jesus answered and said unto him, 'What
I do thou know not now; but thou shalt understand hereafter.'*

*Peter said unto him, 'Thou shalt never wash my feet.' Jesus
answered him, 'If I wash thee not, thou hast no part with me.'*

*Simon Peter said unto him, 'Lord, not my feet only, but
also my hands and my head.' Jesus saith to him, 'He that is
bathed need not save to wash his feet, but is clean every whit: and
ye are clean, but not all.'*

*For he knew him that should betray him; therefore said he,
'Ye are not all clean.'*

*So when he had washed their feet, and taken his garments,
and sat down again, he said unto them, 'Know ye what I have
done to you? Ye call me, Teacher, and, Lord: and ye say well; for
so I am. If I then, the Lord and the Teacher, have washed your
feet, ye also ought to wash one another's feet. For I have given
you an example that ye also should do as I have done to you.
Verily, verily, I say unto you, a servant is not greater than his
lord; neither one that is sent greater than he that sent him. If ye
know these things, blessed are ye if ye do them.'* John 13: 1-17

This passage is about service. The greatest must serve the others.
Those who were students to Jesus, the Master, received his gift as he
radiated it to them in the lowly act of washing their feet.

Feet represent our spiritual foundation. We must cleanse our
foundation, making sure that we are of pure intent, forgiving those who
have wronged us, and reaching out unconditionally. Jesus demonstrated
love by bowing down. We must do the same.

As you express and share your abilities, you begin to recognize
your potential. Jesus is your example. He paved the way. He never said
that he was the only son of God. Rather, he spoke the truth that greater

things you will also do. His example sets the pace. You are to realize the same power. Life affords a wealth of opportunity. As you grasp these and offer your gifts, you fulfill your destiny as a child of God.

You are to become the helpmate to the Universe. The saying that God needs a body refers to the fact that God works through people. To be of highest service in the world requires surrendering your opinions, beliefs, biases, and becoming open to the energy, ideas, and inspiration that are being directed in and through you. As you went through the previous lessons, you prepared to open to a higher, more subtle Spirit, to attain receptivity to the Divine mind so that you can be God's body.

Service is the way you recognize your value, that this earth trip is not just about acquisition and your own learning, but it is about giving as well. As you serve, you become mini-suns, radiating your Light to the world. Sharing Light may be as simple as holding a door for someone or carrying another's groceries. It may be as magnificent as bringing medical help or education to third-world countries. Your service will resonate with you according to your talents. Service is natural. A mother naturally cares for her baby. A person falls down and you naturally help them get up. In both cases, there is no thought of reward.

Service is a great way to get out of your small self. All of a sudden, your problems, worries, and challenges don't exist because you have re-directed your mind elsewhere, to someone or something else. Reaching out helpfully allows you to give the best of yourself. Plus, you get to *see* the best of yourself. Your attention and effort are all placed on a goal higher than ego-gratification. It is like taking a mini-vacation from your small self.

Leo Tolstoy wrote:

Life is a place of service. Joy can be real, only if people look upon their life as a service and have a definite object in life outside themselves and their personal happiness.

If you are not enjoying your life, you can either change your attitude or change your work. Often, a job change is the less desirable alternative. Therefore, look for ways to serve others while you are doing your work.

There is really no job or career that doesn't include service. This means that you can incorporate service into your life, no matter what your occupation. The level of success that each person demonstrates is in direct proportion to his desire to truly serve others. If you are grilling hamburgers and fries, you can do it with the attitude of helping people. If you are an actor performing on stage, you can do it with the intention of providing entertainment, joy, and possibly diversion for your audience. In any case, do what you do with love.

Harry Bullis, former Chairman of the Board of General Mills, encouraged his salespeople to practice this principle. He advised,

> *Forget about the sales you hope to make and concentrate on the service you want to render. As a person focuses on giving and providing service to others, he becomes dynamic, magnetic, and hard to resist. How can you resist someone who is sincerely trying to help you?*

Bullis suggested to his employees: *Start each day with the idea of helping as many people as possible today, instead of making as many sales as possible today.* If they changed their focus in this way, they would have a much easier, more open approach to their customers. They would ultimately make more sales anyway.

Beyond the reward of increasing sales, the person who seeks to help people achieves a happier, easier life and is exercising the highest type of salesmanship. Thus, you see that the opportunity to serve or shine your Light, is present at all times, whether you do sales, change bandages, serve meals, or simply smile at people.

In his book, *The Te of Piglet*, Benjamin Hoff writes:

> *To him who dwells not in himself, the forms of things reveal themselves as they are. He moves like water, reflects like a mirror, responds like an echo. His lightness makes him seem to disappear. Still as a clear lake, he is harmonious in his relations with those around him and remains so through profit and loss. He does not precede others, but follows them instead.*

This is the point that Jesus was making when he washed his disciples' feet.

Self-Expression

As God-Beings, we are in the earth to express ourselves. It is our purpose, goal, and innate urge. It is the path we take to reach conscious soul perfection.

Rudolph Nureyev, the famous Russian ballet dancer, said that work is sacred. Work and self-expression are synonymous. To do what we do with passion, joy, and privilege is powerful. We are in the earth to radiate our Light and to offer our gifts. That could be changing a tire, cooking a meal, playing beautiful music, rocking a baby, adding numbers, or millions of other possibilities. Our work is our gift.

Self-expression, like smiling and radiating peace and joy, releases the love you have inside. If you express joyfully, you magnetize more joy into your life. By the same token, if you perform your duties with resignation or boredom, you magnetize more of the same. Clearly, if you desire a life of inspiration and joy, learning to express from a place of love and passion is crucial.

You can see that there is a cause-effect relationship in this matter of self-expression. If you were to examine a situation, you could trace the thoughts and feelings that contributed to its creation. By connecting the dots meaning, *Thoughts + Feelings = Results*, you will learn the importance of setting up positive causes.

Intention is important. Perhaps you didn't plan the accident that crushed your car, but you may have been thinking about driving a new car. Or, maybe you didn't plan to feel ill, but you did stay up late, drank too much, or ate junk food. No one is a hapless victim.

There is a wonderful story about a British fighter pilot named Douglas Bader who had strong opinions about self expression and intention. This is what he had to say to a fourteen-year-old boy who had lost a leg after a car accident.

> *Don't listen to anyone who tells you that you can't do this or that. That's nonsense. Make up your mind, you'll never use*

crutches or a stick, then have a go at everything. Go to school;
join in all the games you can. Go anywhere you want to. But
never, never let them persuade you that things are too difficult
or impossible.

If anyone had the right to give such advice, it was Douglas Bader.
As a result of an accident while performing foolish airplane acrobatics,
he lost both legs: one above the knee and the other below the knee.
Doctors told him he wouldn't fly again, but he decided otherwise. He
lived his philosophy.

After World War II began, he reapplied to the Royal Air Force
and was accepted. He returned to flying using two artificial legs. He
became a leading ace-pilot, credited with shooting down twenty-two
enemy planes while leading his squadron and participating in the evac-
uation of Dunkirk, the Battle of Britain, and other air battles. He also
became a leading strategist of air warfare and an inspirational leader to
the men he led in battle.

During the war, Douglas was captured by the Germans and
spent three-and-a-half years as a prisoner of war, during which time
he staged several unsuccessful attempts to escape. Like with the rest of
his life, never did his lack of legs keep him from attempting anything.

After he survived internment and the war, Douglas got married.
He was ultimately knighted for his work with the disabled.

Often, we judge disability to be a terrible handicap. Yet Douglas
Bader proved that a person's disability has less to do with his physical
condition than it has to do with his attitude. He took charge of his
attitudes and beliefs, and you can do the same.

We all have disabilities of some sort and we all have the ability to
express our gifts anyway. So, if you are thinking of all the reasons you
can't deliver on your talents, consider the example of Douglas Bader
and do it anyway. As you express your talents and gifts, you will shape
your life.

You have a massive subconscious storehouse of information. As
you become disciplined in practicing the principles expounded in this
book, you will more readily understand the Universal Laws and how
they work. You will discover your power. Every moment, you impact

lives. Express your wisdom to ascend to greater heights of awareness and service as Douglas Bader and others have done.

The world is your schoolroom and self-expression is your teacher. Each person plays a part in the integral scheme of creation and evolution. As you knowingly claim our place and become fully involved, you evolve by opening to experiences heretofore unknown. The possibilities are endless and you are without limit.

You are to align yourself with the Universal Laws. As you do this, you will achieve a new level of dominion. Going back to the disciples, consider each of them as representing qualities that you possess. Notice how they were brought together and educated with one purpose.

This process is identical to learning to manage your mind-body by using consciously directed thought. Establishing control over your mind opens the way to a new sense of leadership. Each person is complete and perfect and complements the whole of humanity. We are One—one Field of Energy, many individuals and one consciousness.

Consider the example of living in an ocean of energy. In this metaphor, the ocean is the Divine Holographic Field or the Universe, God. The ocean is composed of all creation in singular drops of water. Even though each drop has its own individuality, together the drops comprise one living ocean. We are all connected and we are all one because we are all part of this ocean.

When you project love, you send pink energy into the ocean of consciousness, brightening the color tone. If you send gloom and doom, gossip and resentment into the ocean, color turns a dull grey. It is easy to imagine this process by placing a drop of dye in a glass of water. The water changes color. In whatever manner you choose to hold your consciousness, you have an impact. What shall it be? When you enter a room, what energy do you bring with you?

This is what self-discipline is about. Can you afford negativity? Can you chance turning your life and circumstances grey? With discipline, you choose what you want and align to it by providing the coordinating thoughts and feelings. It is fascinating how people want to be beloved, but chose not to love. They may talk about abundance, but continually affirm how poor they are. Get clear. What do you want?

Making mistakes is part of the process. But it is what we do with our mistakes that speak to the depth of our desire and intensity of our commitment for growth. The value of mistakes is that we learn. We process the errors and learn from them. We get up one more time than we fall down. It is that simple.

Because you have moved up the evolutionary ladder and have developed self-consciousness, you also have the responsibility and privilege of creation. No man is an island. You touch and effect every part of creation by your attitudes and actions. As you grow and progress, you are stimulating the growth and progression of all. When new Light enters the consciousness of one, it is present to be seen by all.

Humanity is like the sands upon the beach. Each grain has its place and importance. When one is removed, all the other particles must adjust and shift to fill the void. The total of all the individual particles make up the entire beach. When something is added to the beach, all particles benefit. Without movement of the single particles, the beach is stagnant.

As an important and integral part of the whole, your self-conscious growth raises the consciousness of mankind as a unit. What is given and received by any one individual is ultimately added to all.

Thus, as you clarify self-expression, you add to your essence and wisdom. As you do, you enhance the entire pool of energy for mankind. As you grow individually, all grow collectively. New experiences encourage growth, which in turn, expands expression and prepares you for greater opportunities. This is how you play your part in facilitating evolution.

Humility

The Dalai Lama of Tibet represents a symbol of humility. When asked for what he would want to be remembered, he said, *It is okay if I am not remembered.* In other words, he had no egoic need to be memorialized. His statement truly stands out in a world where we are encouraged to leave a legacy.

Humility is the honest recognition that you are not better and no worse than any other person. Jesus was a humble being. He acknowledged his divinity and, likewise, affirmed the same for every person. This is reflected in his words.

> *Verily, verily, I say unto you, he that believeth on me, the works that I do shall he do also; and greater works than these shall he do; because I go unto the Father.* John 14:12

> *And there arose also a contention among them, which of them was accounted to be greatest. And he said unto them. 'The kings of the Gentiles have lordship over them; and they that have authority over them are called Benefactors. But ye shall not be so: but he that is the greater among you, let him become as the younger; and he that is chief, as he that doth serve.*

> *For which is greater, he that sit at meat, or he that serves? is not he that sits at meat? but I am in the midst of you as he that serves. But ye are they that have continued with me in my temptations; and I appoint unto you a kingdom, even as my Father appointed unto me.'* Luke 22:24-29

In other words, the greatest is not the one who reclines and pretends to be a benefactor when he is only thinking of himself. As the leader, Jesus passes his dominion of God to his disciples.

You are an individualization of God, and you can perform great and wonderful works as Jesus did. There is nothing egoic about this. You were designed for greatness.

True service stems from humility. You must be aware of your value so that you know what you have to offer others. If you don't acknowledge your talents and strengths, how can you offer them to others?

True service operates from a basis of self-esteem. We must know and accept that we have much to offer. Service is a privilege and honor. Jesus did it well and so will you. To understand that all intelligence and talent is an emanation from Spirit makes you humble. In your developing self-awareness, you honor yourself when you realize you are here to channel divine energy in all you do. It is the spirit flowing through you that you express.

Jesus' entire ministry was an act of service for the transformation of consciousness. This is not to say he did not enjoy his work. Quite the contrary, his pleasure in giving was obvious. Each healing opened him to the Father. You cannot observe another person shift in understanding as a result of your work and not feel gratification and joy. That is the true measure of right work: it enriches you.

Service never diminishes you. On the contrary, unconditional giving through service is expansive. You offer what you have to others: skill, knowledge, kindness, time. Then, you allow the others to respond as they choose. Thus, you enjoy the act of giving and are not dependent on the recipient for acknowledgment or gratitude as the other receives your gift. You are free!

Giving unconditional service produces boundless joy and fulfillment. It flows from pure intention. The rewards are always positive.

Small acts of kindness or service can lift the energy and mood of the recipient. Take heed of football player Kurt Warner's comment.

> Sometimes, you don't want to realize it, or you think that an autograph isn't going to do that much, or to stop and say, Hi, doesn't really do that much; but through the course of time, I've realized the impact I can have in whatever way, whatever facet. People are watching, and people do pick up on those things.

Other small acts of kindness have made a huge difference in people's lives. Three-and-a-half-year-old Erika gave all of her Halloween candy to another little girl who was wheelchair-bound and unable to go door to door. Two friends spent an inordinate amount of time and energy removing an injured cat from certain death on a highway. A mother, annually and anonymously, donates food, clothing, toys, and games to a poor family.

An elderly lady, ordering food at a Chinese restaurant, noticed a homeless man rummaging through his pockets to assemble change to pay for an egg roll he had ordered. The woman, who didn't have much herself, bought an additional cup of soup and quietly had it delivered to the homeless man in addition to his egg roll.

So think about it. Who do you know who could use a complement, a love note, a message of appreciation, a thoughtful act? Who needs someone to ease life in some small way? Can you find it within yourself to sing someone's praises, offer a flower, a smile, or a pat on the back? If you want the world to be a better place, it has to start with you. What are you willing to do?

There is a point in our evolution when we must serve. Many call it *giving back*. They are giving back the opportunities and gifts they were privileged to receive. Giving back is part of our spiritual evolution.

Service Through Example

In a previous story, as Jesus washed his disciples' feet, he taught service through example. As we practice serving, we not only insure our evolution, but we bring a whole ocean of people along with us.

But he that is greatest among you shall be your servant. And whosoever shall exalt himself shall be humbled; and whosoever shall humble himself shall be exalted. Matthew 23:11-12

Service, as a tool for self-expression, encourages evolution. When you incorporate the Law of Service into your daily life, you expand your knowledge and expertise, plus open your heart. Freedom and dominion follow. Jesus offered us the example. He practiced, taught, and lived self-control, self-discipline, and self-respect. He explored and directed the Universal Laws to unfold his natural potential. By following this blueprint, he completed his mission. He admonished all of us to do the same.

Every one therefore that hears these words of mine, and doeth them, shall be likened unto a wise man, who built his house upon the rock: and the rain descended, and the floods came, and the winds blew, and beat upon that house; and if fell not: for it was founded upon the rock. And every one that hears these words of mine, and does them not, shall be likened unto a foolish man, who built his house upon the sand: and the rain descended, and the floods came, and the winds blew, and smote upon that house; and it fell: and great was the fall thereof. Matthew 7:24-27

The house represents your mind, beliefs, and consciousness. Building your house on rock means to be strong and stable in the truth. You can construct a solid foundation by understanding Universal Law, by working from pure intention, by leading with love, and by learning from each experience. Then, you will be prepared to stand firm in the midst of any storm, whether it be conflict, challenge, or confrontation. Then, you will accomplish your goal.

You have but to make the decision to follow Jesus' example. If so, the joy, power, and love that were his shall be yours.

As you serve others, you serve yourself. The benefits cycle back to you in the forms of gratification and awareness. Self-appreciation heightens as you see the results of your labor. Jesus explains the principle.

> *If any man serve me, let him follow me; and where I am, there shall also my servant be: if any man serve me, him will the Father honor.* John 12:26

When you offer service without collecting monetary rewards or job-advancement, for instance, you receive internal treasures, such as peace, contentment, and satisfaction. In fact, even when you are materially rewarded, seek out the intangible returns as well. Compensation comes from the act of giving. Giving becomes genuine as you reach out to others as an expression of your inner desire to serve, share, express and grow.

In his book, *Do One Thing Different*, Bill O'Hanlon tells a story about an aunt of a colleague of the great psychiatrist Milton Erickson. This woman's social activities had been drastically curtailed due to disability and illness. She had become seriously depressed, even considering suicide. She lived alone in a large home that hadn't been altered in years. Her one pride and joy was her greenhouse, filled with cuttings of African Violets.

When Erickson met the woman, he chided her for not using her time and talent, her green thumb, productively and in consideration of others. His recommendation to her was to share her gift for growing African Violets with others. He suggested she seek out people who were going through transitions such as births, illnesses, graduations, marriages, and deaths, and bring them plants, along with congratulations or condolences, as the case may be. The woman agreed to do more for other people.

Years later, this woman was immortalized in the *Milwaukee Journal* in a feature that read, *African Violet Queen of Milwaukee Dies, Mourned by Thousands.* The article described the life of an amazing woman, whose caring efforts touched thousands of lives through her trademark flowers and charitable work. She gave her life meaning by focusing on others' needs. In giving service, she enriched her life and the lives of countless others.

I knew a man named Martin who owned a successful flooring store. He kept to himself most of the time and led a quiet life. One Christmas, he felt inspired and decided to step out of his usual routine to do something audacious. This was something he gave himself.

Martin knew about a single mom who was struggling to meet her family's needs. He decided to give her $500 anonymously. So, one night, he put five $100 bills in an envelope, along with a holiday greeting. He commenced to walk up to her house, placed the envelope in a conspicuous location by the front door, then rang the doorbell and ran to hide behind a bush.

The woman answered the door and picked up the envelope. As she opened it, she let out a surprised and happy gasp. She called out to the night air, *Thank you!*

Martin was so excited he couldn't sleep that night. As he told me this story, he beamed with joy. It was apparent that Martin got the greater blessing that night.

India's transformational leader Mahatma Gandhi used this principle well. He states in his autobiography that everything he had ever done was for the purpose of becoming closer to God. He did not require paybacks from the people he served because he received what he wanted through a greater understanding and closeness with God.

Sacred Selfishness

There is a big difference between offering unconditional service and being selfless. In this section, we will explore the difference.

Selfishness is considered a bad word. People run from it. Many will do anything to make sure they are not selfish. They will deny themselves, even sacrifice their happiness and health, in the name of being selfless. But there is a problem with selfless behavior. It results in depletion.

Selfless people tend to operate from the belief that you have the ability to make others happy, which you don't. You can add to their happiness, but you cannot *make* them happy. The easiest way to prove this is to try. Buy them a new car, make their favorite pie, or spend the day with them. Tomorrow they will be unhappy again. Why? Because they have not learned how to make themselves happy. Again, why? Because happiness is not out there in the external world. It is inside—in your heart.

We learn the lesson of happiness by feeling the joy of Spirit. It can be found in the smile of a baby, in a beautiful flower, or in an act of kindness, like holding the door for someone or helping another with packages. Your joy is how you feel. As you feel the inner Light, you experience joy. Joy is everywhere present, no matter what the circumstances are.

Now, getting back to selfishness. There are two kinds of selfishness. The first is called sacred selfishness, which involves giving to yourself. That means doing things that help you feel good and keep your batteries charged. Think about the activities that give you energy. Some possibilities might be reading, walking, yoga, travel, working out, getting a massage, quiet time, meditation, being in nature, friendship, laughter, buying a new hat, taking a nap.

Taking care of yourself keeps your energy high, which, in turn, allows you to have more to give. Taking a day off or taking time out of the day for you is necessary. It creates balance. The bottom line is that when you practice sacred selfishness you have more to give and the quality of your gift is the best.

The second selfishness, called low selfishness, involves taking from people. *I like your shirt, I want it, and I don't want you to have it.* This person is saying, *It's all about me and you don't count.*

Another example would be, *I want you to spend time with me. I don't care if you want to do it or not, or if it is inconvenient.* This person is basically stating, *Just do it. It's your job. I come first.*

Low selfishness can be a way to apply guilt manipulation. *You never call me. I guess you don't care.* In other words, *You are the cause of my loneliness. You are being thoughtless by not tending to me.*

You can see that these two kinds of selfishness are quite different. Low selfishness depletes your energy. Sacred selfishness energizes you and keeps you healthy. Recognizing these patterns will help you decide what is best for you and show you how to set boundaries with yourself and others. You maintain high energy as you set limits.

Jesus gave abundantly to many and he also took time for himself. After teaching a crowd of 5,000, he went off by himself: This was his way of taking care of himself.

As previously stated in Matthew 14:22-24 and in Luke 6:12, Jesus' practice was to dismiss the crowds and his disciples, and go up to the mountain to pray. This is how he recharged his batteries and received instruction from his Source.

Honoring yourself in the same way guarantees your ability to complete your mission, whatever that may be, and it is a powerful model for those around you, as well.

CHAPTER 16

TRANSFORMATION

From time immemorial, we have asked the questions: What is this all about? Who am I? What is the purpose of life?

Through these chapters, you have received many answers. If you meditate regularly, you are aware that the material body is just a vehicle. Who you are is much greater and more dynamic than the small physical form you inhabit. You have discovered that you have a mind, and it manufactures thoughts. You have control over these thoughts. You can say *no* to victimhood, self-pity, judgment, blaming, and unhappiness. You can move into the Light, the Universe, or God to feel the joy of being.

Perhaps you have recognized that you are *always* connected to this vast universal energy and that you are allowing Light to flow through you and express as you. It is possible that you have come to know that the more love you give, the more expanded you feel, and the more love returns to you.

It is true that love is our core. It is our connection to the Universe. It is the reason we are in the earth: to express love. We feel better when we give love because it is our natural state.

So, we move back to the question: Who are we? We are the Power and Presence of God. We are the consciousness of Oneness with all creation. We are perfect harmony, joyful, all knowing, infinitely abundant, and powerful.

We have used our power to create our human experience. In many ways, our involvement in the world of form is the opposite of our pure, natural state. This is because we have externalized our attention on the world and taken on the mental concepts of limitation, powerlessness, and lack of deserving. These concepts have affected and infected our circumstances. These limiting concepts are mental fabrications of the egoic mind. When we hold attention on them, we accept them as real. The maxim: *What you focus on increases.* Therefore, in many cases, these images have shaped our lives.

If we observe these concepts objectively, we can see that they have formed holographic images that have out-pictured in our experience. The people around us, along with media, academia, and religion, have taught us these ideas. We have obligingly accepted their teachings with the naive notion that others know best and that they actually know what they are talking about. Yet, something inside of us does not fully consent to these limiting ideas. That disbelief fuels our search for truth.

In this book, you've read many stories of people who did not accept limitation or disability. They did what they felt was right and succeeded, despite the odds.

If we compare the creation of our human experience with a game such as baseball or monopoly, we can see that the game works as long as the concept and rules developed to play the game are accepted and followed. If, at any point, we decide that we will not accept these rules, the game changes for us.

In the game of life, we have the power to make changes in the way we choose to play the game. For example, if everyone else thinks that the right thing to do is hate their competitors, you can change your own game by deciding that hate is not something in which you wish to indulge. You can choose to love your so-called competition. By doing this, you have not only changed the game but changed your relationship with your competitor and the overall dynamics of your life.

Since fear and anger are human inventions, and since love is the only energy that is real and long-standing, in making game adjustments, you have moved toward being your true Self. You can imagine the dynamic results that would come of making love your dominant mental state in every aspect of your life.

Another diversion from living the truth of our being is accepting the physical form as ruling our existence. We have allowed the size, shape, condition, and beauty of the physical-body form to hold great meaning in how we define ourselves. Since the form itself is limited, since it requires food, rest, touch, and heat/cold for survival, we have believed that *we* are also limited. The error in this thinking could be compared to believing that the car we drive is who we are. We don't define ourselves as a Chevrolet, Jeep, Cadillac, or Mercedes. That is a silly idea. And yet, it is the same silliness as accepting that who we are is a physical form.

When we gaze at a baby, we observe a beautiful essence. We perceive innocence and love. The baby's consciousness is vast and unlimited. Yet, in time the baby will be programmed and accept the concept of limitation. The child will begin to see himself as an imperfect form. His consciousness will be reduced to behaviors and actions. From the moment the child identifies with a name and objects, he takes on the concept of limitation.

If we were observing the process, we would note how the conditioning takes place in the open-minded, receptive infant and child. We would see how the baby gets attention when it is hurt. It is programmed to believe that making noise is a way to get needs met. In school, having many friends is valuable, but if the child were to march to a different drummer, like seeking solitude or foregoing competitiveness, the child might be considered worrisome and deemed negative. We can watch the process of how consciousness takes form and beliefs of limitation become the rule of the day. What we are witnessing is our own progression toward accepting ourselves as small, insignificant beings, which is not truth.

The thing that is important to note in this summary is that the human experience is all made-up. It is a result of imagination. This brings us back to our true nature, which is unlimited.

Consider these ideas:

1. What would happen if you decide to use your imagination in a different way?

2. What would happen if you decide that you are connected to the vastness of Spirit and you begin to make new choices?

3. What would happen if you decide that illness and disability are erroneous concepts, designed to keep you small and powerless, and instead, you chose to imagine health?

4. What if you decide that monetary lack is a *dreamed-up* notion and choose to accept the idea of universal unlimited resources and that you are open to receive them?

5. What would happen if you recognize that love and appreciation are the same thing, same energy, and you make it a point to practice *being love* by appreciating everyone and everything in your life?

6. What would happen if you direct the power of who you are to magnetize a life of joy, expansion, and ever-increasing blessings?

7. What do you think would happen if you make a point of loving your body just as it is, including the blood, glands, organs, muscles, and cells?

What do you think?

Here is an exercise to help you experience your innate vastness. Spend five minutes a day looking into the sky to feel the vastness of what is and *feel* the vastness. Then, close your eyes and imagine joy, abundance, and love flowing into your life as a magnificent waterfall, like Niagara Falls. See yourself receiving, with openness and appreciation, unlimited amounts of money, health, goodness, friends, laughter, and blessings of every kind. Keep a journal of your experiences when you practice this visualization.

In nature, we observe the caterpillar's metamorphosis into a butterfly. The process is unrelenting and timely. The caterpillar cooperates without hesitation. The result: a colorful butterfly that flies freely and adds beauty to the world.

Each of us is a butterfly. We must let go and submit to our personal metamorphosis in order that we may express our divine uniqueness in the world. And in our own way, add beauty.

Take Up Your Cross

As an individualization of God, Jesus, the I AM, continually encouraged his disciples. He attempted to establish unity within the group to insure singleness of purpose. Striving for cohesiveness reflects our attempts to bind our faculties together with one purpose. Our effort is to train our will, imagination, faith, discrimination, zeal, and receptivity in order to work together as one in the same way that Jesus sought to unite his disciples.

The twelve disciples symbolize the major faculties of man coming together under the direction of I Am, the inner authority. To achieve this unity requires discipline.

Jesus was met with excuses, fear, and lack of commitment. He was told by his disciples, *We cannot do the healings as well as you.* This is like a child saying, *I cannot clean my room as well as my parent.* He was asked to explain himself many times in the same way you and I require repetition in our experiences so that we can learn from them. These rationalizations and denials of power represent a cross to bear or a challenge to manage. The crucifixion further illustrates the meaning of a cross to bear.

The story of the crucifixion has puzzled man for over two centuries. A literal interpretation of the events leaves many questions unanswered. How can such destructiveness happen to a man of Jesus' caliber? Does this mean we are meant to suffer? These unanswered questions call for a symbolic interpretation of the crucifixion story.

Esoterically, by its vertical beam, a cross suggests our connection to Spirit and the unlimited possibilities that exist as man works from his potential. The horizontal beam, on the other hand, symbolizes man's identity with the earth. The horizontal or cross-beam represents how the dynamic power of consciousness is inhibited by limited thinking, the ego. We literally interfere with demonstrating the incredible possibilities that exist in the Divine Holographic Field by keeping ourselves earthbound with egoic small-minded beliefs.

Our internal I Am is crucified on the cross of our unwillingness to face our erroneous egoic ways and demonstrate our potential. Jesus experienced his trial with dignity and quiet fortitude. He did not complain. The I Am Consciousness within each of us recognizes the need to crucify old beliefs that get in the way of evolution. It willingly yields to the process with dignity and grace. You see examples of this fortitude in the stories of Mahatma Gandhi, Abraham Lincoln, Edward C. Barnes, Douglas Bader, Nathan Stooke, Wilma Rudolph, and many others.

How does this work? Each of us goes through a personal crucifixion as we offer up the negative thoughts of ego limitation so that we might expand and grow into the vertical possibility of Sonship. Jesus admonished us to take up our cross and follow him. By this, he meant to lift our consciousness. It is up to us to release our limiting ideas and excuses, to lift our awareness to recognize that anything is possible. We are divine energy and potential.

Through our transforming process, we establish alignment with our true Selves, and we are able to use our imaginations, wills, faith, and discrimination with singleness of purpose. This evokes courage to make necessary changes.

We go easy or we go hard, but we all go. *A Course in Miracles* states, *everyone must take the course.* This means that our course in evolution is set. We can embrace it joyfully or fight it. We will still evolve. Accepting change as our destiny and addressing it with an open heart makes earth-life an easier path.

Jesus ascended on the third day. This ascension represents the manifestation of change in consciousness, literally elevating to a higher plane of awareness.

As we give up old ways, we ascend to a new identity. Our new identity is Spiritual Man. All aspects are unified with singleness of purpose. Because we see with our single eye, the intuition, we look past supposed disharmony and recognize the beauty of wholeness.

As Jesus looked past the frailties and maladies of his followers, he saw whole, perfect beings. In our new identity, we are able to perceive the possibility that we can be and do anything. All you need is acceptance and willingness. Remove the crossbeam, the ego, and recognize your unlimited potential.

Jesus' view of perfection allowed him to perceive his persecutors as erring children, threatened by his promise of freedom and power. He did not take it personally that they would want to rid themselves of his example. He knew he was a threat to their way of thinking. That is why he could say, *Father, forgive them, for they know not what they do.* In truth, they did not know the karmic repercussions of their actions and the difficulties they were bringing upon themselves.

On a simple scale, have there been times in your life when you needed help yet refused it even though it was readily available? Your ego considered it weak to accept assistance. Perhaps you were blind to your own need.

That was the condition of Jesus' persecutors. Through Hebrew law, they chose to liberate Barabbas, a known thief, rather than the man who had offered life and health throughout the region. That is the nature of fear and what we must move beyond.

The *Metaphysical Bible Dictionary* defines the name Barabbas as *adverse consciousness, rebellion and hatred, to which man gives himself to oppose the Christ.* This state of consciousness would, if it had its way, destroy the Christ. Do we have this possibility within us? It amounts to resistance.

The people were not ready to receive the Christ. They were operating from a low-energy egoic level that preferred resistance and hate. We have to be ready to let the ego dissolve so we can move to a higher state. Change may seem frightening, but in this case, it is freedom.

What is your cross? What are the old beliefs that have shaped your life and you must release to move on to a greater awareness? Are you ready?

CHAPTER 17

CLAIM YOUR INHERITANCE

To this point, we have examined various factors regarding the path of transformation: Universal Law, self-expression, setting intentions, creating internal unity, and listening to intuition. Let us now consider our inheritance as a child of the Creator and how to claim it.

Jesus used parables to illustrate the workings of Universal Law. Each of these stories unlocks truths relative to personal dominion. In the parable of the prodigal son, which we will explore in depth, we are reminded of the unlimited possibilities for freedom and prosperity when we assume the position of Son to the Father.

The Gospel reiterates we are to do great things. It also teaches that, since God loved the lilies of the field and the birds of the air so much as to provide their needs, how much greater is God's love for us? We are also reminded not to hide our Light as we are to share our talents and gifts. Genesis states that man is to have dominion over all earthly things, which translates to mean that we are to use our imaginations, insights, and wisdom productively. What we ask for, we will receive.

Of course, there is the great pronouncement that love overrules everything. Or, as *A Course in Miracles* describes, *the only thing that is real is love*.

Finally, there is the edict that we were made in the image of God. In other words, we possess the same attributes as our Source.

You claim your inherent nature of love by taking dominion over your thoughts. What you hold in your mind becomes reality. Your thinking makes it so. To say it another way, you are continually declaring the conditions of your life. You have the freedom to decide. You can cave to external factors or seek a higher path and greater possibilities. Transformation or tragedy: you choose your perspective.

Resurrection means that man, possessing like qualities of the Creator, chooses to rise to higher consciousness. Graduating from earth-school is what resurrection is all about. This happens as you elevate your consciousness beyond the ego and the material world to the high vibrational state of love. That was Jesus' message throughout his ministry. Each time you forgive yourself or another, you clear mental space and open to greater brilliance and love. You are truly a brilliant Light.

The world is a great school and playground. You hang out in this vast earth playground, dissolving the illusion of duality, i.e., opposing qualities of bad-good, up-down, fear-love, ego-Spirit. As you realize that you are not the ego, you can let go of all the negativity and silly opinions to assume your true identity of love, which connects all things.

Forgive them, for they don't know what they are doing. Forgiveness holds the key to heaven. It is the way we release the ego-personality and rise to understand the innocence of man. We return to the open, non-judgmental innocence of a child and to the expansiveness and freedom of love.

Each step in the process of transformation and resurrection is necessary. It is important to be clear as you traverse the distance, to know what you want, and to be willing to confront wrong thinking to get it.

Fear is an illusory mental state that you are to move beyond. Love is expansive. You are always choosing one or the other.

Assume dominion in your life by:

1.   Being clear about what you want.

2.   Confront self-induced negativity, fear, and self-doubt.

3.   Take appropriate action; let your intuition be your guide.

Here is a story of a fellow who used Creative Imagination to fulfill every desire. It serves as an inspiration for you to do the same.

Doctor Elmer R. Gates of Chevy Chase, Maryland, prolific in creating useful patents, was one of the great scientists of the world. In his years of cultivating and using his creative faculty, he created more than 200 patents. He developed a unique method by which he would tap into his creative genius, a method that could be adopted by anyone desiring inspired results.

In his laboratory, Gates constructed what he termed his *personal communication room.* It was a soundproof room, meagerly furnished with a table and tablet of paper on which to write. A push-button on the wall controlled the lighting. When Gates chose to tap into his creative imagination, he would enter this room, turn off the lights, and concentrate on the invention he was developing. There, he would sit until ideas relative to his project began to flash across his mind.

There were occasions when his mind was so prolific that he wrote for hours. He wrote until he ran dry, so to speak. In so doing, his creative imagination produced minute descriptions of ideas and principles that were not yet known to the scientific world. This was the manner in which Gates produced his patents. He basically made his living by *sitting for ideas.* He performed this activity for some of the major corporations in America.

The information that came through Gates' mind while sitting in the dark room and it superseded his reasoning mind's capacity. These inspired thoughts came directly from Source. Edison and Gates had their own way of accessing this energy. Yet they shared the use of this creative faculty in developing inventions.

If we depend on reasoning alone, we can often be misled because there may be a misconception in how we perceive information. The content of the reasoning mind is dependent on what we have read, studied, and experienced. The Higher Mind has no such limitations. In working from this creative faculty, the information that comes through will be pure, unfettered, and unlimited.

You can make use of this faculty by stimulating your mind so that you are reaching higher vibrational frequencies. This could be accomplished through meditation, reading inspired work, saying affirmations, using your imagination, or being in nature. Concentrate on the subject you wish to explore. Form a picture in your mind to represent the issue or desired result and hold it until the subconscious mind takes over. Make sure you clear all other thoughts from your mind and wait until the inspiration appears.

Everyone has creative imagination. *Sit* with it and allow your mind to become a channel for inspired thought. Just as for Doctor Elmer R Gates, there are no barriers as to what you can create,.

Know What You Want

Many people don't know what they want of life. They think in terms of *shoulds, ought tos* and *have-tos. I should be married. I am supposed to be responsible. I have to pay the bills. I have to go to work. Shoulds* are not *wants.* They pose as negative guides toward goals that are not of your choosing. They keep you distracted.

Deeply desiring to do something is more powerful than having to do it out of obligation. You may simply wish to make a difference in the world, or you may feel a compulsive, determined drive, or even passion to make a difference. Depending on the strength of your desire, you can just put in a good effort or you can be dynamically spurred to heights of greatness and inspiration.

Heartfelt desire promotes movement that demands fulfillment and insists on responsiveness, whereas *needing to or having to do something* is fostered from fear. It motivates through force and resistance because, deep inside, you don't want to do it.

This is not to say that working from fear is ineffective. Often, it is quite effective. If a wild tiger is chasing you and your best solution is to run, fear can be quite effective in keeping you from the tiger's reach. Yes, you can accomplish other things when you are afraid. It is just that, as you move forward, you are also dealing with the force of resistance. This push-pull minimizes efforts and eliminates joy.

A woman named Grace exemplifies a good example of this principle of motivation that arises *should thinking* rather than heartfelt desire. Grace always believed that being a wife and mother was the only plausible ambition for a woman. Therefore, she locked herself into a situation with a husband and children, only to find that she felt unfulfilled and taken for granted. Had Grace carefully thought out her reasons for creating her wife-mother role, she might have realized that, although there were many benefits to being in that position, there were not enough rewards to fulfill her particular need for expression, visibility, growth, and movement in the world.

Along with handling the responsibilities Grace had already taken on as mother and wife, she now had to regroup and redesign her situation, allowing for additional creative outlets of expression. Perhaps, if she had considered her need for creative expression before she had married, she would have been able to foresee the necessary elements to insure her happiness. Possibly entertaining the activities that brought her the greatest joy would have been a clue.

It is not too late for Grace to resolve her dilemma, but the solution will require creativity on her part, creativity that will balance her responsibilities and desires.

As individuals, we have different needs and desires. It is important to pay attention to our unique requirements before locking ourselves into seemingly irreversible commitments.

Here are some examples of people who knew what they wanted and diligently worked toward it without letting fear, lack of formal training, appropriate credentials, or anything else get in the way.

The students in singer/song-writer Dolly Parton's high school graduating class did not understand her resolve and talent when they laughed at her declaration that she was to be a country western star and sing at the Grand Ole Opera. Years later, Parton thanked them for their disbelief, because it was their ridicule that gave her the determination to go after her goal.

Jules Verne had a vivid imagination and willingly gave it its due when he wrote novels that were deemed unbelievable. Verne felt strongly about the possibilities of the future and decided to put pen to paper and give life to his futuristic imaginings. In his novels, he provided prophetic insights about submarines that traveled under the polar ice cap and spaceships that flew to the moon and beyond. In pursuing his vision of the future, he inspired the creative capacities of scientists who eventually built the extraordinary wonders he envisioned.

Al Haake suffered from acute stuttering. He was laughed at by his classmates at school. They called him out in baseball games just to hear him stutter. He was demoralized, yet these events supplied fuel for his determination to find a way to tackle his problem.

One afternoon, Al heard a U.S. senator speak. The man said, *Look, you can do anything you want to do if you believe in yourself.*

Al wanted to believe he could speak clearly. He read about a man named Demosthenes, a great orator who had put pebbles in his mouth to solve a stammering problem. Al did the same and, ultimately, became a great speaker, too. He was employed by General Motors Corporation to speak throughout the country. He held people spellbound by his clarity, articulation, message, and beauty of speech.

Once you are clear about what you want and decide to go for it, there is no force in nature that can contain you. The Universe complies with your vision. You know how it goes: Ask and it shall be given.

Moving Away from the Light

In the story of the prodigal son, we have a wonderful example of a person leaving his spiritual home, squandering his resources, condemning himself, and almost settling for too little. Here is how the story goes:

A certain man had sons: and the younger of them said to his father,' Father, give me the portion of thy substance that falleth to me.' And he divided unto them his living.

And not many days after, the younger son gathered all together and took his journey into a far country; and there he wasted his substance with riotous living. And when he had spent all, there arose a mighty famine in that country; and he began to be in want. And he went and joined himself to one of the citizens of that country; and he sent him into his fields to feed swine. And he would fain have filled his belly with the husks that the swine did eat: and no man gave unto him.

But when he came to himself he said, 'How many hired servants of my father's have bread enough and to spare, and I perish here with hunger! I will arise and go to my father, and will say unto him, Father, I have sinned against heaven, and in thy sight: I am no more worthy to be called your son: make me as one of thy hired servants.'

And he arose, and came to his father. But while he was yet afar off, his father saw him, and was moved with compassion, and ran, and fell on his neck, and kissed him. And the son said unto him, 'Father, I have sinned against heaven, and in thy sight: I am no more worthy to be called thy son.' But the father said to his servants, 'Bring forth quickly the best robe, and put it on him; and put a ring on his hand, and shoes on his feet: and bring the fatted calf, and kill it, and let us eat, and make merry: for this my son was dead, and is alive again; he was lost, and is found.' And they began to be merry. Luke 15:11-24

We have all turned away from the stability of our Father's house, the Light, and ventured into the earth (materiality) to find our way. Without the connection to something higher, there is a sense of great loss, which would be represented by famine of spirit. Famine is also the shortage of food, which means lack of substance, wisdom, love, or anything.

Internalize the story as relative to your personal journey in life. In your wildest pursuits, you were not progressing. You squandered time, money, and talent, the same way you do when you are not aligning actions with a higher purpose. Nonetheless, by your determination to return to the Father, you, the Son, reconnect with unconditional love, non-judgment, and abundance to your rightful place.

The Father, God, does not even register your self-condemnation. God is focused on the joy of your return. Even when your desire to return is but a thought and not yet executed, God is ready to welcome your home. A popular saying is, you take one step and God takes ten.

In the story of the Prodigal Son, the father, symbolizing God, holds no limits or conditions on his love for his son. There is forever openness and receptivity toward his offspring. This is true of God's love for everyone. You are loved!

244 SET YOURSELF FREE

Finding Your Way Back Home

The story of the Prodigal Son is our story. In various ways, we have wandered from our Father's house, lost sight of our purpose and innate divinity, and disconnected from our Source. Perhaps, we have indulged in self-accusation, too.

After a time, the pain is too great to suffer. Living without higher purpose is heavy and does not produce wisdom. Sense-gratification and ego-gratification result in spiritual deprivation and angst. Over time, our sense of personal value diminishes. These negative feelings must be reversed to develop spiritual awareness and openness. We are urged to return to our Father's house. Waking up to our errors, we begin to seek answers and change.

When a person judges or condemns himself, the assumption is that God also is condemning. We create a human-egoic personality around God. Yet, God is not narrow-minded or vengeful. In fact, there is joy and delight in his son's decision to place Spirit first.

As the story goes, the Son, which is representative of you, is showered with gifts, indicating that by returning your focus to your Source, you open the flow of creative abundance and you are blessed.

The ring symbolizes commitment. The shoes represent protection for your feet, which symbolize your spiritual foundation. The wanderings of the past have gleaned knowledge for you now understand the desolation of life without Spirit. The beautiful robe indicates a new, outward presentation in the world. You are now in exalted in Spirit.

When there is protest, like, *I am a wayward being and undeserving, God*, the Father, pays no attention. It doesn't even register. The truth is that you have returned your attention to Source and nothing else matters, certainly not self-recrimination or guilt. God perceives the son as pure, beautiful energy, in the same way as you would see your child. The focus is on celebrating the Son's return to the Light.

By aligning yourself to the Light within, you are found, and thus, returned to your spiritual home. The lessons of the past help you maintain your focus. The result is prosperity, joy, love, vibrancy, and wisdom. With awareness in place, you remain to work the land and bring forth value and riches. In other words, you are productive and expansive.

Living An Exalted Life

The story of the Prodigal Son is important because it illustrates how, through our disillusionment, we relegate ourselves to a beggar's position instead of living as an exalted being. We divert our attention with dogma and crazy, nonsensical rules, experiencing self-imposed limits and discontent. We can change all that and approach life as it is, an endless opportunity to grow, express, and transform.

In the story, the Son, who represents you-me, left his home to seek adventure. He learned along the way that he was without direction or commitment and, because he focused on sense-gratification, he was lost to the Light. This caused a great sense of lack, whereas living in the radiant realm of love, his father's home, he experienced abundance and joy.

The story is a metaphor for you learning the same thing. When you move away from Love, your life symbolically follows the story with the Son living in low energy, working at the pigs' trough, facing lack and famine. You alive in dark consciousness and without nurturing.

This is a great lesson. You have another option: to live in the realm of Love, no matter what you do, and be fully accepted and adored. Whether your work is collecting refuse, mowing lawns, writing reports, selling widgets, or anything else, it can be accomplished with appreciation, joy, and love.

I once entered a tire shop where the salesman greeted me like I was the most important person in the world. *Good morning. How can I help you?* he said with a big smile and eye contact.

When I informed him of my need, two new tires, he said with enthusiasm, *I would be happy to help you. I know exactly what will work and I will be glad to take care of it for you.* He responded as if my walking in to his shop was the best thing to happen all week. This fellow made his job an act of service. It was clear that he enjoyed helping people.

I thought to myself, *this man is going to be very successful in this business.*

His energy was expansive and welcoming. Who would not want to do business with a person like this?

Needless to say, I bought my tires from him.

Often, we go through life experiences looking for personal affirmation. We finally discover the secret. By giving love, we are loved. By releasing ego-attachment, we are able to move to higher energy, our Inner Divinity, whereby we radiate joy.

This exercise will connect you to Sonship. It is a practice in being bigger than your circumstances. Train yourself to see conditions as opportunities to learn something wonderful. Commitment and consistency to your growth leads to personal expansion and transformation. There are great and amazing possibilities available to anyone willing to do the work.

You are reading this book because you are ready to move beyond a servant's portion and claim the considerations of head of the house. Your household: yourself. This is your heritage.

Claim Your Good

The father in the story of the Prodigal Son says, *Son, thou art ever with me, and all that is mine is thine.* Luke 15:31

It is your privilege to accept these terms. You can choose to see the journey of life as compulsory and venture forth without understanding. Or, you can choose to feel gratified as you work the land and experience life.

To claim your good, you must confront your thought patterns that are rooted in fear. Each time you catch yourself in victim-mode, having to instead of wanting to or getting to, rejoice in your discovery. Then, correct yourself. This is the same celebration engaged in by the father upon the return of his wayward son. You are also returning home.

The father accepts the Son regardless of his wanton behavior or squandering proclivities. You can accept yourself in the same unconditional manner. Set yourself free by affirming your divinity, by making well-intentioned choices, and by using your opportunities productively. You were born deserving. It is your birthright to be free and prosperous in all ways. You can ignore your inheritance by turning away from your Father's house, but it still remains. It is always available and open to you.

Discipline Your Mind

Disciplining your mind means that you are to be ever vigilant to keep your mind focused on what you want. That vigilance indicates diligence, willingness, and purpose in releasing negative thought patterns while replacing them with positivity.

Learning to put aside the ego-chatter of negative opinions and beliefs in order to tune in to the high frequency of Christ Consciousness, involves cultivating the voice of intuition. The story of about Martha and Mary illustrates this choice. Remember, it is a metaphor and has much to say about choice.

> Now as they went on their way, he entered into a certain village: and a certain woman named Martha received him into her house. And she had a sister called Mary, who also sat at the Lord's feet, and heard his word. But Martha was cumbered about much serving; and she came up to him, and said, 'Lord, dost thou not care that my sister did leave me to serve alone? Bid her therefore that she help me.'
>
> But the Lord answered and said unto her, 'Martha, Martha, thou art anxious and troubled about many things: but one thing is needful: for Mary hath chosen the good part, which shall not be taken away from her.' Luke 10:38-42

In this story, Mary took advantage of the opportunity to be with the Lord. She demonstrated self-love by her choice of sitting at Jesus' feet and listening to his words of wisdom. Martha, on the other hand, was bitter because her choice was to attend to her to-do list and she missed out on a glorious opportunity to spend time with the Lord.

This is a perfect corollary to people who choose to tend to their lists of chores rather than meditate, connect to higher energy, or spend time in quiet to restore their energy. Which one are you? Martha or Mary?

We develop our intuitive voice when we take time to listen, whether in meditation or paying attention to our gut feelings.

Jesus prepared his disciples before his crucifixion that they would not be left alone as orphans. He said that he would still be with them in the voice of the Comforter, which is the voice of intuition. He states this to bear witness: Listen to this voice of truth.

> *He that hates me hates my Father also. If I had not done among them the works which none other did, they had not had sin: but now have they both seen and hated me and my Father. But this cometh to pass, that the word may be fulfilled that is writ-ten in their law. They hated me without a cause. But when the Comforter is come, whom I will send unto you from the Father, even the Spirit of Truth, which proceeded from the Father, he shall bear witness of me: and ye also bear witness, because ye have been with me from the beginning.* John 15: 23-27

Jesus provided further instructions to his disciples. The instruc-tions required self-discipline: to love one another, to continue the work, and to ask for what they needed in the name of the Christ. Additionally, the disciples were cautioned to prepare for ridicule, as the world would not understand the changes that were occurring. This was akin to the idea of killing the messenger, for that is what happened when Jesus was crucified. As in most reformations, leaders tend to be misconstrued and misunderstood. Jesus was reiterating this point and, at the same time, encouraging his disciples to be fruitful in their work.

The disciples were admonished to be prepared that, when they left their traditional world, people would tend to hate them because they were different, which made them threatening. People would see them no longer as a part of their tribe or group. The disciples had chosen a different path and they would be discriminated against. Yet, despite it all, there were to love one another and continue to do the work. This edict was not just for the disciples. It is for everyone.

> *No longer do I call you servants; for the servant knows not what his lord does: but I have called you friends; for all things that I heard from my Father, I have made known unto you.*

Ye did not choose me, but I chose you, and appointed you, that ye should go and bear fruit, and that your fruit should abide: that whatsoever ye shall ask of the Father in my name, he may give it you.

These things I command you, that ye may love one another. If the world hates you, ye know that it hath hated me before it hated you. If ye were of the world, the world would love its own: but because ye are not of the world, but I chose you out of the world, therefore the world hates you.

Remember the word that I said unto you, A servant is not greater than his lord. If they persecuted me, they will also persecute you; if they kept my word, they will keep yours also. But all these things will they do unto you for my name's sake, because they know not him that sent me. John 15:15-21

Dear reader, this message is for you as well. When you commence your path of awakening, many will not understand. When you break away from your tribe, or the people you have spent your life with, you are often resented. Many people fight to stay the same and they want that for you, too. When you choose to march to a different drummer, it is often taken as an affront to the established system. All leaders go through this.

Jesus is instructing you to continue to love each person and be fruitful in your practice. In other words, keep going.

Recognizing Distractions to Peace

Ye shall know the truth, and the truth shall make you free.
John 8:32

This passage states that you are really not living a life of freedom and joy until you know who you are, which is energy, light, vastness, joy, and love. When you center your sense of self in the material world, you are deluding yourself into thinking that you are the role you play, the house you live in, the job you perform, the people you hang out with, your golf score, your bank account, etc. In other words, whatever is taking place in your world of form defines who you are.

Form, however, is constantly changing. Your bank account can go up or down, along with your golf score. The people in your life may leave and new ones may enter. The material world is transient and changeable. There are no constants in the earth.

In contrast, who you are is not transient. Your essence is unchangeable and constant. You are the observer, the watcher, the consciousness that is untouched by what happens. Your quest is to learn how to recognize your true essence.

There is a story that illustrates this quest.

A Zen master quietly strolled with a disciple along a mountain trail. The two decided to rest under a large oak tree and eat their simple meal of rice and vegetables.

The disciple, who had not yet learned to calm his mind, interrupted the quietness with a question. *Master, how do I enter Zen?* He was asking how to enter the state of transcendence beyond the physical form. In other words, he sought connection to his inner state of grace, peace, and stillness.

The Master remained still.

The disciple fidgeted as he waited.

He was about to inquire again, when the Master spoke. *Can you hear the sound of the mountain stream?*

The disciple had been so focused on his mental restlessness that he had not heard the sounds around him. Now, he listened for the sound of the stream. It took a while for his mental chatter to quiet. First he heard nothing. As he became more alert, he barely registered a small trickling sound in the distance. *Yes, I can hear it.*

The Master instructed, *Enter Zen from there.*

Gradually, the disciple let his attention drift back to his thoughts. The alert stillness he had achieved was covered over once again by his mental chatter. Before long, he had another query. *Master, I have been wondering, what would you have said if I had not been able to hear the mountain stream?*

The Master responded, *Enter Zen from there.*

Thus, the message is that we can enter Zen, the inner state of transcendence, wherever we are and whenever we wish. It is about releasing our *thinking* patterns and becoming still.

The ego is that part of your contrived self that wants to keep you mentally busy so that, in your preoccupied state, you yield to its mental maneuvering and manipulation. It convinces you by keeping you focused on the outer material world. It convinces you that you are material, that your identity is form. In that way, you do not resist its control, and control you it does.

The ego engages you mentally through your complaining, blaming, judging, self-justification, defensiveness, explaining, being offended, being angry, reliving the past, and fretting over the future. All of these activities keep you locked into the ego in the same way the disciple's anxious mind could not register the mountain stream. You can be so mentally busy that you don't know what is going on. These constant distractions keep you imprisoned and limited.

There is that within you that is bright, alert, and ready to guide you. Place your attention there and listen. Your life will change.

The story of the Zen master reminds you that there is something bigger taking place than your own small mental universe. You can listen to the stillness within. You can enter Zen, *the calmness of Source energy.*

Meditation is a great tool to center your mind and move into Zen. It is an important vehicle to raise your energy and elevate your consciousness. Jesus made a practice of going to the mountains to pray after large gatherings. That was his time for refreshing himself and his way of entering Zen to connect with Source Energy.

> *And straightway he constrained his disciples to enter into the boat, and to go before him unto the other side to Bethsaida, while he himself sendeth the multitude away. And after he had taken leave of them, he departed into the mountain to pray.*
> Mark 6:45-46

Here is an invitation to take rest in the Christ. In this summons, Jesus speaks of refreshing his followers as they take on his yoke. He refers to the peace of turning their attention inward to the stillness.

That is how they connected with their Christ-self and how you can do it, too.

> *Come unto me, all ye that labor and are heavy laden, and I will give you rest. Take my yoke upon you, and learn of me; for I am meek and lowly in heart: and ye shall find rest unto your souls, for my yoke is easy, and my burden is light.* Matthew 11: 28-30

This beautiful passage encourages you to turn to the Christ within to ease your burdens. To live in Christ Consciousness is light and easy.

Affirmation to Claim Your Birthright

Start and complete your day with the following affirmation to claim your birthright. With feeling, say: *I claim my divine birthright as a child of the Creator. I accept responsibility for my life and reward myself generously for my willingness to learn and grow. I open myself to the loving Presence of God, the Universe, and accept my inheritance of wealth, health, companionship, peace, and love. Thank you, Father. And, so it is!*

> *Have faith in God. Verily I say unto you, whosoever shall say unto this mountain, Be thou taken up and cast into the sea; and shall not doubt in his heart, but shall believe that what he said cometh to pass; he shall have it.*
>
> *Therefore I say unto you, 'All things whatsoever ye pray and ask for, believe that ye receive them, and ye shall have them. And whenever ye stand praying, forgive, if ye have aught against any one; that your Father also who is in heaven may forgive you your trespasses.'* Mark 11:22-25

Have faith. As you pray, believe that you will receive your answer. Continue to forgive any and all who cross you, and you will be forgiven, as well.

CONCLUSION

T he original question was: *If God is love, how can there be a holocaust?* I might add, how can there be war, murder, racial and ethical division, or any other act of hatred?

I have wandered far and wide to discover the answer. This question was the original motivation that began my search for answers, and now, we are at the end.

This is what I now know as truth: God is love and God is in every person. Indeed, we are individual sparks of God Energy, and we have the ability to shine our Light and share our Love in amazing, incredible ways. This is our path and our destiny.

Along the way over these millenniums, we have chosen to focus away from our Inner Light. We developed the idea that we are separate from our Creator. We have focused on our small material bodies, our separate lives, and a wide divergent set of beliefs and opinions. We have forgotten to pay attention to our feelings and listen with our hearts.

We have created a virtual prison by limiting our self-identity to the ego, the personality, and we have let it define us. In this ego state, we have looked *out there* and seen differences rather than noticing how similar we are. We all love our families. We all have the same needs and desires. We all are trying our best.

The idea that we are all connected in the sea of cosmic energy got lost because we could not fathom it with our small instruments, the eyes, and our narrow-minded focus. Our five senses have been our connection to *reality* and reality appears small.

When we turned from the Light, we made up the idea of separation and dualism. *You must be wrong so I can be right. You must be bad so I can be good.* The ego becomes unquenchable and out of control. The Light is blocked. We are in darkness.

The dualistic ideas of right wrong, good bad, perfect imperfect, and me-me-me drown out the inner intuitive voice of God. That is when a person decides that the construct of the world is all that matters. That is when it gets dangerous, when nations are destroyed because others don't fit the *perfect* pattern, or when people are thrown into gas ovens because they have the *wrong* lineage. A crazy man verbalizes a nation's insecurities, and soon he has followers who let fear and separation destroy goodness, accomplishment, prosperity, and kindness. He is the manifestation of a mind filled with anxiety and fear. He becomes the voice of the people. It has happened many times.

Materialism blinds. The inner Light is blocked. Millenniums of erroneous thinking cloud the truth. Connection is lost. The Light is still present, but we are no longer aware of it. When love is lost, only fear and separation exist as mental constructs.

The answer is to keep our focus on God, the Light, the Universe, our Creative Essence. In every day, in every way, listen with your heart. Pay attention. Put *love* first. Ask, *How can I serve in the greatest way today?*

Love the crazy little differences that illustrate how creative the Universe is in that every snowflake is of its own design and so is every person. Revel in it. You are playing in the sandbox of life. Make sure you don't dot all your i's and don't cross all your t's. Live an expanded life. Have fun! Let there be Light!

Here are Jesus' guidelines:

I am the resurrection, and the life: he that believeth on me, though he die, yet shall he live; and whosoever live and believeth on me shall never die. Believest thou this?' John 11:25-16

Ye have heard that it was said, Thou shalt love thy neighbor, and hate thine enemy: but I say unto you, love your enemies, and pray for them that persecute you; that ye may be sons of

*your Father who is in heaven: for he maketh his sun to rise on
the evil and the good, and sends rain on the just and the unjust.*
Matthew 5:43-45

God holds no prejudice, and you need not either.

The Great Commandments

*And one of the scribes came, and heard them questioning
together, and knowing that he had answered them well, asked
him, 'What commandment is the first of all?'*

*Jesus answered, 'The first is, Hear, O Israel; The Lord our
God, the Lord is one: and thou shalt love the Lord thy God with
all thy heart, and with all thy soul, and with all thy mind, and
with all thy strength.*

*The second is this: Thou shalt love thy neighbor as thyself.
There is none other commandment greater than these. And the
scribe said unto him, Of a truth, Teacher, thou hast well said that
he is one; and there is none other but he: and to love him with
all the heart, and with all the understanding, and with all the
strength, and to love his neighbor as himself, is much more than
all whole burnt-offerings and sacrifices.'* Mark 12:28:33

Okay. Got it! We are to put God first. Love your neighbor as
yourself. Forgive. Let go. Surrender. That pretty much says it.

I wish to you the best. I hope you receive the truth in this book
and live an exalted life!

Much love, many blessings!

Jean Walters

ABOUT THE AUTHOR

Jean Walters is a Saint Louis based teacher of self-empowerment principles for over thirty years. She has studied metaphysics extensively and applies universal principles to every area of her life.

Walters has written weekly and monthly columns for major St. Louis newspapers and publications and been published as a freelance author all over the United States. Besides *Set Yourself Free: Live the Life YOU Were Meant to Live*, she has written, *Be Outrageous: Do the Impossible: Others Have; You Can Too* and *Dreams and the Symbology of Life*.

Her radio show, Positive Moments, was syndicated on 110 stations across the nation and she has been a featured guest on many radio and television shows, even being referred to as "The Dream Lady" on several stations. This is in response to her ability to interpret listeners' dreams over the air.

Walters has designed and presented classes and workshops in empowerment, meditation, building communication skills, universal laws, dreams interpretation, strengthening intuition, and creating spiritual connection for many organizations, colleges, universities, spiritual groups, and businesses around the Midwest. She continues to offer her services to empower others.

From her office in St. Louis, Missouri, she works with people around the world as a Transformational Coach and Akashic Record reader (psychic). She has performed over 35,000 readings with the emphasis on providing insight regarding personal growth, life purpose, strengthening relationships, and moving through obstacles. She has been presented with "Best Psychic in St. Louis Award" for the last eight years.

Jean's mission is to lead people to the Light—to encourage, guide and assist others to live freely and express from their Highest Selves.

www.spiritualtransformation.com

jean@spiritualtransformation.com